THAT NIGHT
AT SURIGAO

Life on a Battleship at War

M. ERNEST MARSHALL

THAT NIGHT AT SURIGAO

ABOUT THE COVER

The cover design was created from two photographs taken from the album of Lt. Robert Baumrucker. The top image is the battleship *U.S.S. West Virginia* (BB-48) as she appeared in Puget Sound Navy Yard following her repairs and modernization. The bottom photograph was taken from the same album but it lacked a date or legend. Clearly identifiable, however, are Robert Baumrucker, seated fourth from the left, and Thomas Lombardi, seated on the right end.

For information about special discounts for bulk purchases, please contact Sunbury Press, Inc. Wholesale Dept. at (855) 338-8359 or orders@sunburypress.com.

To request one of our authors for speaking engagements or book signings, please contact Sunbury Press, Inc. Publicity Dept. at publicity@sunburypress.com.

FIRST SUNBURY PRESS EDITION
Printed in the United States of America
August 2013

Trade Paperback ISBN: 978-1-62006-243-2
Mobipocket format (Kindle) ISBN: 978-1- 62006-244-9
ePub format (Nook) ISBN: 978-1-62006-245-6

Published by:
Sunbury Press
Mechanicsburg, PA
www.sunburypress.com

Mechanicsburg, Pennsylvania   USA

CONTENTS

DEDICATION

This book is dedicated to the Officers and Crew of the battleship, *U.S.S. West Virginia* (BB-48), and to the memory of Lt. Robert Owen Baumrucker, U.S.N.R., for his devoted service during World War II - an unsung hero no more.

ACKNOWLEDGMENTS

That Night at Surigao is an odyssey that reveals what life was like for the men who served on a battleship in the Pacific Theater of Operations during World War II. Numerous resources were used to synthesize this account of wartime naval life and the author gratefully acknowledges the contributions of those who made it possible. Mike Mullins, Curator for the *West Virginia Association*, provided contact information for a number of the ship's veterans who gave valuable oral histories relating to their service time. Without these leads to the crewmembers, there would be insufficient information for this work. Mullins also stood shoulder-to-shoulder with me in the National Archives in College Park, Maryland, as we photographed several thousand pages of ships' records, including Deck Logs, Action Reports, War Diaries, Damage Reports, and photographs that had been held classified since the 1940s.

A central element around which this narrative is built is the written record of Lt. Robert Owen Baumrucker, U.S.N.R. Baumrucker maintained a diary for over three years, as he served on three battleships, knowing that it was against Navy regulations to do so, and that its discovery would lead to a court martial. As the ship's Intelligence Officer, he was authorized to obtain classified photographs in the conduct of his duties and to carry a camera. He collected copies of numerous classified images that he labeled and organized in his personal photograph album. Baumrucker was deceased already when research for this manuscript began but, as fortune would have it, he had remanded his diary and photograph album, along with other documents, to his niece, Ms. Judith Kroos of Boise, Idaho. Baumrucker's nephew, Mr. John Fort, provided additional personal records from this uncle's collection. These were of particular value regarding his post-war years and helped to resolve a number of mysteries generated by the diary.

I am especially grateful to the women and men who work within the National Archives in College Park, Maryland. These young people are aware that they protect the precious history of our country and they take great pride in their work. Specific mention is due Nathaniel S. Patch, Archives Specialist, United States Navy/United States Marine Corps. It was through these dedicated people that I was able to access the Deck Logs, War Diaries, Action Reports, Damage Reports, and other records of the battleships, *U.S.S. Mississippi, U.S.S. Tennessee,* and *U.S.S. West Virginia.* Not everything found in these documents was self-evident. Robert E. Osmon, Captain, U.S. Navy (Retired), and graduate of the U.S. Naval Academy, gave generously of his time and expertise to assist with the understanding of many of the details of Navy life that were encountered in the ships' records.

Presented later is a photograph of the Japanese flag that was removed from the body of the *kamikaze* pilot who crashed his plane into the *West Virginia*. The flag contains inscriptions in Japanese that were written by different hands. Japanese language scholars at the University of Virginia in Charlottesville provided translations of these writings. This task was made difficult by the fact that the written form of the language has evolved since the 1940s. A collaborative effort among several Japanese linguists was required to unravel the meaning of these inscriptions. The author is grateful to the following for their eager and devoted assistance with this task: Steve Mercado; Mieko Kawai, Lecturer in Japanese language; Michiko Niikuni Wilson, Professor of Japanese Language and Literature, Director of Japanese Language Studies, Department of East Asian Languages, Literatures and Cultures, University of Virginia. Additional translation assistance was given generously by a contact of Mike Mullins who preferred to remain anonymous.

A special level of gratitude is expressed to Dr. Dorothy Potter and Dr. Clifton Potter, Professors in the Department of History, Lynchburg College, Lynchburg, Virginia, for on-going advice and editorial assistance with this manuscript. Important recognition is due Mr. Steve Bozeman, United States Marine Corps veteran of two tours in Vietnam. Mr. Bozeman is highly active in veterans' affairs and is at the heart of such activities in Lynchburg, Virginia. He assisted greatly through his successful efforts to locate and contact veterans of World War II who are living in the Lynchburg area.

Gratitude is expressed to Richard T. Lombardi of Dublin, Ohio, whose father, Thomas Lombardi, was assigned to the *U.S.S. West Virginia* at the time of the attack on Pearl Harbor. Lombardi was an officer and eyewitness observer of the attack, and an active participant in the events that took place that day. Richard generously provided a copy his father's detailed personal account of the attack that he recorded within days of the event. Lombardi and Baumrucker met in Bremerton, Washington while the *West Virginia* was being repaired and modernized following her sinking at Pearl Harbor. They served together for much of the remainder of the war.

I was privileged to meet and/or interview a number of veterans who served on the battleship *West Virginia*. Their oral histories provided valuable insights into what life was like on a World War II battleship. Among the veterans interviewed were: Charlie Loving from Roseland, Virginia; John Parks Tazewell from Wilmington, Delaware; George Donald Gackle from Kulm, North Dakota; Joseph Variot from Detroit, Michigan; James Dennis O'Neill from Southfield, Michigan; Jerry Hudson Porter from Cisco, Texas; and Robert G. Wilson of La Canada, California.

The title, *That Night at Surigao*, was taken from an article by the same name in which Lt. Baumrucker described the details of the famous Battle of Surigao Strait as he experienced them. His contribution to this historic event was the culmination of his formal Navy education, dedicated personal training, and arduous drilling while at sea. The events of that night never left him as he sought official commendation from the U.S. Government for himself and his men for their actions at Surigao Strait. The wartime battle of ships turned into a post-war battle of paper.

INTRODUCTION

With the bombing of Pearl Harbor by the Japanese on 7 December 1941, the United States entered its second global conflict. The war spanned the two great oceans, multiple continents, numerous governments, and involved tens of millions of people, both combatants and non-combatants. These hostilities introduced new technologies for the movement, supply, and support of troops, and for the destruction of the enemy. Waging war on such a scale required some of the greatest logistical feats in the history of mankind. By the war's end, correspondents and historians were already at work attempting to sort out and record the complex events of this struggle. Because of the nearly overwhelming nature of a war so vast, early historians understandably painted pictures of the military clashes with broad strokes. The war was defined in terms of campaigns, naval battles, invasions, and engagements of large armies. Often, these events were depicted by red and blue arrows, representing opposing forces, drawn across continents, oceans, or countries, on maps with broad scope and little detail. Six and a half decades from the end of the Second World War, as veterans are dying at an increasing rate, there has been an intense effort to reduce the details of these struggles to the levels of the individuals who fought them. Detailed accounts of the movements of large armies, brigades, divisions, and even smaller military units, do not capture the experiences of the individual soldiers who were integral parts of the larger picture. It is interesting, and necessary, to read the exploits of the battleships and cruisers in the epic campaigns of the Pacific war, but it is understood intuitively that these great ships were inert objects until brought to life by the combined efforts of the individual sailors who served on them.

In 2008, I retired from the practice of medicine and returned to my hometown of Lynchburg, Virginia to pursue my other passions, writing and photography. Whether in my studio or walking the streets with camera in hand, my primary photographic interest has always been people. On November 10, my wife looked up from her newspaper to inform me that there would be a gathering of veterans for a special ceremony the following day in downtown Lynchburg at Monument Terrace. I had known Monument Terrace since my childhood. It is the iconic face of Lynchburg and the great gathering place for the city. Its one hundred thirty-nine steps rise steeply to connect Church Street with Court Street. The staircase is interspersed with terraces that contain memorials to local heroes who died in every American war from the Civil War to Vietnam. This is the natural place for the city to honor its soldiers, living and dead, on each Veterans Day. My wife was suggesting that this gathering of veterans might be a rewarding photographic opportunity for me. She was right. There I saw soldiers of all ages and generations, many in the uniforms they wore during their active service time and others in their American Legion attire. There was a color guard of old veterans with flags and parade rifles. The camera I carried proved to be an unofficial passport that allowed me to move freely about the crowd, and around the ceremonies, capturing images of its participants. When the old veterans of World War II and Korea saw my camera lens pointed in their direction, they noticeably straightened their spines as much as they could in an attempt to "stand tall" and look "military." I was genuinely moved by this gesture. The sense of military pride that had been instilled in them over sixty years ago had never left them. The photographic outing was a success. These old warriors had produced some stunning high contrast black-and-white images. Whether standing in the color guard, clutching their rolling walkers, or sitting in wheel chairs, these soldiers, sailors, marines, and airmen from ages gone by radiated their sense of pride at having served in uniform.

Later that night, as I sat in my study editing the digital images that I had shot, it occurred to me that there was an opportunity to combine the visual record of these men with their stories. I was introduced to Steve Bozeman, a former Marine who was a veteran of two tours in Vietnam. Steve had become the focal point of all veterans' activities in the area. It was clear to everyone that Steve cared deeply about the veterans and they were drawn to him like a magnet. I discussed with Steve my desire to capture oral histories from as many veterans as I could in the central Virginia area. He prepared a list of veterans and their contact information for me and supplemented it as he learned of more veterans in the area. I made appointments with each of them to meet in their homes. There I recorded the oral history of their lives leading up to and following their military service. I photographed much of their wartime memorabilia and compared images of them taken in their military youth with photographs that I took of them as old men. Steve knew most of these veterans well enough to know who was still fit for his age and whose health was failing. He guided me to the men who needed to be interviewed most urgently. Indeed, a number of these people have died since my original interviews.

I started this project with no clear idea of where I was headed with it. I just went to it with a sense of needing to capture the stories before so many of the veterans were lost to us. One interview gave me a sense of direction that I needed. My interview with Charlie Loving launched me on a fascinating multi-year journey that has not yet ended. Loving was born and raised in rural Nelson Country, Virginia. Upon entering the Navy, Loving was assigned to duty on the battleship, *U.S.S. West Virginia* (BB-48). The *West Virginia* was sunk during the Japanese attack on Pearl Harbor. Repairs began immediately. The ship was re-floated and sailed to Bremerton, Washington for extensive repairs and modernization. Loving met the *West Virginia* at Bremerton, near the end of her repairs, and he sailed aboard her for the duration of the war in the Pacific. He and I conducted our first interview in his home, sitting at his dining room table while his wife sat quietly listening in the living room. Loving's memory of the remote events of the 1940s was excellent. He used a number of pages of notes that he had written decades earlier, when memory was still recent to the events, to refresh his recollections. On the rare occasions when memory and notes failed him, he made no effort to invent parts of his story line or to speculate. He seemed to enjoy telling his story, often smiling or laughing at certain memories, but, as he traced his time line, he came to an episode that piqued my interest. On April 1, 1945, as the Battle of Okinawa commenced, Loving and a shipmate (now deceased) were at their battle stations manning a fire hose near an aft gun turret when a Japanese *kamikaze* plane crashed into the O2 deck. Because the bomb the plane carried did not detonate, Loving was able to visit the crash site for a close examination of the wreckage and to collect a souvenir that became a closely guarded personal treasure. He managed to keep this item secret from probing officers who knew of its existence. When I asked how he managed to do that aboard a ship at sea, Loving's usually crystal memory clouded momentarily as a grin appeared on his face and a gleam in his eye. There were some things this old sailor just wanted to keep to himself - and that was fair. I also sensed a bit of paranoia from him. He stated that he knew it was a violation of Navy regulations for sailors to collect souvenirs. It is not likely that this was true, but it was an impression under which he operated. He gave a sense that, all these decades after the fact, if the government knew he had the item, they would take it and he might be subject to some punishment. My attempts to reassure him were unsuccessful. His souvenir was the pilot's body flag. It was in remarkably good condition and I was able to photograph it but it never left his vigilant sight.

I learned later from the Deck Logs of the *West Virginia* that, while the *kamikaze* plane's bomb did not detonate, the plane killed four sailors who were manning a 20 mm gun pit. These men were buried at sea, but no official record accounted for the body of the Japanese pilot. Loving had no knowledge of the disposition of the pilot.

Curious about the ultimate fate of the pilot's body, I sought out other members of the crew who might have first hand knowledge of the *kamikaze* incident. Various histories recorded the successful *kamikaze* attack against the ship, but further details were lacking. I turned to Mike Mullins, Curator for the *West Virginia* Association. While he lacked any documentation of the fate of the pilot's body, he invited me to attend the 2009 reunion of the ship's veterans to be held in Charleston, South Carolina, with the hope that some of the former crew would have knowledge of the episode.

The reunion was held September 13 through 17, 2009 in the Quality Suites hotel in Charleston, South Carolina. Mullins had reserved meeting rooms for socializing and for displaying memorabilia on tables arranged around the walls. There was hot coffee and iced tea. One could purchase tee shirts and baseball caps with the *U.S.S. West Virginia* emblazoned on them. The proceeds from the sale of these items went to the *West Virginia* Association. This was my first face-to-face meeting with Mullins. He politely introduced me to a number of the veterans and alerted them that I was interested in interviewing them. Not one declined. As I moved about the lobby of the hotel and the large meeting room, I saw small clusters of men standing around or seated at small tables, chatting. I approached a number of these groups cautiously, expecting to hear the old boys recounting tales of their WWII experiences only to find that they were chatting about grandchildren, vacations, and fishing. It occurred to me then that, perhaps, they had long ago tired of retelling Navy stories. Thoughtfully, Mullins had arranged a table in a quiet corner for me to interview the veterans individually. While I recorded some interesting experiences of service on the battleship, I did not find what I was seeking - first hand knowledge of the fate of the Japanese pilot's body. I interviewed one veteran who had assisted with the removal of the pilot's body from the wreckage of the plane, but he could report only that the body had been taken below decks, and that he did not know where or what happened "below." He speculated, as a few others did, that the body was "dumped over the side" of the ship.

Following the reunion, Mullins provided me the name and contact information for James O'Neill, a veteran crewmember whose poor health had prevented him from traveling to the reunion from his home in Michigan. I conducted a telephone interview with O'Neill and received a follow-up hand written letter from him in which he described his involvement with the *kamikaze* pilot. As the opening phase of the battle of Okinawa was raging, O'Neil

3

was serving as a "volunteer stretcher-bearer." He pointed out that, at that time, on the *West Virginia*, the duty of stretcher-bearer was a volunteer service. In the conduct of his duties, he was a participant in the disposal of the pilot's body and offered his detailed first-hand account of the proceedings (described later).

I began to feel a small, but growing, sense of fulfillment in my quest to walk in the footsteps of the individuals who had fought this naval war, but I also felt that there was a final element to be provided for completion of this episode of the *kamikaze* attack - the report of an officer. Once again, Mullins provided a valuable lead. He informed me that Lt. Robert O. Baumrucker was the Intelligence Officer for the *West Virginia* at the time of the Okinawa campaign and the *kamikaze* attack. Baumrucker survived the war and married, but too late to produce children. He died of natural causes on 24 April 1999. Mullins was aware that Baumrucker's niece, Judith Kroos of Boise, Idaho, was in possession of his wartime diary, photograph album, and other memorabilia from the war. Multiple telephone and electronic mail conversations with Ms. Kroos have resulted in the formation of a long-distance friendship based upon her devotion to the memory of her uncle and his wartime experiences. This devotion is more than personal adoration - it is an open window to the life of a Navy officer as he served on three battleships during the war. Generously, Ms. Kroos entrusted me with the permanent care of Baumrucker's hand-written diary, his typed version of that diary, and his photograph album, along with other miscellaneous documents of interest. These documents and photographs form the core of much of this narrative history of life on a battleship at war.

Having Baumrucker's journal is good fortune. Keeping a diary on a warship was not without significant risk. Baumrucker knew that, for security reasons, it was against Navy regulations to maintain one, and that its discovery would result in a court martial, and the end of his Navy career. I believe the observations and accounts found in this diary are reliable, largely because they reflect the events recorded in the ship's Deck Log. Serving as Intelligence Officer, Baumrucker was uniquely positioned to be aware of events that were not known generally to the other officers and crew. He also had collateral duty as Fire Control Officer for the ship's huge 16-inch guns and was skilled in the use of the ship's radar - an innovation struggling to find its place in modern naval warfare. After the war, he was regarded as a reliable historical reference for Prof. Myron Smith's histories of the *U.S.S. West Virginia*[1,2], and he had written communications with historical novelist, Herman Wouk. I have spent many hours copying and pouring over several thousand pages of the Deck Logs, Action Reports, War Diaries, and Damage Reports of the ships on which Baumrucker served. These accounts are in accord with the events in his diary. Thus, Lt. Baumrucker's record became a "diary-within-a-diary." This provides a unique opportunity to reach to the level of the individual while simultaneously examining the larger picture through the diary of the ship. Baumrucker was present for most of the major campaigns in the Pacific following Guadalcanal. While serving on the *West Virginia* as both Intelligence Officer and Main Battery Fire Control Officer, he was the key person on the key ship at the most famous naval battle of the war - the Battle of Surigao Strait. He witnessed one of the first reported successful *kamikaze* attacks of the war, and was present as a *kamikaze* plane crashed into the *West Virginia*. While his diary covers military matters, it is replete with social notes, and documents his liberty time skiing, fishing, and dating. The diary records his awareness of the wartime deaths of close friends, and addresses clearly interpersonal tensions and conflicts among officers serving together on a battleship at war.

Conventional histories of battles deal with the actions of ships as if each was a living entity unto itself. The approach taken here was to combine ships' records with the Baumrucker diary and photograph album, the Lombardi memoir of the attack on Pearl Harbor, other official Navy documents, and several oral histories from surviving crewmembers of the *West Virginia*, in order to gain insights into the wartime lives of the *individuals* who gave life to the battleships. It is not the purpose of this work to repeat the history of World War II or to recount the details of its battles. Some historical material has been introduced for the purposes of context to offer a temporal backdrop for the contents of the Baumrucker diary. An old adage, whose author remains unknown, states that war is long periods of boredom punctuated by moments of sheer terror. It is my belief that this narrative presentation of the diary of Lt. Robert O. Baumrucker, U.S.N.R., along with supporting documents, is a unique opportunity to examine the daily life of a Navy officer during World War II - both on duty and at liberty-sixty-eight years later.

-M. Ernest Marshall

CHAPTER 1
Pearl Harbor

In December 1941, Thomas Lombardi was an Ensign assigned to the battleship, *U.S.S. West Virginia* (BB-48). The *West Virginia* was moored in Pearl Harbor outboard of the battleship, *U.S.S. Tennessee* (BB-43), at berth F-6 with forty feet of water beneath her. On 6 December, the island paradise enjoyed a typically beautiful day with temperatures in the mid- to upper sixties, and a gentle breeze that carried the pleasant smell of the ocean. Lombardi was a graduate of Syracuse University – class of 1933 – where he distinguished himself as a leader on multiple levels. He was Captain of the football team, President of the Student Body, and was seated *stroke* on the crew team.[i] In his Navy uniform, he was a dashing figure who could have been sent from central casting in Hollywood. Lombardi was off-duty that fatal weekend and, as a magnificent day melted into a beautiful evening, he and eleven fellow officers from the *West Virginia* went ashore for a relaxing and entertaining night at the Officers' Club, with cocktails and dinner dancing under the stars.[3] So lovely was the evening that they temporarily lost track of time as they found it difficult to separate from their dates. Lingering too long over their "good nights" caused them to be late returning to Pearl Harbor. When they got back to Pearl, they found that they had missed the last boat back to the ship. Consequently, they had to wait for the first boat out the next morning, and they were forced to spend a restless and uncomfortable night trying to steal what sleep they could at the boat landing.

The next morning, Sunday, 7 December, just as the 7:55 a.m. boat that would take them out to the *West Virginia* was making its landing, they noticed a flight of dive bombers beginning its descent over the Naval Air Station off to their left. They thought it strange that their airmen would be practicing bombing runs on a Sunday morning, especially at such an early hour. As they watched, they saw bombs being released from underneath the planes, followed shortly thereafter by the sounds of explosions as the bombs hit their targets. Almost simultaneously, a plane flew over them en route to battleship row. It was easy to spot the bright red circles on the undersides of the wings and torpedoes slung underneath the bellies of the aircraft. Immediately, they realized what was happening – the Japanese were attacking Pearl Harbor.[4] From that moment, things began to unfold before them rapidly. What they were seeing must have seemed unreal because, instead of seeking cover, they "stood there in the open, and watched one by one, the Jap torpedo planes come over [their] heads, headed for battleship row."[5] The planes were coming in low. Lombardi estimated that they were flying at about one hundred feet altitude and at less than one hundred knots. "We could have hit them with a baseball."[6] When the planes got

---

i The *stroke* is the rower seated closest to the stern of the boat. This is the most important position in the boat because the *stroke* rower sets the stroke rate and rhythm for the rest of the crew. A good stroke is a rower who can remain calm and level headed while simultaneously being highly competitive. In 1978, Lombardi was named a Syracuse Letterman of Distinction.

Ensign Thomas Lombardi was called to active duty 1 November 1940. This photograph was taken of him standing on the Signal Bridge of the U. S. S. West Virginia (BB-48) on 1 December 1941, just a few days before the Japanese attack on Pearl Harbor. Lombardi was both witness to and active participant in the events of that day. [Photograph courtesy of Mr. Richard Lombardi.]

to within about one hundred yards of the ships, they dropped their torpedoes. Lombardi estimated that the enemy planes were coming in about every twenty seconds, and the surprise of the attack was complete because "by the time our people realized what was happening, a good share of the damage had been done."[7]

At about 0755 hour, while Lombardi and fellow officers watched from shore, Lt. (jg) Frederic H. White and Lt. Claude V. Ricketts were finishing breakfast in the wardroom of the *West Virginia* when they heard the Fire and Rescue Party being called away by bugle. White ran to the quarterdeck. When he got there, the first thing he saw was a Japanese plane over a ship ahead of the *West Virginia* from which a column of water and smoke was rising.[8] He ran forward, stopped at the Deck Office, and sounded the general alarm just as the first torpedo struck the ship. Heading to his battle station, he noticed that there was no one in charge of the anti-aircraft battery on the boat deck where crews were manning the guns. He stopped and took charge of the battery and ordered the crew to break out the ready service ammunition, form an ammunition train, and get the starboard guns firing. By the time this effort got organized, three or four torpedoes had hit the ship causing water and oil to be thrown over the decks. The ship began to list badly and, when it got to about twenty-five degrees, the oil and water made footing very precarious. Because of the severe list, the guns on the port side could not be elevated sufficiently to fire. Consequently, the port side gun crews were sent to the starboard side to assist there. The air to the guns had gone out which meant that the guns had to be depressed for loading by hand. When the ammunition in the ready service boxes was expended, White went below to determine if more ammunition could be brought up. On his way down, he picked up some hands from the secondary battery and formed a working party to follow him below. The water was rising on the port side of the ship, and there were many injured men in the water with others lying on the deck. White ordered his detail to evacuate the injured while he made his way to the secondary battery. He found Ensign Thomas J. Ford in charge of the battery but it was not engaged at the time. White directed these men to join the effort to evacuate the injured from the second and main decks. He then returned to the anti-aircraft battery and reported to Lt. Cmdr. Doir C. Johnson that more ammunition could not be brought up, and he informed him of the situation below deck.

***

When the action began Lt. Ricketts left the wardroom right behind Lt. White. Ricketts climbed the ladder to the starboard side of the quarterdeck. As he reached the quarterdeck, he felt the ship being hit:

She was shaken some but I was not knocked from my feet. I thought then that instead of actual hits the vibrations might be caused by bombs falling close aboard.[9]

Taking in the sights before him and making his assessments of the situation, he went to the starboard side of the boat deck and saw that the anti-aircraft battery there was being manned. He ordered Ensign George M. Hunter to open fire as soon as possible and, because he was the senior officer in the gunnery department aboard, he then made his way to the Fire Control Tower only to find that it was locked, forcing him to break his way in. Almost at the same time, the Captain appeared as the ship was listing rapidly and severely to port. Ricketts asked, "Captain, shall I go below and counterflood?" to which the Captain replied, "Yes, do that."[10] Ricketts had served previously in the Damage Control Department, and that experience formed the basis for his quick recommendation to the Captain. On his way below, he picked up Boatswains Mate 1/c Garnett S. Billingsley to assist him. They made their way to the main deck and aft on the starboard side, and down to the second deck through the escape scuttle[ii] in the hatch in front of the office of the Executive Officer. He found the hatches in this area to be closed with the escape scuttles open. Wounded men were being brought up through forward hatches. The ship began to list so heavily that it became impossible to walk on the linoleum decks without holding onto something. They reached the third deck by using the ladder at frame 87 starboard and went forward to the first group of counterflood valves. Billingsley went aft to get a crank for operating the valves and, when he returned, he was accompanied by Murrell B. Rucker, S. F. 1/c and Arnold W. Bobick, M. M. 1/c, who were shipfitters from Repair III. Ricketts and Billingsley started counterflooding at B-163 while the other men moved to other valves. When Ricketts felt assured that counterflooding was well underway, he told Rucker to counterflood everything on the starboard side until the ship was on an even keel. It did not take long for the excessive list to port to decrease.

Later, Rucker told Ricketts that "he had not received any orders previously to counterflood the ship but he and Bobick decided that they should anyway and they actually opened the valves to two voids in Repair III."[11] Ricketts proclaimed in his written statement later, "This action on their part, in my opinion, showed excellent initiative and judgement."[12] Near the end of this exercise, Ricketts encountered "a considerable number of men...in the starboard passageways on the third deck and I ordered them forward to A-420 to supply ammunition. From information received shortly afterwards I don't believe these men ever got to A-420."[13] He reached the anti-aircraft battery on the boat deck to find that all the ammunition from the ready boxes had been expended. He formed an ammunition train and opened the hatches as necessary. When the hatch to the third deck A-420 was opened he found it to be flooded. They closed the hatch and abandoned any further attempts to obtain ammunition. The men who comprised the ammunition train were then set to work evacuating wounded from the second deck.

***

Jerry Hudson Porter, born in Cisco, Texas, enlisted in the Navy in 1940 at eighteen years of age. His parents were deceased and he was living on his own. He saw the Navy as an opportunity – "Looked like a pretty good deal so I signed up."[14] The Navy trained him as a machinist. When he finished his training, he was shown a list of ships that needed men with his skills, and he was allowed to pick his assignment. He asked to go to the *West Virginia* because it was a "big ship. It intrigued me."[15] He was aboard the *West Virginia* at Pearl Harbor and, on 7 December 1941, he was on Mess Duty. His regular duty assignment was in the after engine room but, when on "special detail," such as Mess Duty, he was relieved of his regular duties. The crew ate "family style" and, that morning, the section of men assigned to him had finished eating breakfast and he was washing dishes when the attack came. He heard what sounded like a bomb

---

ii A "scuttle" is a small opening in a wall, deck, roof, or larger hatch that is fitted with a cover that can be opened to allow access to or escape from a compartment. When closed, it makes the compartment watertight.

exploding and he thought the sound had come from Ford Island near the seaplane hangars. Other explosions followed. Initially, he thought, as did so many others that day, that these explosive sounds were the result of the Army conducting exercises although the timing for such a thing was most unusual. "What's the Army doing on Sunday morning playing war games?"[16] Very shortly, the alarm was sounded for "battle stations."

When "battle stations" was sounded, men on "special detail" – such as mess duty – were expected to collect in the center motor room as "dead heads" – "we had no particular job – just get out of the way."[17] In extremis, in the event of injury or death to crewmembers, the "dead heads" could be assigned to other duty stations as replacements. Porter got about halfway to his battle station when the first torpedo hit. "I did a 'Donald Duck' in mid-air and came down on one knee...got up and started running again. Another one hit. Managed to keep my footing that time."[18] As he got to his battle station, the ship began to list badly:

> The lights went out. We lost telephone communication so we were pretty much isolated in the dark except for battle lighting. Must have been about twelve of us down there...I don't know how much time went by... seemed like an eternity but probably on the order of fifteen minutes at most. And the ship listed rather badly and we assumed – I did – that it might capsize. But they counter flooded and saved the ship from capsizing, so we righted somewhat and settled to the bottom, and someone from up above opened the hatch, and told us the word was to abandon ship. So, we all left the boiler room and closed the hatch, and worked our way up to topside to [the] quarterdeck...And that's when I saw the holocaust that was going on with the Arizona. When I got to the quarterdeck, the mid-ship of the *West Virginia* was totally engulfed in flames [and] the Arizona was almost obliterated from view [due to] smoke. I'm not really sure the Arizona had blown at that time because, just about the time we got up there, we saw dive bombers coming right at us and a bunch of us ducked into the nearest door we could find to avoid the strafing and we were in there, I think, probably about ten to fifteen minutes, and I think possibly during that time is when the Arizona blew. [On deck,] word was passing around [the] *West Virginia* crew to go to Ford Island. So, I crossed over [to] the *Tennessee*, and a bunch of us grabbed a row boat and rowed it over to the beach. I saw some of the men dive into the water with that oil...I thought, 'That's not such a sensible thing to do.' That's why I didn't jump in the water.[19]

They opted to use one of the rowboats.

As Ricketts abandoned his efforts to obtain ammunition, he received word that the Captain was seriously wounded and in urgent need of assistance. He sent Ensign Edmond Jacoby and Seaman Lester W. McKnight, S. F. 2/c, forward to get a pharmacist mate to the Captain on the flag bridge. Ricketts then went to the flag bridge himself where he found Ensigns Vail and Delano with the Captain. The Captain was lying in the starboard doorway leading to the Admiral's walk. Lt. (jg) White was quick to join them. Ricketts then dispatched Vail to the boat deck with orders to send all of the anti-aircraft crews over to the *Tennessee* to assist the fighting from there. The Captain had a serious abdominal wound. It appeared that the wound was caused by a piece of metal shrapnel resulting from a bomb hit on a turret on the *Tennessee*. Chief Pharmacist's Mate Leslie N. Leak used a first aid kit to dress the wound the best he could. This was woefully inadequate treatment for such a deep wound, but there was nothing else that could be done at that time. The Captain was placed on a cot and moved under shelter aft of the conning tower. He was there when the second air attack came. Lacking a stretcher, the men used an eight-foot long wooden ladder to carry the Captain. He was lashed to the ladder and lines were attached to each corner so that they might lower him over the side of the conning tower down to the boat deck. This plan was made impossible by heavy smoke pouring up over the bridge and boat deck forward, as a result of a fire that had started in the galley. The boat deck needed to be evacuated. Ricketts searched for a safe avenue of escape, but the fire had spread to the life jacket stowage under the after part of the bridge, and flames were emanating from a bomb hole in the port side of the flag bridge deck. As Ricketts cleared out the signal flag bags that had caught fire, the men that he had posted with the Captain were forced to leave him in order to go up for air. The ladder was not working out very well as a substitute stretcher, so the men began to look for a knife to cut the Captain free. When Ricketts returned to the Captain, he found him still partially conscious. He directed White and two crewmen to unlash the Captain from the ladder and take him aft. The Captain was taken to the port side of the navigation bridge, where there was no fire, and comparatively little smoke.

***

From the outset of the attacks, the view from shore was somewhat different from that aboard the ship – devoid of the details of the struggles of the men still on the *West Virginia*. From where they stood, Lombardi and his fellow officers noted that the *Oklahoma* was the first ship hit, followed almost immediately by the *West Virginia*. "Then, it seemed, the air became full of planes, and it was hard to follow the rotation of hits – they were all getting it."[20] Within moments, the *Oklahoma*, hit by three torpedoes, listed to port and slowly turned over – "[a] heartbreaking sight."[21] The *West Virginia* had been struck by two 15-inch armor-piercing bombs and from five to seven torpedoes to her port side. Lombardi watched the *West Virginia* list to port and "for a time it seemed that she, too, was going over, but she seemed to settle low in the water, and stayed upright."[22] Later, Lombardi would learn of the quick thinking and valiant efforts of the men who counterflooded the ship to save it from capsizing.

In his after-action account, written only days after the attack, Lombardi recalled,

> The air was full of explosions – torpedoes hitting, bombs exploding, planes screaming overhead – all Hell was breaking loose. About this time – only five minutes had elapsed – the destroyers and cruisers at 10-10 dock opened up with their guns, followed shortly by the guns of the battleships...The noise was now terrific – more planes had appeared, and more of our guns had opened up. Time [was] 8:05. Suddenly, with a roar one can never forget, the Arizona blew up – horrifying sight.....The flame a solid sheet of vivid orange covering the spot where she had been, reached the height of 500 feet. A bomb, probably from a high altitude bomber, had pierced her and exploded in her magazines. The explosion

was terrific – she never knew what hit her. Almost immediately thereafter, one of the Jap torpedo planes blew up, apparently from a hit in her gas tank. She was about 500 feet off the landing, flying low. Where there had been a plane, was a big piece of flame, which plummeted into the water and went under so quickly, it barely made a splash.[23]

According to Lombardi, "There wasn't a single American plane in the air."[24] The *West Virginia* had a meager twenty-five rounds of 5-inch ammunition per gun and that was expended in short order. Because the *West Virginia* and the *Oklahoma* were outboard of the *Tennessee* and the *Maryland*, they protected these latter ships from torpedo strikes, but high altitude bombers hit the *Tennessee* with two bombs and one bomb landed on the *Maryland*. The bomb that struck the *Maryland* landed on the forecastle and went all the way through the ship causing her to settle by the head. Fortunately, the two bombs that fell on the *Tennessee* were duds. Lombardi and his best friend, Bert English, were left wondering why they had not been "swept off" by strafing.[25] During a lull in the action, two other friends, Ens. Eugene ("Gene") Lamiman and Ens. William ("Bill") M. Hodges, caught up with them. They all got into the boat and headed out to the ship. As they got approximately halfway across the channel, they saw incoming Japanese planes that were targeting the *U.S.S. Pennsylvania* that was still in her dry dock. They scored a direct hit with one bomb, but several others missed their mark and hit two destroyers – the *U.S.S. Downes* (DD-375) and the *U.S.S. Cassin* (DD-372) - that were in the dry dock ahead of the *Pennsylvania*. The destroyers caught fire, but quick thinking dock tenders flooded the dry dock to extinguish the flames before they could damage the *Pennsylvania*. The two destroyers were capsized and converted into a "pile of iron in the bottom of the dock."[26][iii] Bombs and torpedoes were striking ships of all sizes, but there was "still not an American plane in the air."[27]

As the officers approached the *West Virginia* in their small boat, they passed close aboard the overturned *Oklahoma*. They found her surrounded by a thick layer of floating oil, and they heard cries from men who were struggling in the water. They rescued two sailors who were clinging to the side of the ship. "They were so blackened with oil, we could hardly distinguish them in the water."[28] Lombardi kicked off his shoes and donned a life preserver, thinking that he would have to "swim for it" at some time or other. "At the time, I was wearing a white tux coat, and tux trousers – a fine uniform for battle!!"[29]

They arrived at the bow of the *West Virginia* to find her awash on her port side. As they stepped aboard her, they were met with an "inspiring sight."[30] The *Nevada* had gotten underway and was moving down the channel with "every gun blazing away and spitting flame."[31] They cheered as she passed by them. The *Nevada* was attempting to clear the channel to get to open water but, as she made the bend, "the Japs cut loose on her."[32] She was struck by a torpedo and by a bomb. Fearing that she might sink and block the channel, Signal Tower instructed her to go no further. She beached herself on the far side of the turn and settled to the second deck.

As Lombardi and his small band of officers landed on the *West Virginia* they became aware that fuel oil was leaking from tanks that had been struck by torpedoes. The oil had caught fire and was engulfing the ship in a curtain of

---

iii Observers at the time believed that the *Downes* and *Cassin* were totally destroyed, but both destroyers were subsequently refloated, repaired, and sent back into the war.

dense, black smoke. The forecastle was awash to port. Everything abaft the foremast was obliterated by the thick smoke. All was hodge podge – the decks were littered with clothing, bedding, injured personnel, and debris. I just stopped there, rooted in my tracks – was this the same neat-as-a-pin, proud ship I had left the night before?[33]

Quickly now, they were catching up on the details of the struggles that were taking place on the ship while they had watched from shore.

The first person Lombardi encountered aboard ship was Archie Kelly, one of the Ensigns. "His uniform, formerly white, was the color of the Ace of Spades."[34] Kelly informed Lombardi that all of the guns were out of commission and that the ammunition hoists were jammed or flooded.

The ship was out of action completely, with water up to the level of the main deck. The call to abandon ship had gone out 10 minutes previously. The torpedoes had ripped out her port side, and she had gone down almost immediately. Now she was resting on the bottom.[35]

Now, Lombardi's mind was "all confusion – I just couldn't believe what I was seeing. The immediate problem was the removal of the wounded, so we turned to on that job."[36] He came across a pair of sea boots lying on the deck that, as luck would have it, were his size. He quickly slipped the boots on and found them to be a great relief on the hot, oil soaked deck. With the interior of the ship filling with smoke, the men used gas masks to keep themselves from choking. Men were being brought up from below that were suffering from "concussion shock." They had been in the vicinity of the torpedo hits and were stunned by the force of the blows. Lt. Comdr. T. T. Beattie "put in [an] appearance and asked if the forward magazines had been flooded."[37] James G. ("Spud") Crawford, Chief Turret Captain of #2 turret, answered that they were under water. The after magazines had been flooded when the first torpedo hit. As they were completing these assessments, the second air attack started. Lombardi remembered that the first attack had consisted mostly of dive bombers and torpedo planes, but this follow up attack involved strafing runs and high altitude bombing. The high altitude bombers flew at approximately eight thousand feet with six planes to a formation. The guns of the *Tennessee* next to them went into action. Lombardi "watched the gun crews – they were really putting out the steel. Ordinarily 18 rounds a minute is considered fast for A.A. guns, but it almost looked like those boys were putting out half again that amount."[38] Once again, there was incredible noise resulting from the mixture of guns and bombs all around them. Lombardi believed that it was this attack that produced the bomb hits on the *West Virginia*, the *Maryland*, and the *Tennessee*. He thought, "the Japs were out to finish the job."[39]

"It was maddening to sit there so helplessly – nothing to fight with, and the ship gone."[40] The attack ended after approximately fifteen minutes, and they went below to finish removing the dead and wounded.

Gazing aft, Lombardi saw that the smoke had lifted on the starboard side of the ship. The sailors on the forecastle were either going over to the *Tennessee* or getting into boats that were coming alongside to off load crew. He decided to go aft to examine the situation there, and found Lt. Comdr. J. S. Harper, Ensign Hank F. Graham, and Ensign Jonathan T. Hine attempting to fight the fire that was coming up the quarterdeck hatches. Lombardi joined the struggle by commandeering half a dozen men who were in the area and directing them to hook up several fire hoses to the *Tennessee*. Later, he could not recall where they got the hoses or how they hooked them up without proper tools, but the fire was spreading the entire time, and the hoses helped only to "keep a slight damper on the flames."[41]

Astern of the *West Virginia*, the *Arizona* was "a blazing inferno."[42] The water all around them was covered with burning oil. The wind was blowing in their direction, and it carried the floating sheet of flames up onto both the *Tennessee* and the *West Virginia*, "but smart thinking on the part of the [men on the] *Tennessee* saved the situation. The *Tennessee* turned on her engines at slow speed and the wake thus produced by the propellers held back the burning oil."[43] Lombardi later recounted, "The flames did reach us several times, burning the after end of the Tennessee. The flames damaged us too, but a few extra fires at that point didn't matter much."[44] Lombardi and his men closed all the hatches on the quarterdeck in an effort to confine the fire below, and then worked their way up to the boat deck to do the same. The task was made difficult by flames coming up the hatches, making them red hot and impossible to handle, but "by various means,"[45] they got them closed. Having done all they could with the hatches, Lombardi turned his attention upward to the bridge, and he became aware of the struggle that was taking place with the Captain's body. He saw Lt. Ricketts, Lt. White, Signalman Siewart, and two boatswain's mates carrying the Captain up the ladder. He started for the ladder to lend a hand but found it impossible to get there. The oil stowage fire was engulfing the base of the mast in flames that were "rising by the second,"[46] and he came to the sudden realization that "those men up there were trapped – they couldn't get off."[47] He called up to Ricketts to ask how things were going. "His coolness was amazing. He said they were carrying the Captain's body to the lee side, and were going to get off – how he didn't know."[48]

Finally, fatigue began to settle over Lombardi "what with only 1 ½ hours sleep the night before, all the excitement, lungs full of smoke, etc."[49] He discovered a line lying on the deck and asked Ensign Hank Graham, who was with him at the time, to climb the crane. He located a heaving line and tied the nozzle of a hose to it. From his perch atop the crane, Graham was able to sling it up to the bridge. They then tied the heavy line to the smaller one. The men on the bridge pulled it up and made it fast. Ricketts instructed the men to use the line to move to the crane, and to relative safety. While they were dealing with the lines, another man had climbed up beside Graham. Lombardi was able to get a live hose up to him. The water from the hose was directed at where the men were standing on the bridge, and it succeeded in suppressing the flames. As these maneuvers were being carried out, Leak reported to Ricketts that the Captain had died. Leaving the Captain's body on the bridge, the men came down the line hand-over-hand. The last man down was Lt. White. "He was so weak, he almost let go halfway over, but he caught again, and made it. He collapsed when he hit the deck."[50]

The entire ship was now in flames. The men had managed to hook up about ten water hoses, but they turned out to be "pretty small antidotes."[51] The closing of the hatches proved to be of significant help, but when the deck became uncomfortably hot, the men were forced to return to the quarterdeck. The third attack came just as they reached the quarterdeck. Lombardi estimated that this attack lasted only five or ten minutes "but we watched those boys on the

Tennessee. They were a great sight – every man at his post, no one flinching – everyone giving everything he had."[52] Apparently, the Japanese had different targets for this attack as the *West Virginia* was spared further insult. Mr. Ricketts, Hank Graham, J. T. Hine, Mr. Beattie, Lombardi, and about ten seamen were the only men left aboard the *West Virginia* now. "Why we didn't get out of there I don't know."[53] These men continued to fight the fires and remained aboard until relieved properly by other fire fighting parties. They fought the fires until 3:00 that afternoon. On being relieved, they left the ship.

[We] looked back at a sorry sight. The California was awash, the Oklahoma's keel was all of that ship that showed above water, the West Virginia was covered with heavy black smoke, the Nevada was awash, the Oglala was lying on her side, and the Arizona – or what was left of it – was a roaring blaze. It wasn't until two days later that the fires were brought under control.[54]

Lombardi made his own private mental damage assessment:

Considering the Wee Vee's[iv] damage – seven torpedoes and two bombs – we were fortunate. Our total loss didn't exceed 100 men, altho ironically enough, the Captain was one of the two officers killed.[55]

***

Ordered to abandon ship, Porter and the small band of men he was with, left the deck of the ship, climbed into small boats, and rowed to land, as instructed. When they reached Ford Island, they were told to report in to the Marine Barracks. Subsequently, from there, the *West Virginia* crewmen were told to report in to the Officers' Club. Shortly after mustering at the Officers' Club, they were returned to the ship to help fight fires. They remained there until relieved around dusk by a replacement detail. After being relieved from their fire fighting detail, the men were transported to the Navy recreation center where they were issued a mattress and a couple of blankets. They took these to the bleachers in the recreation arena and spent the night there.

In the aftermath of their experience of being plunged into darkness inside the ship that was listing and threatening to capsize, Porter remembered a sense of fear but there was "no panic:"

I was one of the junior men on my boat but we had some senior Petty Officers there and, of course, we looked to them for leadership – and they seemed to be calm, and, I thought, if they're calm, I'm OK.......There was a great feeling on my part of disbelief – this is happening, I know it's happening – the ship's getting rocked by....torpedoes...and the mind doesn't want to accept this. We know that it's happening – it can't be, but it is.[56]

***

After leaving the *West Virginia*, Lombardi and his group of officers landed on Ford Island and mustered at the Naval Air Station. "It was a sorry afternoon,

---

iv "Wee Vee" was the affectionate name for the *West Virginia*, playing off the initials.

and what made it worse, we were all certain the enemy would be back that night."[57] It seemed logical to the men that the Japanese would return to follow up their initial advantage with a "knockout blow." In preparation for the return attacks, machine gun nests and other gun emplacements were established in the Yard. Tensions were running "fever high. The men at the guns had itchy fingers, waiting for the expected assault."[58] Lombardi ended up at the barracks with Ed Jacoby and Tommy Thompson – "weary, foggy, and sore mentally and physically."[59] The three of them lay on the grass in front of the barracks near one of the guns. They tried to get some sleep but were prepared to help out with the gun if needed. Except for occasional catnaps, they found it difficult to sleep. By now, mosquitoes, combined with the nervous expectation of another attack, made it impossible to get any meaningful rest. Around 10:00 p.m., a machine gun in the distance opened fire.

> Almost instantly, the other guns took it up, and in a split second the air was filled with the roaring guns. It was just like a prairie fire – the one gun provided the spark which kindled a roaring blaze.[60]

Searchlights came on all around the area. The lights, combined with the tracers from the machine guns, "formed an almost unbroken arc, with the apex in the sky."[61] Suddenly, six airplanes appeared. "The shower of steel going up was almost solid – even a bird couldn't have gotten thru."[62] Two of the planes went down in flames. It was learned later that these were American carrier based planes trying to land. Lombardi wrote later, "A shame – but it was hard to stop anyone from firing. The pitch was too great."[63]

The Japanese did not return for another attack.

***

In the aftermath, Lombardi and the other men tried to pull together the events of the day. During the first phase of the attack, Ens. Roman Leo ("Lee") Brooks had the deck of the *West Virginia*. He reported that he had seen an explosion on the *Oglala* across the way and believed her to be on fire. He called away the Fire and Rescue Party, but rapidly unfolding events established what was happening and he sounded General Quarters. The men with whom Lombardi spoke admitted that they did not know what was happening at this time. They believed it to be another drill until a strained voice over the loudspeaker announced, "This is real – it's an Air Raid – no _____."[64] It was then that the first torpedo hit. With the ship keeled over to port, they had difficulty getting out what little ammunition was available. The fourth torpedo hit just as the available ammunition was expended, and the call came to abandon ship. All communications and lighting circuits had been shot away.

In Lombardi's turret - #1 – the men stood fast, and only left their positions when the water started to rise in the Lower Handling Room. His division lost two men – Mann, Gunner's Mate and Burgess, Seaman second class. He never learned their fates. The two were seen leaving the turret when the ship was abandoned, but no one could account for them after that. "They may have decided to swim for it and had dived overboard, to be picked up by some ship going to sea. Hope so anyway – they were good boys."[65] They had not been accounted for when Lombardi was transferred to the Naval Air Station four days later. In spite of his best wishes for these "good boys," Seaman 1st Class Charles

W. Mann and Seaman 2nd Class John Edwin Burgess, Jr. would be listed among those killed in the December 7 attack.

Throughout all of the other events of the day, Lombardi had been searching for his "room-mate and best buddy," Ens. Harold W. Sears, but he could find no one who knew what had become of him.[66] As it turned out, Sears had had quite an adventure of his own. He and Nicholas – one of the pilots – had left the ship early to go hunting in the hills behind Aiea. When the attack started, they ran out of the hills, down to the landing, and hopped into a launch, ending up on the *U.S.S. Phoenix* (CL-46). The *Phoenix* was a light cruiser that escaped damage during the Japanese attack. Shortly after noon, she headed out to sea. Ensign Sears asked the Commanding Officer of the *Phoenix* if he needed a turret officer, but he received a negative reply. When the ship passed near the *West Virginia*, Sears jumped over the side and was picked up by a passing motor boat, which he commandeered in order to make his way back to the *West Virginia*.

***

In his written after-action report, Lt. Claude V. Ricketts gave high praise to the officers and men of the *West Virginia* for their conduct and devotion to duty that day.

> The personnel that worked with me on the bridge I cannot commend too highly. They carried out every order promptly and enthusiastically, even when it meant danger to themselves. They did not attempt to abandon the bridge until ordered to do so. These personnel were: Lieut. (jg) F. H. White, Ensign V. Delano, Siewart, A. A., C. S. M., Leak L. N., CPHM, and Miller, Mack D., Matt, 2c. Two or three other men, signalmen, I believe, were also present. Lieut. (jg) F. H. White is to be especially commended for his great help, many suggestions and disregard of personal danger. Ensign Graham and Ensign Lombardi provided us a means of escape by passing us lines from the starboard crane and by directing the fire fighting on the after side of the mast structure.[67]

Ricketts commented also on the conduct of Captain Bennion.

> The Captain deserves the highest praise for his noble conduct to the last. Although in great pain he kept inquiring about the condition of the ships, whether or not we had any pumps running, etc. He was particularly concerned about the fires on board and the oil on the surface of the water. I assured him that everyone was doing everything possible to fight the fire and control the damage. He did not want to be moved and after the fire started kept insisting that we leave him and go below. For a short time after he was wounded it would have been possible to move him down, but his wound was so serious I knew he would be better off with as little handling as possible. Leak concurred with me in this opinion. However, when the fire broke out around the after part of the bridge structure I moved him regardless, because of the suffocating smoke and approaching fire.[68]

While praising the conduct of the officers and men, Ricketts did not attempt to glorify his own actions. The only criticism that he had of anyone's

17

performance he leveled at himself. In a thoughtful addendum to his report, he stated,

> Looking backwards I can see that I should have utilized more time between the first and second attack in attempting to get ammunition to all machine guns. It might have been possible to get some from the TENNESSEE for the after guns. Also I should have broken out marines with rifles and their ready ammunition. Such action might have helped repel the second attack.[69]

Lombardi, however, had nothing but praise for the conduct of Ricketts. Lombardi wrote: "Lt. Ricketts was a pillar of strength all day. He should get a D. S. C.[v] for his work – he certainly merits it, doing a marvelous job throughout the action."[70] Lieut. (jg) White's after-action letter to the Navy Department ended,

> Lt. C. V. Ricketts deserves the highest commendation for his exemplary inspiration and leadership. Had he not counter flooded, it is almost certain the West Virginia would have capsized as did the Oklahoma. His presence of mind, cool judgement and complete disregard of personal safety are an inspiration to all hands.[71]

Lombardi ended his after-action memoire of the attack on Pearl Harbor with the following:

> It will be a long time before one forgets the picture, hears the drone of a plane without looking for a bomb, or gets the smell of burning oil out of his nostrils. The courage of the men was outstanding and something to marvel at. They showed the stuff they were made of that day, and this country can well be proud of its youth. They met the test in this, their first baptism of fire, and to a man, they have everything it takes. Whoever said that American manhood was decadent should have been there that day to see those boys carry on. When the time comes to meet those yellow men on a man to man basis ------Lord help the Japs!!!!![72]

***

On the morning of 8 December, Porter and the men who spent the night in the recreation arena were mustered into work details. Porter was sent with a group of men to the grounded *Nevada*. The ship had lost power and calm thinking NCOs got their men back to the practical business of running ships. The work detail was sent aboard the *Nevada* to unload her refrigerators of a large supply of sides of beef that would spoil if not retrieved before the temperature rose. This task of removing the beef from the ship and transferring it to refrigerators ashore took the entire day.

The *West Virginia* had been wounded severely but, unlike her Captain, she would survive and return to the fight. Plans were set into action to repair the ship. A patch was placed over the damaged area of her hull, and the water was pumped out. She was refloated on 17 May 1942. As the repairs began, the ship came under close scrutiny, and it was confirmed that she had taken a total of seven torpedo hits. During the repairs, workers found the bodies of seventy

---

v "Distinguished Service Cross".

sailors who had been trapped below deck when the ship sank. Once temporary repairs were completed, the *West Virginia* sailed under her own steam to Puget Sound Navy Yard at Bremerton, Washington, where she would be rebuilt and modernized. She would emerge from this rebuilding to play a major role in the war in the Pacific. By the time her repairs were completed, over a thousand men – officers and crew – would join her at Bremerton to infuse new life into her. Among these were Thomas Lombardi and Robert Baumrucker.

CHAPTER 2
Baumrucker

Robert Owen Baumrucker was born 30 July 1909 in River Forest, Illinois. He attended Dartmouth College in Hanover, New Hampshire, graduating with the class of 1931 and with a Bachelor of Arts degree with a Major in English. By traditional criteria, he was not a stellar student. He was graduated three hundred ninety-one in a class of four hundred fifty-eight students. His academic record, however, was not an accurate reflection of his intellect or abilities. His experiences in the Navy, reflected in his diary, leave one with the image of a young man who was very intelligent, highly motivated, inquisitive, athletically fit, and always functioning at a high energy level. He possessed remarkable problem-solving abilities.

There was an unlikely episode during his freshman year at Dartmouth that gives a better glimpse into his resourcefulness than does his transcript. Baumrucker was an experienced skier. He combined his innate cleverness with his athletic prowess to become the winner of the world's first modern slalom ski event. This accomplishment was revisited in a February 1984 issue of *Ski* magazine and again in the Winter1996 issue of *Skiing Heritage*.[73],[74] Morten Lund wrote the former article about Baumrucker under the title, "Slalom Gets Its Start – While FIS and the British feuded about the rules, a wet-behind-the-ears Dartmouth undergrad won the world's first modern slalom." An excerpt from the article read:

> *New York artist Andy Warhol once said that 'Everyone will be famous for 15 minutes'. If that is so, then the quarter-hour of R. O. Baumrucker came on March 9, 1928. On that day, Baumrucker won what was the first slalom race in the world ever to be run under internationally accepted rules. The race was held at Dartmouth College in Hanover, N. H., a place on the far fringes of the world ski-racing scene, an improbable site for an historically significant ski competition. The reasons the race was held there were many but, first and foremost, it came about because of the presence of Dartmouth professor Charles A. Proctor.*
>
> *Father of (and sometimes confused with) Dartmouth's 1928 Olympic skier Charles N. Proctor, Professor Proctor directed the intercollegiate Winter Sports Union, the most influential body in Eastern U. S. racing, as well as inspiring much of Dartmouth's ski-racing program. On that March day in 1928, Professor Proctor set a series of poles on the northwest side of Balch Hill near the college and timed participants in the annual Dartmouth 'interclass' winter competition.*
>
> *R. O. "Bob" Baumrucker was a freshman who had some experience skiing but had never run a slalom. Nevertheless, determined to go out and do battle for the freshmen, he 'boned up' on the race in the classic collegiate way - by going to the library and studying the pictures (he couldn't read the German text) of the newly published Wunder Des Schneeshuhs. There, the first-ever rapid-sequence action ski pictures*

featured Hannes Schneider, famed director of Austria's Arlberg Ski School. Armed with his new knowledge, Baumrucker strapped on his $16 Northland skis and ran the course faster than any other eligible student. Proctor declared him the winner.

Now, this was an epochal event. It was the first instance in which time alone determined a slalom winner in the U. S. – all previous races had also counted style points. It was the first slalom race in the world run under rules approved by skiing's international ruling body, the Federation Internationale de Ski (FIS).

Robert Baumrucker's interest in skiing did not end there, nor did his need to study photographs. In just a few years, he would find himself studying photographs of a much different nature, and matching himself against the clock in the much deadlier contest of war.

Following graduation from Dartmouth, Baumrucker joined the Cleveland, Ohio offices of the advertising firm of McCann-Erikson, Inc. While there, he enlisted in the U. S. Navy Reserve on 1 April 1942, and awaited orders to be called to active duty. As an English Major in college, with a penchant for writing, he decided to record a wartime diary. He did this with full knowledge that it was against Navy regulations. His handwritten record was maintained in a commercially available *Perpetual Date Book*. The book was small, measuring six inches tall, three-and-a-half inches wide, and one inch thick. Its pages contained only the month and date with no year. After completing a notation for 31 December of a given year, the diarist returned to page 1 (January 1), drew a horizontal line under the first entry for that date, and began notes for a new year. Consequently, the first page has an initial entry that reads, "1942 - Starts July 23", to indicate the date he began making entries. The first entry read, "1942 - July 23 - Left River Forest for the West Coast - Mom and Dad saw me off at the station." Because of the perpetual organization of this diary, 1 January contains entries for 1942, 1943, 1944, and 1945. The small size of the journal lent itself to easy concealment, yet the perpetual format necessitated brief entries. There is no evidence that anyone was aware of Baumrucker's journal during the war, and no court martial proceedings were initiated for this cause. Each brief entry contained enough fact to serve as a reminder of a larger memory in future years. After the war, he sought permission from the Naval Historical Center to publish his journal, but he was cautioned to avoid referring to it as a diary. He transcribed his hand-written version into a typed copy, and gave it the rather intriguing title:

LIFE ON THE MISSISSIPPI, THE TENNESSEE AND THE WEST VIRGINIA being a diary of activities on these three battleships during World War II, reconstructed from notes held cryptic while at sea so as not to divulge information giving help and comfort to the enemy and including certain social events occasioned during brief periods on the beach by Fire Control Division Officer Robert O. Baumrucker, USNR, who made his way from junior lieutenant to junior commander despite encounters with some unsympathetic and even unfriendly senior officers at critical points in his career.[75]

The meaning behind the enigmatic title becomes clear as one examines the detailed contents of the diary in combination with a number of post-war documents. His first diary entry was made coincident with his orders to active duty:

22 July 1942 - "Completed 60 days of indoctrination at Tower Hall, Chicago, where we learned how to salute but not who, plus a full course of instruction on running lights at sea. Orders for San Francisco, with four days delay, to pick up transportation to USS Mississippi wherever she may be.[76]

***

The *U.S.S. Mississippi* (BB-41) was a *New Mexico*-class battleship. She was six hundred twenty-four feet long with a beam of ninety-seven feet five inches. She had a displacement of thirty-two thousand tons and a draft of thirty feet. Her speed was twenty-one knots. The ship was armored with twelve 14-inch guns, fourteen 5-inch guns, four 3-inch guns, and two 21-inch torpedo tubes. She carried a crew complement of one thousand eighty-one men. The *Mississippi* had been escorting convoys in the North Atlantic prior to the Japanese attack on Pearl Harbor on 7 December 1941. Two days after the attack, the *Mississippi* left Iceland for the Pacific Ocean and arrived in San Francisco on 22 January 1942.

The *Mississippi*'s journey from Iceland to San Francisco may have been less arduous than Baumrucker's journey from his home in River Forest, Illinois to meet up with the ship. He left his home on 23 July by train to Los Angeles, arriving there three days later. Baumrucker was a person with boundless energy. He knew how to live the "good life," and he enjoyed the company of people. Opportunities to travel - even to California - would be punctuated by side trips, often seeking out friends, or the pursuit of pure entertainment. After unsuccessful excursions to San Diego and Santa Ana in search of friends, he returned to Los Angeles and checked into the famous Ambassador Hotel.[vi] This magnificent hotel, with its art deco style, housed the famous Cocoanut Grove restaurant and nightclub that were frequented by numerous celebrities. The hotel had hosted the Academy Awards and, on a number of occasions, served as the venue for fund raising events during the war. The great hotels, restaurants, and nightclubs throughout California were very friendly to servicemen and women during the Second World War. The film industry was particularly generous to those in uniform. It was not unusual for actors, producers, directors, or studio administrators to buy drinks or meals for complete strangers in uniform. Their generosity often extended to inviting servicemen to visit studios or location shoots where movies were being made, giving the opportunity to meet many of the most prominent film stars of the day.

Baumrucker learned that the Officers' Club in Los Angeles maintained a dating service, and he was quick to take advantage of it. Not only did he enjoy the company of beautiful women, he liked being seen with beautiful women. He could not accept boredom or inactivity for very long, and he had a need to be around people constantly. These characteristics may not have been unique to Baumrucker. It is likely that many servicemen, knowing that time stateside was

---

vi The Ambassador Hotel would be the site of the assassination of U. S. Senator and Presidential hopeful Robert Kennedy by Sirhan Sirhan in 1968. The hotel would be demolished between late 2005 and early 2006.

short, felt the need to take in as much entertainment as possible. The atmosphere of cities like Los Angeles and San Francisco was electrifying, as the streets, hotels, restaurants, and nightclubs swelled with the infusion of so many young people in uniform all seeking the same things. In the minds of many was the unspoken possibility that they might not return from the war.

Thinking that he was about to enjoy his last few days before joining the *Mississippi*, Baumrucker filled those days - and nights - with multiple dates, running with friends, living off good food and drink in the finest restaurants, and sightseeing. On 29 July, he toured Walt Disney Studio where he previewed *Der Feuhrer's Face*, a cartoon starring Donald Duck. This was an anti-Nazi propaganda movie in which each of the Axis leaders was depicted as a member of an "oom pah" band. Hirihito was portrayed playing a sousaphone, with Goring on piccolo, Goebbels on trombone, and Mussolini on bass drum.[vii] Encounters with film stars and movie moguls were frequent occurrences in Los Angeles, and Baumrucker made note of their names in his journal. On 31 July, he returned to San Francisco, checked into the St. Francis Hotel, and, characteristically, ran into old friends – this time from Tower Hall. He reunited with Marshall Field, Bennie Moe, Bob Taft, and others.

Eager to get on with his trek to war, he reported in for duty on 1 August "as per my orders, but was told the Mississippi was about to shove off and there was not time to get aboard."[77] He was advised to "check in" in a week for possible transportation to the ship. Apparently, the ship had not been informed of the four days delay in his orders. Later that afternoon, he and a group of friends watched the battle line of ships that included the *Mississippi* going under the Golden Gate Bridge. Thus began a series of delays for him as he struggled to make it to his first ship assignment.

With at least a week's free time to kill, he returned to Los Angeles, thinking that there were more interesting things to do there than in San Francisco. As before, he checked into the Ambassador Hotel and quickly began lining up dates through the Dating Service and tracking down his numerous friends. After a morning of swimming at the hotel, he and friends, Heidtman and Blackman, did an afternoon tour of Columbia Studios where they met actors, Fred Astaire and Rita Hayworth, who were rehearsing "You Were Never Lovelier." This 1942 Columbia Pictures release was a musical comedy set in Buenos Aires and starred Fred Astaire, Rita Hayworth, Adolphe Menjou, and Xavier Cugat. It was an entertaining and elegantly made film that contained no wartime theme.

Growing impatient, he wrote to Commander Armstrong in San Francisco on 7 August. He informed Armstrong that he was available if Armstrong had transportation for him out to the *Mississippi*. Otherwise, he "was doing OK in LA."[78] Later that day, he amused himself with a tour of Columbia's Ranch Studio, where he encountered Randolph Scott "sitting alone in his Lincoln convertible during a break in filming."[79] Although still acting, Scott had tried to get a commission in the U.S. Marine Corps, but he was denied because of a prior back injury. He did, however, appear in a number of war movies including *To The Shores of Tripoli, Bombardier, Corvette K-225, Gung Ho!,* and *China Sky.* Baumrucker also had a long talk with actor, Glenn Ford, "but didn't know who

---

vii "Der Fuehrer's Face" was released on 1 January 1943 by Walt Disney Studios and distributed by RKO Radio Pictures. In 1943, the film won the Academy Award for best Animated Short Film and in 1994 members of the animation industry voted it one of the fifty greatest cartoons of all times.

he was."[80] Later that year, in December 1942, Ford interrupted his acting career to volunteer for duty in the U.S. Marine Corps Reserve, where he served as a photographic specialist with the rank of Sergeant.

The following evening, he took a "stag tour" of Hollywood with his friend, Blackman. On this outing, they discovered the *Beachcomber's* Restaurant, where they partook of at least one *double-zombie*, the famously potent cocktail, invented by Don Beach.[viii] It consisted of 1 part white rum, 1 part golden rum, 1 part dark rum, 1 part apricot brandy, 1 part pineapple juice, 1 part papaya juice, ¼ part 151-proof rum, and a dash of grenadine. The ingredients were mixed in a shaker with ice, poured into a glass, and topped with the high-proof rum.

On 10 August, his growing impatience caused him to telephone San Francisco to check on the status of things with regard to his transport to the *Mississippi*. A Chief Petty Officer told him to relax, that they would get in touch with him when they had transportation out to his ship. After three more days of fine food, fine alcohol, fine ladies, playing bridge, and relaxing with friends, he "finally cracked – this is no way to fight a war so I checked out of the hotel and took a train to San Francisco to investigate."[81] Making a personal appearance got him no better results than his previous phone calls. He was "told not to bother them, they'd get me to the ship in time,"[82] so he decided to go to Lake Tahoe where he checked into the Tahoe Tavern. At the Tavern, he met and befriended Carlos and Roberta Maas. These were good acquaintances. This new friendship was to produce numerous adventures and much entertainment during his shore time to come. Skiing and fishing were Baumrucker's two greatest leisure-time pleasures. While he would fish anywhere, anytime, for any kind of fish, he was particularly fond of trout fishing. The Maas' arranged for him to have an outing at Tahoe where he spent the day fishing for mackinaw trout. So passionate was he about fishing that he wrote articles for wildlife magazines on the subject. In subsequent articles, he supplemented his text with photographs taken of his fishing adventures at Lake Tahoe and in the Truckee River. Fishing and partying with the Maas' kept him entertained for a few days before he once again grew impatient with the Navy, and he took the train back to San Francisco where he was told once again to call back in yet another week. Knowing there was nothing more he could do, he connected with some friends from Tower Hall and hopped a bus headed to northern California, where they killed time touring redwood logging operations, the Noyo Fisheries, and anything else that caught his limitless fascination. Finally, on 26 August, while surfcasting with friends in Carmel, his long-awaited phone call came from San Francisco.[83]

He reported in on 29 August and was told that there would be a ship out to the *Mississippi* within days. Another delay but, at least, he was getting closer. He filled this short void with more sightseeing. Other ships coming into port

---

viii Ernest Raymond Beaumont Gantt, born 22 February 1907 became the 'founding father' of tiki restaurants and nightclubs. This led to his being known as "Don the Beachcomer". During WWII, he served in the U.S. Army where he operated officer rest-and-recreation (R&R) centers. His friend, Lt. Gen. Jimmy Doolittle, ordered him to open R&R centers for airmen of the 12th and 15th Air Forces in Capri, Nice, Cannes, the French Riviera, Venice, the Lido, and Sorrento. After the war, he moved to Hawaii to continue his business ventures. He died in Honolulu 7 June 1989.

were a constant fascination for him. The *U.S.S. Chester*[ix] had been out to sea when Pearl Harbor was bombed and she had already been in a number of engagements by the time Baumrucker visited her. She had taken a hit from a bomb during one of her campaigns. He visited the *S.S. Coolidge*, a luxury ship that had been converted into a troop transport vessel that could carry five thousand men. As he toured the *Coolidge*, he could not have known that this would be the last time she would see port in San Francisco.[x]

Baumrucker reported aboard the *S.S. Antigua* on 3 September 1942 and was assigned a cabin with Bob Boylan. An unexpected luxury, the *Antigua* was a chartered cruise boat "with elaborate menus and four to a table at meals."[84] He spent his last night ashore with Boylan, enjoying "a Lou Gehrig movie with Gary Cooper."[75] In *Pride of the Yankees*, released in March 1942, Cooper played the role of baseball great, Lou Gehrig, who died of a neurological disease known as amyotrophic lateral sclerosis (ALS). The next day, they were en route to Hawaii, passing under the Golden Gate Bridge at 1220 hours. The *Antigua* was in a convoy of five ships and two destroyers. There was some training along the journey. On 5 September, the gun crew underwent firing practice – "not very reassuring."[86] Ever the fisherman, he borrowed a spinner and line from the crew and trailed it over the stern. The next day, the destroyer escort "goes over the horizon on a 'submarine' contact."[87] Leisure time on the *Antigua* was particularly relaxing because a layer of frustration had been lifted from him – he knew he was getting closer to the *Missisippi*. With no duties to perform, he spent his day sunbathing on a hatch cover and got into some poker games in the evening. The following day brought more firing practice and "the other [destroyer] goes over the horizon. Do they know something we don't?"[88] With no other indications of impending danger, he pursued more sunbathing and games with the crew – "as if we were paying tourists."[89] Baumrucker and Boylan dubbed the mate who woke them each morning, "Sunshine," because of his habit of awakening them by singing, "You Are My Sunshine."

Both of the destroyers had gone over the horizon on 9 September and, on the evening of the eleventh, Baumrucker noted "lengthy blinker messages from [the destroyers] far into dusk."[90] His imagination must have gone into overdrive as he watched these frenetic visual communications between destroyers on a submarine hunt. Fortunately, no harm, or even further alarm, resulted from this activity.

---

ix The *U.S.S. Chester* (CA-27) was a heavy cruiser that supported the reinforcement landing on Samoa in January 1942 and took part in the raid on Taroa in February 1942. Retiring under heavy air attack, she was struck by a bomb and returned to Pearl Harbor for repairs. Subsequently, she took part in the Guadalcanal-Tulagi raid in the Battle of the Coral Sea in May 1942. After an overhaul in September 1942, she returned to the south Pacific to take part in the operations in the Solomons where she was struck amidships by a torpedo but made it to Espiritu Santo for repairs. Based on the history of the *Chester*, it is likely that Baumrucker saw her in port for her general overhaul and not for specific repair of bomb damage. The *Chester* continued to serve throughout the war, including the bombardment of Okinawa. She was scrapped after the war.

x In October 1942, while entering the harbor at Espiritu Santo, she struck two friendly mines and sank. The Captain was one of only two men lost. Five thousand three hundred forty men got off the ship safely. The ship remains on the bottom of the harbor lying on her port side.

CHAPTER 3
The "Missi"[xi]

"The 'Missi' in a blow." The battleship U. S. S. Mississippi was Lt. Baumrucker's first ship assignment. She and the friends he made aboard her would always hold a special place in his heart. The "Missi" had been on convoy patrol in the Atlantic prior to the bombing of Pearl Harbor. Two days after the attack, she left Iceland to join the war in the Pacific. This photograph was taken of her during that voyage and sent to Baumrucker by a former shipmate after he had been transferred to the U. S. S. Tennessee. He received this photograph in a mail delivery of 23 June 1943. [Photograph taken from Baumrucker's album.]

On 12 September 1942, en route to Hawaii, the *Antigua* raised Koko Head at dawn. Baumrucker's frustrating journey continued as he discovered that the *U.S.S. Mississippi* was not in port. However, accustomed to filling time, he reported in to the District Office, and then paid a visit to Marshall Field who was aboard the *U.S.S. Enterprise* (CV-6). The *Enterprise* was an aircraft carrier that already had had a busy year by the time Baumrucker visited her. She had been involved in the campaigns of the Gilbert and Marshall Islands, and Wake Island in February, Midway in June, the Guadalcanal landings in August, and the Eastern Solomons in late August. She would take part in the battle of Santa Cruz in October, and the Naval Battle of Guadalcanal in November 1942. By the end of the war, the *Enterprise* would have been involved in every major campaign in the Pacific but two, and she would become the most highly

---

xi The "Missi" was the affectionate name given to the *U.S.S. Mississippi* by those who served aboard her.

decorated ship of World War II - but, today, she was simply the temporary floating home for Marshall Field. A few hours' visit with Marshall, and he was on his own again. Never having difficulty finding diversion, he wound up at the famous Moana Hotel. After the bombing of Pearl Harbor, the Moana – known as "The First Lady of Waikiki" – became a site for R&R for soldiers, sailors, and Marines. Full of men and women in uniform, she was a perfect venue for partying when on liberty. By the Moana's own history, she became "the last stop on American soil for those headed to war – not knowing if they will come back – and it's the first stop on American soil on their way back." That he spent the night sleeping in one of the Moana's bathtubs,[91] speaks to his success in locating a suitable party. The next day, he decided to move into the comparative comfort of the Bachelor Officers' Quarters.

On the fourteenth of September, Baumrucker's long trek to meet up with the *Mississippi* came to a successful end. The "*Missi* came in and we boarded her at dusk - me saluting a duty belt, as taught at Tower Hall, but it turned out to be a messenger instead of the Officer of the Deck."[92] Lesson one, learned. He would adapt quickly, and learn the details of the many duties required of an officer on a ship at sea, and at war. He was very comfortable at sea. Favorite past times in his youth had prepared him for this level of ease on open water. Whether fishing on a lake from a rowboat, or sailing in the Caribbean, he loved the water. And, where there was water, he would fish. Settling in aboard ship, he wrote, "This took 54 days since I had my orders. Lots of mail waiting."[93] The next day, they got "underway on the Missi at last, but just across the harbor to dry dock for a general check up."[94] Baumrucker noted that this was the same day that the *U.S.S. Wasp* (CV-7) "got it in the Solomons."[95] The aircraft carrier, *Wasp*, was part of the escort for transports delivering Marines to reinforce Guadalcanal. She was torpedoed by a Japanese submarine and sank.

Something of an unusual nature surrounding the *Mississippi* was unfolding in the international press. Baumrucker, sitting aboard the *Mississippi*, clipped newspaper articles containing German claims of the sinking of the *Mississippi* by torpedoes off the coast of Africa.[96] Newspapers around the world carried the false German claim. Except that one would be dealing with the loss of human lives, these reports were something of a comedy-of-errors on the part of Adolf Hitler and the Italian government. As reported by one newspaper:

U.S. Battleship Sunk, Says Axis
Washington Silent on Italian Claim
Berlin, Oct. 6 (German Broadcast Recorded
By United Press in New York.)
An Italian military communiqué issued in Rome said today Italian naval forces had sunk the United States battleship Mississippi off Freetown, South Africa. The battleship was sunk by an Italian submarine, the communiqué said... There was no confirmation of the Italian claim from any American or Allied source. The U.S. Navy Department declined to comment.
In a special communiqué Rome Radio added that the *Mississippi* was hit by four torpedoes from the large, ocean-going *Barbarigo* which also had been credited months ago with sinking a battleship of the 32,000-ton *Maryland* type. (That sinking likewise was never confirmed by Allied Authorities.)

The *Barbarigo* attacked the Mississippi 630 miles off the Africa coast, the first communiqué said. In supplementary communiqués the position of the sinking was moved closer to the African shore - to about 300 miles off Freetown - and the ship was designated only as "of the Mississippi type."

They added that the vessel was hit all four times in the bow.[97]

A newspaper report from London, dated 30 October 1942, served to clarify the Italian claims. It disputed Ensio Grossi's claim to have sunk a battleship of the Maryland-Mississippi class. Grossi had actually sunk a merchantman when he claimed to have sunk the battleship. Grossi was honored by Adolf Hitler and Benito Mussolini for the "sinking." Informed sources also said Grossi missed the British corvette *Petunia* with four torpedoes October 5 when he claimed the sinking of another Maryland-Mississippi class battleship. Chancellor Adolf Hitler had awarded Grossi the Knight's Cross with the insignia of the Iron Cross, 7 October 1942, and the Italian Navy had awarded him the *Medaglia d'oro al valor militare*.[xii] One can only speculate what humor these reports evoked among the officers standing on the decks of the *Mississippi* in Pearl Harbor.

It was at Pearl Harbor that Baumrucker received his first assignment. He was assigned to the gunnery department, "F" Division, main battery fire control, 1st section. While the *Mississippi* was still in dry dock, he spent his days alternately between standing routine deck watches and taking brief liberty ashore. On 21 September, he was standing anti-aircraft watch in Sky Forward, the highest forward position on the ship for visual observation, when he noticed the arrival at Pearl of the *Saratoga*, the *South Dakota*, and the *New Orleans*. The aircraft carrier, *Saratoga* (CV-3), had been struck by a torpedo from a Japanese submarine while patrolling east of the Solomons. After temporary repairs were made, she sailed to Pearl Harbor for permanent repairs. The battleship, *U.S.S. South Dakota* (BB-57), had been en route to Tonga when she struck an uncharted coral pinnacle, suffering significant damage to her hull. She was also sailing into Pearl for repairs. Baumrucker's journal notation of spotting the *New Orleans* coming into the harbor appears to have been a case of mistaken identity.

Baumrucker did not use all of his liberty time to go ashore. With his new duty assignment in the gunnery department, he used liberty time to familiarize himself with the components of his new responsibilities. He spent time with drills in the plotting room, and struggled for some days to learn how to use the [analog] computer there, before he learned that there was actually a manual to assist him. One liberty day was spent checking every optical instrument on the ship. By all rights, he could have been ashore relaxing with his friends, but his drive to learn his assigned duty - to be prepared - overrode the desire for fun. This characteristic drive to excel in the performance of his duties resulted from a blend of his innate curiosity about how things work and his awareness that

---

xii After the war, it was declared that Grossi was not entitled to the decoration once it was learned he had fired in vain at the British corvette, *Petunia*. The *Barbarigo* was a *Marcello*-class submarine in the Italian navy. In 1943, it was converted into a transport to carry materiel between Germany and Japan, but it disappeared while on her first such mission. The date was estimated to be sometime after 16 June 1943. The Brazilian-born Enzo Grossi died in Argentina 11 August 1960.

the life of his ship could depend on how well he executed his duties, especially in Fire Control. He would be ready. Eager himself to get to sea, his eyes were often trained out to sea, taking note of battle-experienced ships returning to Pearl Harbor. Lacking naval combat experience, he kept track of the U.S. warships that were sunk or damaged in the Pacific Theater. Visual assessments of the wounded ships that returned to Pearl Harbor for repairs were but a small taste of his war to come.

The first of October, the *"Missi"* got underway for firing practice. Anti-aircraft practice consisted of firing at sleeves towed by airplanes or firing at drone planes. They drilled at General Quarters and fired the big guns of the main and secondary batteries. Bombardment practice was directed at Kahoolawe, the smallest of the eight main Hawaiian Islands. This island was taken over by the military after the bombing of Pearl Harbor, and was used for training exercises that included ship-to-shore firing, and the testing of torpedoes. Standing anti-aircraft watch in the ship's 'Sky Forward' proved largely unpleasant for Baumrucker. While he had a marvelous panoramic view from there, he was "in miserable stack gas" for hours at a time.[98] The early days of October emphasized the need for on-going training. On the 9th, Baumrucker recorded, "The 5" battery fired too steep, and an eight inch piece of shrapnel landed at my feet."[99] While humorous on a superficial level, it is obvious that being struck by a piece of metal that size could be seriously injurious, if not fatal. Thus, the need for further drilling. Eyes out to sea, he noticed "flares and flashes over the horizon that night."[100] While the source of these was not known, they could have conjured visions of naval combat far out to sea, or they could have been the result of other ships conducting night training exercises. From his vantage point, he had no way of knowing. On 10 October, the *Enterprise*, with Baumrucker's friend, Fields, aboard, headed southwest over the horizon. This was the same day that the *Mississippi's* spotting plane crashed. This mishap brought death closer to Baumrucker's world, and the non-combat crash illustrated how mere preparations for war could be fatal.

On the twelfth of October, Baumrucker was headed to the Officers' Club for some liberty time when he stopped to examine the *U.S.S. West Virginia* that was still undergoing temporary repairs. He noted that she was "still badly beat up."[101] As he surveyed the damage, he had no way of knowing that his destiny would be tied to that noble vessel. He finished out the month with more routine deck watch duties, firing practices off shore, and brief trips ashore on liberty. A level of routine had definitely been established. He continued to take a keen interest in the exploits and fates of any and all American vessels in the Pacific. He made note that the *U.S.S. Hornet* (CV-8) and the *U.S.S. Porter* (DD-356) had been sunk. The aircraft carrier, *Hornet*, had seen action in the battle of Midway and in the Solomon Islands. While participating in the Battle of Santa Cruz Islands, she took bomb and aerial torpedo hits that resulted in her destruction. After American ships tried unsuccessfully to scuttle her, Japanese destroyers finished the job with four torpedoes. The destroyer, *Porter*, was torpedoed during the Guadalcanal campaign. Early reports attributed this to a Japanese submarine but, subsequently, it was believed that the torpedo that struck her had come from a friendly American torpedo plane. Fatally wounded, she was sunk by another American destroyer, the *U.S.S. Shaw* (DD-373).

November 1942 started the same way that October had ended – routine duties. His diary entry for 9 November contained the mysterious entry, "Had some kind of talk with the exec but don't remember what it was. When does the war start?" [76]The tone of the comment suggests that Baumrucker had some untoward interaction with the Executive Officer of the ship. It is very unlikely that he would not remember the nature of that interaction. The Executive Officer was the second highest-ranking officer on the ship. It is more probable that he omitted from his diary the nature of the exchange so that, if his diary were discovered, it would not contain anything suggesting insubordination to a superior officer. This journal entry was the first suggestive evidence of Baumrucker having problems with superiors. If he thought the war starting would end such conflicts, he was mistaken.

From combat experience, the Navy had learned that the paint it used on its ships constituted a fire hazard, and, consequently, the crew was set to work chipping it away - "miserable duty. Incessant hammering, day and night."[103] On 12 November, he recorded, "San Francisco and Buchanan damaged by Jap air off Guadalcanal." The *U.S.S. San Francisco* (CA-38) was a heavy cruiser that was in action during the naval battle of Guadalcanal when a Japanese aerial torpedo missed her, but the plane that dropped the torpedo crashed into the aft of the ship, swung around her, and fell into the ocean. The *San Francisco* made her way to Espiritu Santo for initial repairs. During the opening phases of the naval battle of Guadalcanal, the *San Francisco* accidentally targeted the light cruiser, *U.S.S. Atlanta* (CL-51), and opened fire. Her gunfire caused extensive damage to the *Atlanta* and killed Admiral Scott, along with most of the crew of the bridge. The *Atlanta* had been hit by an estimated nineteen 8-inch shells before the *San Francisco* realized her mistake and ceased firing on her. Mortally wounded, the *Atlanta* was sunk by a demolition charge.

While still at Pearl Harbor, there was sufficient free time for Baumrucker to finish writing a manuscript titled, "Fair Weather Fishing."[xiii] This would be the second article of his to be published in *The Southern Sportsman*. It was a light-hearted account of his journey from River Forest, Illinois to meet up with the *Missisippi*. He began the article,

> This has been written in short snatches, some of it hundreds of feet in the air, as my battleship drives on through the sea and coveys of flying fish skim out of the way and finally flip down behind a wave crest.....And now as I revise it in port, the chipping hammers[xiv] are going like crazy, yard workmen are swarming over us for repairs, and my perspective is such that I wonder if its apparently trivial content will interest you who are free to go fishing more or less whenever you want.[104]

His text was populated with a number of photographs of his fishing adventures during his trek to California to meet his ship. His facetious ending claimed,

> ......the only fish I've seen have been long silver ones,[xv] streaking at me under a row of bubbles, straight as an arrow. There have been bigger, black ones,[xvi] too, that I don't see because I'm at battle stations down at

---

xiii A copy of this article is included in an Appendix.
xiv This is reference to the hammers that are chipping the paint from the ship's surfaces.
xv Reference to torpedoes.
xvi Reference to Japanese submarines.

the controls. But know they're there. Have you ever felt a depth charge rock a ship?

Such articles are testimonial to his love of fishing, his penchant for writing, and his need to have his time filled with activity.

On his return from a swim at Waikiki on 15 November, a Navy Yard air alert was sounded. All ships went to General Quarters, shorelines were removed, and "we stayed up until 7 AM waiting for an air raid to materialize. Guadalcanal jitters?"[105] A couple of days later, he returned from a trip around Ford Island to learn that he and a number of other officers, "had completed their training period, evidently,"[106] and were ordered to the *U.S.S. Tennessee*, "just as it looked like we might be getting into a war."[107] Instead of war, it was to be off to Bremerton.

During the attack on Pearl Harbor, two bombs struck the *Tennessee*. They damaged two of her four gun turrets and she suffered further damage from the oil that was burning from the sunken *Arizona*. Following temporary repairs at Pearl Harbor, she sailed to Puget Sound Navy Yard at Bremerton, Washington for further restoration. After about six months of cruising the west coast of the U.S. and a brief stay at Pearl Harbor, she returned to Bremerton for more

Lt. Robert Owen Baumrucker aboard the transpot, S. S. Antigua. At the time of this photograph, he was en route from the U. S. S. Mississippi to his new assignment with the U. S. S. Tennessee. [Photograph taken from Baumrucker's album.]

extensive modernization. Baumrucker was under orders to join the *Tennessee* in Bremerton.

The *"Missi"* was his first ship assignment. His detachment from her must have been accompanied by great disappointment – an emotion that was not expressed in his journal. Certainly, he must have believed all along that his assignment to the *Mississippi*, with all the subsequent training, would lead to his being deployed south to the war with this vessel, and with the men with whom he had been training. The *Mississippi*, along with the friends he made aboard her, always occupied a special place in his heart. In the months and years to come, he never missed an opportunity to visit her when she was nearby, and enjoy a reunion with his former shipmates, but the war needed him elsewhere.

On 29 November 1942, "Detached from the Mississippi. A few for the road at the Officers' Club, then a wild ride into Honolulu with a couple of drunken Kanaka taxi drivers called Freddy and Charley. Checked in at the Moana, but no sleep because of a wild storm."[108] The next day, he reported back aboard the transport *Antigua* with "Sunshine Gus". "Underway and seasick, of all things, in a bad roll."[109] He became aware of the sinking of the *U.S.S. Northampton* (CA-26), a heavy cruiser that took two torpedoes to her port side and sank during the Battle of Tassafaronga. This ship would play a prominent role in Herman Wouk's novel, *War and Remembrance*. Following the war, Baumrucker found cause to correspond with Wouk regarding the historical details in one of his novels.

CHAPTER 4
The *Tennessee*

December 1942, while en route to San Francisco, "Everyone still a little green, but we got a little sun on the familiar hatch. Ira Wolfert showed up, beating his gums about Guadalcanal."[110] Wolfert was a war correspondent that would be awarded the Pulitzer Prize in 1943 for his reporting of the Battle of Guadalcanal. For reasons that are not clear, Wolfert got under Baumrucker's skin on a regular basis, but, on many other occasions, Baumrucker seemed to enjoy his company. It is likely that Baumrucker was drawn to Wolfert because of his gregarious personality, but his loquacious boasting could have been hard to long endure. From some unidentified source, Baumrucker got the impression that Wolfert's accounts of Guadalcanal were suspect. In his diary, he recorded, "....it was discovered [Wolfert] had been far behind the lines with his head between his knees and wrote his first person stories from interviews with others."[111] Diary entries over the ensuing days contained the lines, "Wolfert's bull sessions pretty fascinating, nevertheless,"[112] "bull sessions continuing,"[77] and "Wolfert still talking."[78] It is quite possible that Baumrucker was dealing with, and suppressing, some envy that Wolfert had experienced combat, while he had not.

Lt. Baumrucker at liberty spending an evening with Bobbie Lee, his most frequent companion when ashore in San Francisco and Los Angeles. [Photograph from Baumrucker's album.]

The *Antigua* had docked in San Francisco by noon on 6 December. Baumrucker checked into the Maurice Hotel, made phone calls, arranged dates with familiar women, and began to enjoy the nightlife again. As usual, he crammed as much activity as he could into the few days available to him. He got to see "You Were Never Lovelier", starring Fred Astaire and Rita Hayworth, the film he had seen in production back in early August. He saw Bobbie Lee, a beautiful and frequent companion when he was in San Francisco, and he ran into Roberta Maas from Lake Tahoe. Baumrucker never seemed to be alone. On the rare occasions that he was absent company, he sought out and found it. His journey to meet up with the *Tennessee* was launched on 10 December as he caught the 5:00 p.m. train to Seattle. The train ran very late, forcing him to check in to Bremerton by phone, and spend the night in Seattle. When he logged aboard the *Tennessee* on 12 December, she was still in dry dock undergoing her modernization. He moved into the Bachelor Officers' Quarters and "had a few" at the Officers' Club with new shipmates.[115] He met the Captain and the Executive Officer the following day, and was assigned to "F" Division again, this time under Bill Hasler. "Looks like I'll get plotting room duty on the main battery computer."[116] The MK8 Rangekeeper was an electromechanical analog computer that was responsible for tracking a target, predicting the position of the moving target, and correcting gunfire to hit it.

The ship was the site of frenetic activity as its skeleton swarmed with yard workmen, and was filled with sounds of the howling of blowers, riveting, and construction noises of every nature. Given his geographic location, and the sense that he would be in the area for some time while the ship was being repaired, Baumrucker sent home for his ski clothes. While away from his own family, he was able to enjoy some family life ashore in Seattle, including the Christmas holiday, with the Nickum family. He devoted a great deal of time to studying the rangefinder setup for the *Tennessee*, and he began a handbook on the ship's optics. He had caught "the collateral duty of Optical Officer as well as the officer for the soda-fountain-to-be."[117] Dating in Seattle took on a different flair as he encountered women who shared his love of skiing. His first ski date was with a woman named Mary, and it consisted of a ski weekend. He spent the weekend in her home and was entertained by her family as they all got acquainted. Baumrucker's friend, Luke, was paired with a date named Lynn. As it turned out, Baumrucker and Lynn knew each other from skiing at Sun Valley.

When he returned to Bremerton, following his ski weekend, he "caught a Security Watch on the empty hull."[118] Life at this time at Bremerton was largely stress free, as he carried out his routine duties, studied diagrams on target designating systems, and continued to socialize with a number of women in Seattle. Baumrucker told his diary that all of his dates were not "successful," but, while enjoying the company of a number of women, he continued to see Mary on a fairly frequent basis.

Among the more mundane assignments he had at Bremerton was barracks duty. He attended inspections of the barracks with the Captain at times, and made certain that life in the living quarters for the enlisted men was orderly. On 21 February 1943, he wrote,

More of that lousy barracks duty with super-numerary Trade School assistant gun boss. He thought a little newspaper boy needed to shape up and called him to attention and said, 'Do you know who I am?' When the boy - about 12 - said no, he said 'I'm Bruce Richardson Ware III', and the boy said 'No S _ _ _!'[119]

By referring to him as "supernumerary" and a "Trade School" officer, Baumrucker was showing his dislike for this officer and, perhaps, most Naval Academy graduates. It was not uncommon for friction to exist between the formally trained Naval Academy officers and the more practically, on-the-job-trained Reserve Officers. He would use the term "Trade School" frequently to refer to Academy graduates and always in a demeaning manner. He had another interaction with a superior officer on 23 March. This time, it was with the Captain, but as with the previous encounter with the Executive Officer, his diary entry remained vague about the nature of it. He "had a meeting with the captain and he forwarded a letter to the Bureau but I don't remember what it was about."[120] It seems highly unlikely that one would have a meeting with the Captain and not remember its nature. Because Baumrucker continued to be discrete in his diary about most of his meetings with superiors, one cannot assume that all of them were of a negative nature. The issue of promotion was on Baumrucker's professional horizon, and it may have been that this was the subject of his discussion with the Captain. On 8 April, he "had another spirited talk of some kind with the exec."[121] On 4 May, Baumrucker continued his course of discretion as he told his diary that he got "word from the exec from the captain over some matter I have forgotten - maybe that March 23 dispatch to the Bureau. The Exec had been filling his time nagging several reservists and I think I went to bat for us."[122]

Practical training, including firing practice, increased as the time to put to sea drew nearer. In mid-April, Baumrucker ran into Kippen, a former shipmate from the *Mississippi*. Kippen was in Bremerton for a change of duty. Through Kippen, Baumrucker was able to catch up on news of his friends aboard the *"Missi."* Kippen, however, was "very depressed because his wife left him for another guy."[123] Days later, he encountered Wilson and Hancock, friends from Tower Hall. They were serving aboard the *U.S.S. Chincoteague* (AVP-24), a seaplane tender. "They have been in Seattle ever since we left Tower Hall almost a year ago. Who hasn't?"[124]

With time in port getting shorter, a number of officers sought as many opportunities as they could find to get shore leave – usually to spend time with wives or girl friends. It was common practice to switch watches with fellow officers in order to get shore leave for special time - all to be reciprocated. On 6 May, Baumrucker "took an extra watch to accommodate a chap who wanted to get ashore to see his wife; even though these things never seem to get reciprocated I knew I'd like the same in a day or so."[125] Two days later, as the ship was about ready to get underway, he tried to shift duty with the "trade school boy" whose watch he had stood on 6 May, for a last date with Mary, "but the exec wouldn't permit it."[126] After the executive officer went ashore, "that coyote Ware suggested I now try to get permission from the Command Duty Officer, the head of the snipe department. But he said no. Mary had broken a date and was waiting."[127] A day later,

The Exec had heard (from where but Ware?) that I had tried to get ashore and we had another little talk - this time in front of a lot of enlisted men. He said he'd write the Bureau that I wasn't qualified for my promotion -

in fact, that I be knocked down. I apologized for any appearance of misfeasance, that it was very important that I got ashore and pointed out that there were several instances where Regular Navy Officers had done the same thing. Also, that I wished I had gotten to know him better by spending more time at the Officers' Club bar. He then sort of apologized, and said he wouldn't write the Bureau after all, since he remembered when he was young, too! At a time like this![128]

In the end, Baumrucker did not get ashore to see Mary on this occasion.

The ship got underway on 11 May 1943 for trials in Puget Sound with an escort of PT boats. Baumrucker busied himself with repeated rangefinder calibrations and drills. A couple of days later, they returned to Bremerton, but only four days later they were back in Puget Sound for the first firing of the ship's anti-aircraft guns. Underway in Juan de Fuca, the Main Battery plotting room drills continued as Baumrucker noted that the drills were "very rugged." The day seemed better when a mail delivery arrived. Mail from home was always essential to the happiness of the crew. As they headed for the open sea, they did the first Main Battery test fire. En route to Long Beach in late May, they had a "very fouled up comedy of errors in main battery firing: misfires, no buzzer signals, etc. Then we couldn't even track properly."[129] As they continued to drill en route, things began to improve steadily. They arrived at Long Beach on 31 May, but "only those with good alibis get ashore."[130]

CHAPTER 5
Alaska

On 1 June 1943, the *Tennessee* was at anchor in Long Beach. Baumrucker – and likely most of the officers and crew – had made the logical assumption that they would be deployed further south into the Pacific to join the war there, but such was not to be the case. "Great loads of foul-weather clothing start coming aboard, so we know we're not bound for the South Pacific!"[131] They got underway at 1730 hours en route to Adak in the Aleutians. On 3 June 1942, in bad weather with poor visibility, Japanese carrier-based bombers attacked Dutch Harbor on Unalaska Island. Perhaps due to the poor weather conditions, little damage was done. On 6 June and 7 June 1942, they invaded Kiska and Attu, respectively. The campaign to recapture these possessions began in May 1943. The *Tennessee* was being sent to take part in this effort.

Baumrucker's promotion papers to senior grade arrived and "the exec tells me I got away with something that was previously unheard of in the Navy. Where had he been?"[132] This final diary entry relating to his promotion may shed light on the nature of the previous conversations with the Captain and the Executive Officer. While the content of those interactions with his superiors may have slipped his mind before they made it into the diary, it is quite possible that the Executive Officer – who was in a position to influence the process – might have been holding the prospects of promotion over Baumrucker's head to manipulate him in some manner. Over the next couple of days, he underwent medical and dental examinations in support of his promotion. Subsequently, he was commissioned full lieutenant. Having cleared that hurdle, Baumrucker utilized the journey to Adak to continue his rangefinder calibrations, and to hold rangefinder examinations for his men along the way.

A week later, still en route to Adak, Baumrucker suspected, but could not confirm, a radar jamming. Problems with radar were not uncommon during this technological era. It was still a relatively new technology and given to interference from a number of external influences, including atmospheric phenomena, and it was not always a simple matter to distinguish a "real" pip on the screen from an artifact. Someone spotted suspected torpedo tracks coming toward the ship, and sent the ship to a fast General Quarters. Many of the men got trapped by Condition Zebra[xvii] before they made it to their battle stations. Hatches and passageways were locked to provide maximum watertight security to the ship. Men could be trapped in passageways on their way to battle stations, and would have to remain there until "Condition Zebra" was lifted and the passages were unlocked. False sightings of torpedo tracks were frequent

---

xvii "Condition Zebra" is one of three "Material Conditions of Readiness". "Condition XRAY" provides the least amount of protection and is set when the ship is in no danger of attack – e.g., when a ship is at anchor in a well-protected harbor. "Condition Yoke" provides a greater degree of safety and water integrity. Condition Yoke is set when at sea or when in port during wartime. "Condition Zebra" provides the highest degree of subdivision and watertight integrity to the ship. It is the maximum state of readiness for the ship's survivability. It is set immediately and automatically when General Quarters is sounded, but at other times, the Commanding Officer determines the material condition to be set.

events throughout the war but each suspected sighting had to be taken seriously. On 8 June, "Snuffy Smith in Spot I reports a large number of masts coming over the horizon and we start tracking. Tension is relieved when he starts identifying them, one by one, as friendlies joining up with us."[133] Uncertain radar signals, suspected torpedo tracks, unidentified surface vessels, and unidentified aircraft were all reasons to send the ship to General Quarters to be prepared for whatever unfolded. Unfortunately, frequent calls to General Quarters caused increased tensions among crews, and contributed to physical and emotional fatigue. Yet, it had to be done for the safety of the ship.

The *Tennessee* made a radar entrance into Adak in a dense fog. They were aware that there were many ships around them, but they could not see them visually. The infrequent use of radar for this maneuver carried with it a certain risk of collision, but on this occasion all went without incident. Baumrucker did not allow the fog to deny him the opportunity to fish over the side from the quarterdeck. From Adak, they began patrolling the Bering Sea to the north and west of the Aleutians, and they joined up with twenty-eight battleships, cruisers, and various other ships. What should have been routine cruising did have its moments. On 13 June, while steaming in column in a dense fog, the *Santa Fe* –a *Cleveland*-class light cruiser - reversed course and cut across the bow of the *Tennessee*, passing by about twenty-five feet abeam to starboard. "We wondered why."[134] While no explanations for this near incident were forthcoming, it did illustrate that moving ships about the ocean in fleets was fraught with hazards that were not imposed by the enemy. It was just the nature of service on a warship. Against that backdrop, Baumrucker had the soda fountain make up a batch of very dark chocolate ice cream. After all, he had been given the collateral duty of officer-in-charge of the soda fountain, and this was a good opportunity to exercise his authority in the role.

While still cruising in the Bering Sea on 14 June, Baumrucker reflected on an unexpected friendly gesture from Ware. In the service, it was not uncommon for an officer to keep the insignia of his previous rank after getting promoted. When a friend, or someone who was respected, got promoted to that previous rank, an officer would give him his old insignia as a gesture of friendship or respect. This was considered an honorable act. Baumrucker would never have expected to be the object of such a gesture from Ware but,

> For some reason Ware had given me his old shoulder boards when I made full lieutenant. I lost one of them from my khaki blouse this day. I also dropped my glasses on the deck of the director and smashed them to bits. Win some, lose some.[135]

The following day brought another near incident, as three *suspected* torpedo tracks were reported headed for the ship, and Condition Zebra was set, but there were no impacts. On the sixteenth, as a destroyer went over the horizon on a submarine contact, dropping depth charges, Baumrucker commented, "It would be too bad if they got us so soon after all the work done on us."[136] While on mid watch in Main Battery Plot the next day, he began reading *Berlin Diary*, the first hand account of the rise of the Third Reich, and its road to war, as witnessed by the American journalist, William L. Shirer, a radio reporter for CBS. The contents of this work provided much of the material for Shirer's landmark book, *The Rise and Fall of the Third Reich*. The same day, with no

J. N. "Woody" Woodall served aboard the U. S. S. Tennessee and proved himself a talented artist. This cartoon was one of Baumrucker's favorite because it captured the frenetic atmosphere in Main Battery Plot. Baumrucker is represented on the extreme right of this figure. [Photograph from Baumrucker's album.]

explanation offered by the diary, the *Tennessee* left the formation of most of the other ships. While still in the Bering Sea on 21 June, Baumrucker had another untoward interaction with a superior officer, and he shared it with fellow officer, Bill Hasler:

> Had a talk with Hasler regarding organization issues. A report of a surface contact had come in on the previous midwatch and I waked the crew in the director to train out so we could track it. The officer there, senior to me, had objected to taking 'orders' from me - but for practical reasons - Hasler agreed that this was necessary. The officer in Spot I was not qualified for the watch in Plot.[137]

Wisely, the identity of this officer was not revealed in the diary.

On return to Adak, the *Tennessee* anchored in the outer harbor, but inside submarine nets. Leaving the ship on official errands, Baumrucker caught sight of "our old friend *Antigua*." He went aboard her, and "had a snort with the mates."[138] Mail came aboard, and it was with both pleasure and pride that he received a picture of the *"Missi"* from a former shipmate. The photograph showed the *Mississippi* in a "heavy blow" en route from Greenland to the Pacific following the 7 December attack. Suspected enemy submarine contacts and torpedo tracks were becoming commonplace but, a couple of days at Adak, a particularly strange episode unfolded. A submarine contact was picked up *inside* the nets, and Condition Zebra was set, while destroyers depth-charged the waters. Later the same day, Baumrucker went ashore and picked up some scrap aluminum from a crashed plane. The depth charging was still going on when he returned. When the depth charging continued into the next day, with no visible results, he made the terse comment in his diary, "Must be fish."[139]

"Woody" Woodall was a capable sketch artist aboard ship. He made several drawings of life aboard ship that delighted Baumrucker. In particular, he enjoyed Woodall's sketch that captured the frenetic atmosphere within Main Battery Plot. It contained caricatures of Baumrucker and other identifiable officers. When he went ashore with some men from the division, he made arrangements to have photostatic copies made for his shipmates. While ashore on 28 June, he went with a small group of men out past the Japanese prisoner of war camp to a lake, where they fished off a raft and caught a few silver trout. A feeling of relative inactivity was catching up to him, and it became increasingly difficult to find different ways to fill his time with amusement or industry. Back aboard ship, he fell into a new pastime - late night poker - that resulted in a lot of lost sleep. Finally, near the end of June, his thoughts turned back to memories of life in Seattle.

July 1943 started in a routine and uneventful manner. On 9 July, they learned that their next operation was to be a landing on Kiska, and "all available time was spent on planning for it."[140] On the tenth, the ship was headed east back to port when, suddenly, all the ships reversed course and headed west at full power, with all lights below deck turned out in order to divert power to the engines. The next day, four enemy surface contacts were picked up west of Attu, and the fleet headed out to intercept them. They launched themselves into this potential encounter with a sense of excitement over engaging the enemy at sea for the first time. It came as a disappointment to Baumrucker that friendly planes had gotten to the targets before the ships could reach them, causing the American ships to reverse course back to port. "The dope wasn't clear as to just what happened, but we felt robbed of some easy main battery targets."[141] On a larger scale, what they did not realize fully was that they had just had a glimpse of the future of naval warfare, as air power was replacing the ancient practice of ships firing on ships. The significance of this would become clearer to them as they got deeper into their war. The *Tennessee* was the first ship to enter Dutch Harbor, escorted by a tug with a band playing on the deck. Life in Dutch Harbor was quiet, and Baumrucker turned his attention back to fishing. He soldered some single fishhooks together to make trebles, and went ashore to try them out. The Chief Fire Controlman from Plot accompanied him, and they watched others fishing in a canal, and made an unsuccessful attempt to catch some fish in a nearby river. They wandered up into the hills where they caught a "funny little rock rabbit" that they took back to the ship as a mascot for the division. But, before returning to the ship, Baumrucker reserved some fly fishing tackle at the recreational center for his next liberty. With so many men from the several ships going ashore to relieve their boredom by fishing, there was a shortage of gear to be found. Back aboard ship on 18 July, Baumrucker and his roommate, Mac, both tired, decided to go on a "new regime - less poker and more sleep."[142] Only one day later, however, "The new regime collapses; what else is there?"[143] Still trying to amuse himself during this quiet war, and pursue his love of fishing, he was one of a dozen men who took a whale boat about eight miles up the shore to fish. They arrived to find that the crew of the *Idaho* had gotten to the recreation center ahead of them, and, what tackle was left, was far too heavy for trout. The *U.S.S. Idaho* (BB-42) was one of the battleships that took part in the assault on Kiska. With "millions of salmon spawning in the bay," and the men from the *Idaho* - "and our exec" - "catching many trout in the stream,"[144] Baumrucker and friends returned to the ship with an urge for fishing that went unfulfilled that day. Back aboard, he wrote home to have his own fly-fishing tackle sent to him.

The ship got underway for Kiska on 23 July. This time of year, "It [was] daylight almost all night long - no darker than a foggy day all night."[145] Two days en route to Kiska, they "changed course to try to intercept another surface contact, but couldn't locate it. These radar 'pips' were either a Jap trick or an atmospheric phenomenon - not actual targets."[146] Although Baumrucker's diary does not mention it, there was another incident resulting from the ship's radar. Radar was still a fairly new technology that was often unreliable. A new Task Group was formed for the impending attack on Kiska that included the *U.S.S. Tennessee* and the *U.S.S. Idaho*. On 27 July 1943, while eighty miles west of Kiska, the ships began to pick up a series of unknown radar contacts ("pips"). The ships opened fire on the "contacts," firing a combined five hundred eighteen 14" shells. Unfortunately, there were no hits on enemy vessels, and Imperial Japanese Navy records revealed later that there were no Japanese ships within two hundred miles of the site. History later recorded this little known incident as "the battle of the pips."

Their patrolling off Kiska ended on the thirty-first, and they headed to the north side of the islands, and an approach to a preliminary bombardment of Kiska. The bombardment began on 2 August 1943. Baumrucker recorded, "A long day of preliminary bombardment at long range. No return fire nor sign of activity ashore."[147] After returning to Adak for more ammunition, he and Mac "decide on a new regime [of more sleep] for sure."[148] Three days later, he proclaimed, "Gross failure of new regime when Mac and I get into considerable trouble [at poker] with another Mac and it takes all night to get even."[149] By 9 August, there were increasing signs of the impending assault on Kiska, as he attended numerous meetings aboard ship with Aleutian scouts and with people from other ships. While on watch on the tenth, he witnessed two P-40 fighter planes crash overhead the *Tennessee* - two more non-combat fatalities. On that same watch, he also spent time looking at old friends on the *"Missi"* through the rangefinder. They got underway for Kiska, a tiny island twenty-two miles long and one and a half mile wide. The Japanese invasion of this island on 6 June 1942 had been a diversionary tactic as part of their plan for the Battle of Midway. Combined U.S. and Canadian forces planned to invade and retake Kiska on 15 August 1943. The invasion force consisted of nearly thirty-five thousand troops and ninety-five ships, including three battleships and a heavy cruiser. On the fifteenth, Baumrucker was up early for the bombardment. Following the shelling of Kiska, they were all surprised to hear of "the speedy advances of our troops - no opposition."[150] On the sixteenth, there were still no signs of Japanese resistance ashore. "There [were] rumors that a dog and warm fire site were found but the island has evidently been abandoned. Was that dog putting up all the flack the Army fly boys were reporting?"[151] It was determined later that, knowing the allied invasion force was approaching, the Japanese had removed their troops under cover of a dense fog without the allies noticing. Things fell quiet again. Two days later, Baumrucker sent their mascot - the "funny little rock rabbit" - ashore because the "noise of the bombardment was spoiling his disposition."[152] Baumrucker now busied himself in the Fire Control Workshop, making bracelets, pins, and spoons for his nephew out of the aluminum that he had taken from the crashed Japanese plane.

With the Kiska operation finally over, the *Tennessee* was headed south. On 24 August, the *Tennessee* got underway for the "lower 48 [states]."[153] They were under the Golden Gate Bridge on 31 August, and tied up to a pier near the Bay Bridge. Almost immediately, Baumrucker started placing phone calls to make dates ashore in San Francisco. While his diary is replete with the first names of the people with whom he socialized or dated, he offers very few last names and avoids too much detail about the individuals. Perhaps he thought he was omitting information that could be interpreted as providing "intelligence" to the enemy, should his diary be discovered, or perhaps his gentlemanly nature prevented him from recording intimate details of his dating life. He repeatedly demonstrated the ability to orchestrate dates with multiple women - often on a given night. Throughout this, his relationship with the Maas' appears to have been a genuine friendship that was enduring - at least for the span of the war. Whenever they encountered one another, the Maas' provided rich entertainment for Baumrucker. He connected with his friend, Bob Chambers, while in San Francisco on this shore leave. By 17 September, Baumrucker confided to his diary, "The Mary situation falling apart."[154] He never defined the "situation," but she had been a frequent companion of his while on the west coast. The next day, Mary visited him on the dock, and he arranged for Bob Chambers to take her out. He then "saw an unhappy Mary aboard the train to Oakland"[155] the next day, whereupon he phoned Alice.

With the *Tennessee* moving south to warmer climes, he shipped his ski gear back home to Illinois, and the fishing gear that he had requested while he was in the Aleutians arrived. After three weeks of alternating ship duties with liberty, he and the *Tennessee* got underway for Long Beach and firing practice at sea. Anchored at Long Beach, he went into town where he made connections with Bobbie, Alice, and Virginia. On 30 September, Baumrucker reported in his diary an incident that must have provided some measure of satisfaction. "Bruce Richardson Ware III falls off the catwalk returning drunk from liberty."[156] The last few days of September, and the early days of October, he spent a lot of time with Virginia, escorting her to such places as Ken Murray's Blackouts. These live variety shows were performed at the El Capitan Theatre on Vine Street in Hollywood. They also dined at the Hilton Roof and took in movies. The relationship with Virginia became somewhat stranger, the longer he saw her. On 5 October, after a day of firing practices off Catalina, he returned to Long Beach for a date with her.

> I couldn't find her at the apartment where she said she lived. [She] ran up to me a block away, we visited with some of her elderly 'friends' and there began to be some confusion among her various most interesting anecdotes.[157]

A couple days later, while taking her to Chinatown for dinner, her stories began to get even more confusing. Later that evening, he took her to the Ambassador Gardens and Casino, where he "got the redo that she [was] really Captain Musick's daughter."[158] This had to be quite a revelation for Baumrucker, who must have been familiar with Captain Musick's reputation. Musick was an early commercial pilot who worked for various airlines after World War I. He was renowned for opening up access to New Zealand with his bold and skillful long distance flights. He was on a flight out of Pago Pago on 11

January 1938, when he encountered mechanical problems, and his plane exploded in mid-air. He was regarded widely as the most famous pilot of his time, and now, Baumrucker was faced with the claim that he was dating Musick's daugher. In any event, he did not record any of his impressions upon hearing of this connection between Virginia and Captain Musick.

He was awakened early the next morning to get underway for the New Hebrides. En route to Hawaii, they drilled at General Quarters, and conducted anti-aircraft firing practice. Upon arriving at Pearl Harbor on 15 October, Baumrucker spotted Bob Boylan's new ship, the *Lexington*. The *U.S.S. Lexington* (CV-16) was an aircraft carrier that earned the nickname, "The Blue Ghost," because her hull was painted dark blue. She was the only aircraft carrier not to wear camouflage. He phoned his friend, Lowell Dillingham, and contacted a woman by the name of Alice Kelly, who had been recommended by a secretary in his former office. "She was having about six dates per night."[159] A reader of the diary is left wondering, "What constituted a 'date?'"

CHAPTER 6
Tarawa

Leaving Pearl Harbor, they got underway for the New Hebrides on 21 October 1943. There were numerous civilian correspondents aboard the *Tennessee* for this trip. The day after setting sail, Baumrucker learned that their next operation was to be Tarawa, in the Gilbert Islands. The invasion of Tarawa was to be the first U.S. offensive in the Central Pacific Theater. Tarawa was the eastern-most in a series of island conquests needed by the U.S. for the establishment of air bases from which attacks could be launched against the strongly defended Marshall and Marianas Islands. Baumrucker's "combat" experience to date had consisted only of shore bombardments of landmasses that turned out to be devoid of any enemy. He had no way of knowing the gravity of events that would unfold on Tarawa. With no apparent sense of trepidation over the impending campaign, he spent the next several days amusing himself by making a fishing tackle box and a fishing rod. He arranged his tackle box to hold trout flies, and puzzled to himself by writing, "Trout flies?"[160]

Gilbert Bundy was an International News Service artist who was aboard the *Tennessee* for the Tarawa campaign. He was a watercolor artist and illustrator who specialized in high society and glamour subjects, especially beautiful women. In addition to producing illustrations for advertisers, he published his images regularly in such magazines as *Judge, Life, Esquire,* and *The Saturday Evening Post.* He was married and had one daughter when he decided to leave what appeared to be a safe and comfortable life to volunteer to work as an artist in the South Pacific for Hearst newspapers. En route to Tarawa, Bundy used his art to capture the essence of life aboard a battleship. Baumrucker befriended Bundy and, after dinner on the evening of 25 October, he took him on a tour of a gun turret, and into Sky 2 to stand the watch as a concert was being broadcast to the gun mounts over the phones from the director. This was a strangely peaceful calm ahead of the storm that loomed over the horizon.

Also aboard the *Tennessee* for this mission to Tarawa was war correspondent Robert Sherrod. Sherrod had been the editor of the *Saturday Evening Post.* He had previously covered the campaign in the Aleutians, and was present for the invasion of Kiska. When the U.S. decided to open the Central Pacific campaigns, Sherrod was transferred to cover the story:

> The Central Pacific sounded more exciting than anything I had seen in the war against Japan. In the first place, it would give us a chance to exercise the naval might which I could see building up all around me - for Kiska we had 135 ships......The Central Pacific, which is at least ninety-five percent water, seemed an ideal place to use all this Navy.....And there would be no snow or fog in the Central Pacific. I was sick of Aleutians weather. I was tired of flying in airplanes which took off in a little hole in the fog, hoping to find another hole in the fog at the end of the journey, tired of groping my way through tundra-covered

mountains without being able to see more than thirty feet in any direction.[161]

Once the battle for Tarawa was over, Sherrod wrote a brilliant and moving narrative of the campaign that became a classic book on the subject. His narrative began, however, with the journey to Tarawa aboard what he called the *U.S.S. Blisterbutt* (pseudonym for the *U.S.S. Tennessee*).

On 26 and 27 October 1943, Baumrucker made two terse and disturbingly unemotional entries in his diary.

26 [October] - En route Efate. Munson crushed to death because he had been sleeping in the wrong place when the main battery was elevated. Pilot Chapman lost when his plane didn't catapult correctly. Further unhappiness from tetanus shots.[162]

It seems incomprehensible that he could refer to the tetanus shots as "further unhappiness" in the wake of the horrible deaths of two men: "27 [October] - En route Efate. Munson buried at sea."[163]

These were two more deaths within Baumrucker's awareness, but, as yet, not one was combat related. These deaths all served as notice that, when moving thousands of men around the globe in warships, even if a single shot in anger is never fired, men will die.

Sherrod was witness to the death of Pilot Chapman and the death of Munson. While Baumrucker's diary contained simple unemotional notations of these deaths, Sherrod's accounts were more detailed and moving:

The Blisterbutt hadn't had a fatal accident in fourteen years and she had had only four men killed by the two bomb hits she received at Pearl Habor. But one day on the way to Tarawa, via Base X,[xviii] her luck ran out. Two men were killed in unrelated accidents.

That she should have lost an officer and a man in one day's accidents was blamed by some superstitious sailors on the fact that a junior-grade lieutenant who had been on the ill-fated carrier Hornet lost his lucky dollar on that day which happened to be about one year after the sinking of the Hornet.

The ship's senior aviator, Lieutenant Harry P. Chapman, Jr., a quiet popular Virginian, was the first casualty. He stepped jauntily up the quarterdeck ladder, wearing his blue, long-billed flyer's cap. His little patrol plane, an OS₂U Kingfisher, was already being warmed up, for launching off the catapult on a routine patrol. The plane was trundled over the catapult. It was lifted onto the long catapult by a crane. Chapman climbed into the cockpit and started revving up the engine.

But the plane's underside had been insecurely fastened to the catapult slide. When the overhead cable was released, the little OS₂U started falling off the catapult toward the starboard side of the deck. I was standing only twenty feet in front of Chapman. I could see the look of horror in his eyes when he realized what was happening. He started to rise up out of his seat. Then he realized it would do no good to try to jump. He settled back, waiting for the crash.

---

xviii Writing in a time of war from the deck of a battleship, he was careful to avoid naming strategic locations.

"TWO HANDS could do the trick but they all grabbed the line and ran up the deck. That's mail coming aboard far out at sea."

Artist Gilbert Bundy was aboard the U. S. S. Tennessee as she sailed toward Tarawa. He used his art form to capture the essence of life aboard ship. This cartoon emphasizes how important mail from home was to the crew. Beside the copy of this cartoon in his photograph album, Baumrucker wrote, "We are en route to landings at Tarawa with a number of correspondents aboard. Gilbert Bundy, whose cartoons I had long enjoyed in The New Yorker, is seated next to me at mess and we become good friends." [Photograph from Baumrucker's album.]

Several sailors who were standing underneath tried bravely to hold the plane in position by main strength. They jumped out of the way just in time. Amid a rending of metal and glass the plane crashed back into the deck. The gunwales (side plates) which rose eight inches above the deck's perimeter, cut into the cockpit. The engine was knocked out of its frame. The plane toppled into the water.

As we pulled away from the floating wreckage - battleships do not stop in wartime - we could see one figure bob up. The rear-seat radioman was safe, but there was no sight of Lieutenant Chapman.

Within five minutes one of our destroyers was racing to the wreckage, where it put a boat over. The destroyer stayed at the scene for forty minutes. A diver went under the plane, cutting his arm severely on a piece of jagged aluminum. But nothing was ever seen again of Chapman.[164]

Sherrod offered a lengthier and even more moving account of the death of sailor Munson:

A young sailor named Kenneth Munson unaccountably had chosen to sleep under the loading platform of a main turret gun. When in the darkness of early morning, the big gun was elevated, the platform crushed the seaman under the weight of its eighty tons. It was a wonder that any spark of life remained in him. I saw him in the sick bay an hour before he died, when medical corpsmen were feeding him oxygen to keep him alive. He cracked a joke, and there was a flicker of a sad smile on the faces of the three men about him.

Above all other things, Seaman Munson told the chaplain, he wanted to live. But he never had a chance. The doctor's report read: crushed pelvis, urethra, one lung punctured, belly wall punctured and intestines and liver forced up through the hole in the lung, skull fractured, brain probably full of hemorrhages. He was not in pain; the great physical shock of his mangling had mercifully put young Munson beyond pain.

Before he died the seaman, who had allowed himself to be listed on the ship's roll as a Protestant, revealed that he had been baptized and reared a Catholic. Through the Catholic chaplain, who told him that his time to die had come, the seaman made his peace with his God. He died at eight o'clock that night.

Quite a few days would elapse before the Blisterbutt reached port, so it was not feasible to hold the body for burial on land. Neither was there any reason for night burial - sometimes when casualties are heavy burial-at-sea ceremonies are held quietly and with brief prayers at night, lest the morale of the crew be disrupted by the sight of many shipmates going over the side for the last time. Preparations were made to bury the sailor at sea next morning at ten o'clock.

The body was clothed in the uniform of the day; blue dungarees. It was weighted by two five-inch shells (approximately one hundred pounds). It was sewed in canvas by the sail-maker, but the ancient custom of taking the last stitch through the nose of the deceased was omitted. Nor were coins placed in his mouth, as custom dictated when sailors believed it was necessary to pay the boatman Charon for the body's passage across the river Styx.

The ceremony was brief, since we were sailing through submarine-infested waters, but it was impressive. Some time before ten o'clock on the day of the funeral two wooden carpenter's horses were placed on the starboard side of the quarterdeck. A detachment of armed Marines, distinguished from the sailors in blue by their khaki uniforms, stood at attention next to the horses. The ship's band stood aft of the Marines, their backs to the sea. Still further aft, about seventy-five officers faced forward. The most spectacular sight was the thousand or more dungaree-clad sailors who swarmed over the turret armor and out to the very ends of the big guns of the battleship, over the air-defense stations, the anti-aircraft turrets and guns, and the superstructure. It is doubtful if a dozen men on board had ever before seen a burial at sea. Everyone was there except those whose duty at that moment was to keep the ship running and the guns manned.

At 0940 the chaplain went below to the sick bay to bless the body, in the presence of the pallbearers, who were selected from the gunnery

"WITH THE TAR bubbling between the planks and the tropic sun beating the color and life out of everything, the cool foam seemed to welcome the boy."

Seaman Munson had a habit of sleeping in a main battery turret. One morning, the guns were elevated unexpectedly crushing Munson under their weight. He died fifteen hours later. Gilbert Bundy captured the burial at sea service with this cartoon. [Photograph from Baumrucker's album.]

division of young Munson, who would never fire his big gun at Tarawa. The blessing was the 129th Psalm, which begins:

Out of the depths have I cried unto Thee, O Lord;
Lord, hear my voice.
and ends:
Eternal rest grant unto him, O Lord.
And let perpetual light shine upon him.

The pallbearers carried the body aft, the stocky chaplain, Lieutenant Charles Covert, walking beside it, praying, 'Come to his assistance, ye Saints of God! Meet him, ye Angels of the Lord. Receive his soul, and present it to the Most High. Eternal rest grant unto him, O Lord!, and let perpetual light shine upon him.' When the pallbearers reached the portside aft they had considerable difficulty lifting the body up the narrow ladder through the hatch, up to the quarterdeck. The band was softly playing Nearer My God, to Thee. The body, covered by a large flag of the United States, was carried by the pallbearers across the quarterdeck and placed on the two wooden horses.

Now the service proper began. The hundreds of grave-faced men uncovered as Chaplain Covert, wearing a black cassock and white-lace surplice and black stole over his khaki officer's uniform, stood beside the body and prayed, almost inaudibly, for perhaps ten minutes, 'Enter not into judgment with Thy servant, O Lord; for in Thy sight shall no man be justified, unless through Thee he find pardon for all his sins...Lord, have mercy on us...Christ, have mercy on us...Lord, have mercy on us.'

.....Though the prayers in themselves followed the Catholic ritual almost as closely as if the funeral were being held on land, the chaplain interpolated some reference to the vast ocean whose bosom would receive *the young sailor's body. 'O God, through whose mercy the souls of the faithful find rest, be pleased to bless this watery grave. Send Thy Holy Angel to keep it; and loose from the bonds of sin the souls of all whose bodies lie beneath the waters of this sea, that they may ever rejoice in Thee with Thy saints...'*

At the end of the prayers the pallbearers lifted the flag, holding it a few inches above the canvas shroud which enveloped the sailor's body. The outboard carpenter's horse was removed and, tenderly, the pallbearers lowered the sailor's feet.

The Marine Guard, which had already about-faced toward the sea, snapped smartly to 'Present Arms!' More than a thousand officers and men brought their right hands to their forehead in a farewell salute as the American sailor moved off the stretcher from underneath the flag and silently disappeared into the sparkling waters of the Pacific. Father Covert made the sign of the Cross, and said, 'May the blessing of Almighty God, the Father, Son, and Holy Ghost descend upon you and remain forever. Amen.' The Marines brought their rifles to 'Order Arms!'

The Marine captain barked, 'Ready! Aim! Fire!' The first volley from the Marines' Garand rifles cracked over the waters. Then a second and a third. The bugler sweetly sounded Taps, which is as stirring a piece of music as ever was written.

The band played Onward Christian Soldiers. The officers and men stepped from the deck into the bowels of the ship, back to the business of war. That afternoon the padre said a mass for young Munson.[165]

Gilbert Bundy captured the spectacle and feeling of this burial at sea in an ink drawing (figure 6).

***

The *Tennessee* continued its journey to Efate, and on 28 October 1943, she crossed the Equator for the first time. It was customary in the U.S. Navy for a ship to conduct a "Shellback" ceremony when a ship crossed the Equator. This was an initiation for those aboard who were making the crossing for the first time. The *Tennessee's* mission schedule, however, could not be interrupted for such a ceremony on this occasion. On 2 November, they joined up with other ships sailing for the same destination. Baumrucker had a "pleasant evening bull session"[166] on the ship's fantail with some New Zealand pilots who were going to guide them into the Betio Atoll. This was necessary because they had no reliable charts of the area. Betio was a long, thin triangular-shaped island on the western side of Tarawa Atoll in the Gilbert Islands. Betio's point was to the east, and the base of its triangular outline was on the west. The lagoon of the atoll lay to the north and east. The northern coast lay in the shallow waters of the atoll, while the southern and western sides were bordered by deep water. Because of the deeper waters on the south side, there were no good landing areas there. The logical approach for an amphibious assault was from the shallow lagoon side of the island. To deter an attack from this side, a huge wall had been constructed across the lagoon just inside the high water mark. Machine gun posts and pillboxes had been established on the inner side of the wall. From these positions, the Japanese defending the atoll could fire on anyone or anything coming over the wall. A long pier projected from the western end of the island that allowed the off-loading of cargo ships. Robert Sherrod wrote that, en

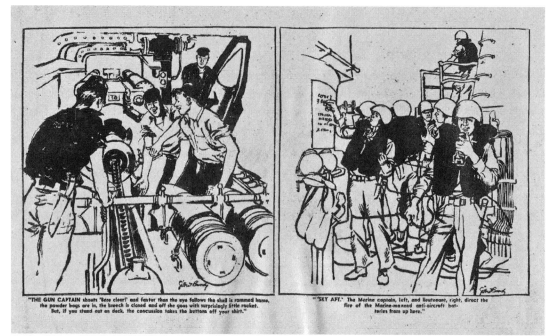

Left: "The GUN CAPTAIN shouts 'Bore clear!' and faster than the eye follows the shell is rammed home, the powder kegs are in, the breach is closed and off she goes with surprisingly little racket. But, if you stand out on deck, the concussion takes the buttons off your shirt."

Right: "'SKY AFT.' The Marine captain, left, and lieutenant, right, direct the fire of the Marine-manned anti-aircraft batteries from up here." [Drawing by Gilbert Bundy; Photograph from Baumrucker's album.]

route, once the correspondents had been informed that their destination was Tarawa, four of them were assigned to the transport that would carry the Second Battalion of the Second Regiment of the Second Marine Division. These included artist Gilbert Bundy, Associated Press correspondent, William Hipple, Fox Newsreelman, Don Senick, and Sherrod. This battalion was given the assignment of hitting the center of the landing area with another assault battalion on either side of them.

They reached Efate Harbor on 5 November. The beauty of the island did not escape Baumrucker's notice, and he almost got ashore on liberty, "but the captain got cold feet on [the idea of] liberty when he heard a more senior officer on another ship wasn't allowing it."[167] On the seventh, they got underway cruising off Efate for drills for the Tarawa bombardment. A curious diary entry for 8 November read, "A marine on a transport jumped overboard to avoid the trip to Tarawa. Maybe he knew something."[168]

With some quiet time while cruising off Efate, Baumrucker read an article in *Time* magazine that confirmed the anecdotes told him by Virginia, except that the article stated that Captain Musick had no children. Always getting the most out of his leisure time, he enjoyed a little unsuccessful fishing from the quarterdeck for cockeyed pilots[xix] before they got underway for Tarawa on the twelfth. On the way, Baumrucker busied himself with rangefinder calibrations on a daily basis. He knew that this equipment and the skills to use it would be

---

xix Cockeyed pilot is a species of salt water fish (*Glyphidodon saxatilis*).

vital in the days to come. Approaching Tarawa, they became aware increasingly that they were closing with the enemy. On the seventeenth, a group of Japanese planes located another allied task force approximately twenty or thirty miles from the *Tennessee*. On his 2000 to 2400 hour watch, Baumrucker saw the Japanese planes surround the other task force with flares, but they did not appear to see the *Tennessee's* group. On the eighteenth, Baumrucker declared, "All checked out and ready."[169] The following day, they passed the island of Tarawa on his watch. Japanese searchlights were trying to find them, and they sent "unintelligible blinker signals."[170] Baumrucker was tracking an unidentified in-coming target with this radar but, when it got almost in range, the radar went out. Fortunately, the light cruiser, *U.S.S. Santa Fe*, just ahead of the *Tennessee*, and a destroyer took it under fire. The target disappeared.

On 20 November 1943, the assault began with a heavy bombardment of Tarawa. This was the largest invasion force yet amassed for a single operation in the Pacific. It consisted of seventeen aircraft carriers, twelve battleships, eight heavy cruisers, four light cruisers, sixty-six destroyers, and thirty-six transports. Baumrucker commented that this was "obviously not another Kiska as we take return fire and silence shore batteries."[171] The landing parties had difficulties on the reefs. During his mid watch in Spot 1, there were Japanese planes overhead but the ship held its fire. The bombardment continued all day on the twenty-first and into the twenty-second. On the twenty-second, two destroyers located a submarine close by while the *Tennessee* was in the precarious circumstance of being dead in the water in order to provide 5" ammunition to a number of destroyers. Depth charges from two destroyers brought the submarine to the surface between them and the *Tennessee*. Baumrucker recorded in his diary that "our 5" battery sinks it."[172] This, however, turned out to be a case of the "fog of war". The official records of the *U.S.S. Tennessee* do not substantiate Baumrucker's claim. The Operational Remarks from the War Diary of the *Tennessee* dated, 22 November 1943, recorded a brief but detailed account of the incident with the submarine.

1748 [hour] Japanese submarine surfaced on starboard beam. Opened fire with 5"/38 battery at range 11,500 yards. 1748 [hour] MEADE and FRAZIER opened fire on submarine. 1749 [hour] Ceased firing, 21 rounds 5"/38 common projectiles expended. Approximately two hits scored on target by this ship. 1750 [hour] Changed course to 180° T and PGC. FRAZIER rammed submarine. 1754 [hour] Submarine sank stern first at 90° angle. FRAZIER launched whale boat to pick up survivors.[173]

The entry was made and signed by H. G. Smith, Jr., Lt., USN.

Baumrucker's diary for 23 November 1943 contained the single, simple claim, "The occupation is completed and we are cruising off shore."[174] Neither he nor anyone else aboard ship could have known the type of hell experienced by the Marines on Tarawa. At the time of this operation, Tarawa was the most heavily fortified and defended atoll that U.S. forces in the Pacific had invaded. In his book on the battle for Tarawa, Robert Sherrod wrote:

Betio had been declared 'secured' at 1312 [hour] on the fourth day, seventy-five hours and forty-two minutes after the first Marines hit the beach.....What I saw on Betio was, I am certain, one of the greatest works of devastation wrought by man. Words are inadequate to describe what I saw on this island of less than a square mile. So are pictures - you can't smell pictures.[175]

It became apparent very shortly after the battle that the Marines had lost over one thousand men dead and over two thousand six hundred men wounded. Sherrod reported that the Second Battalion that he accompanied ashore suffered sixty percent casualties. In the aftermath of the battle, there was controversy over the wisdom of capturing Tarawa. As expected, the commanders involved in the operation defended their decisions.

The following day, the *Tennessee* went south across the equator to Abemama, an atoll in the Gilbert island group, to protect two hospital ships. Ahead of them, on 21 November, the submarine, *U.S.S. Nautilus*, had landed a small force of Marine Amphibious Scouts on the island to secure it, and, four days later, the surviving Japanese defenders committed suicide. At Abemema, the *Tennessee* encountered the *Nautilus*, which had been gathering intelligence, including photographs of islands such as Tarawa, Makin, Abemama, and others in the area. She was at Tarawa in November gathering updated data on weather and surf conditions. As it turned out, it was the *Nautilus* that the *Santa Fe* had targeted and taken under fire on 19 November. Baumrucker's diary had mentioned the "target" coming under fire by the *Santa Fe* and a "destroyer." The "destroyer" was the *U.S.S. Ringgold* (DD-500). When she fired on the *Nautilus*, her first salvo of 5-inch shells put a hole in the *Nautilus'* conning tower, but the

"A REALISTIC RELIEF MAP of Tarawa was set up in the ship's wardroom and day and night there was a crowd studying the island's details over and over before the battle."

"A REALISTIC RELIEF MAP of Tarawa was set up in the ship's wardroom and day and night there was a crowd studying the island's details over and over before the battle." [Drawing by Gilbert Bundy; Photograph from Baumrucker's album.]

Betio Island: Baumrucker wrote, "The bombardment begins on November 20. We have no navigational charts and only photos like this to guide our shots." [Photograph from Baumrucker's album.]

shell did not explode. The *Nautilus* was able to submerge, disappear, make temporary repairs, and withdraw. Happily, she was not sunk. The *Tennessee* returned to Tarawa on 25 November to cover additional landings on the island. Cruising off Tarawa on the thirtieth, they saw the natives beginning to return to Betio from the other islands in their small sailing vessels.[176]

On 2 December 1943, a Marine colonel, who had been ashore on Tarawa during the battle, came aboard the *Tennessee* to inform the ship's officers of what had transpired on the island. As much as he wanted to hear it, Baumrucker could not get off his watch because the officer who was scheduled to relieve him attended the talk in his place. On the third, the island was finally well secured, and the *Tennessee* got underway for Pearl Harbor. The ensuing week was uneventful as Baumrucker caught up on casual reading and sleep when not on duty. They made Pearl Harbor on 12 December. There he ran into Layer and another shipmate from the *Mississippi*, and caught up on their news. He also ran into Gilbert Bundy, whom he had not seen since Bundy left the *Tennessee* to go ashore with the Marines at Tarawa. His understated diary entry on the encounter read, "Also saw Gil Bundy who had started ashore at Tarawa but got hung up on a reef for many hours with dead marines aboard. Made date with Alice Kelly."[177]

In his book, Robert Sherrod gave a detailed account of what Bundy had experienced off Tarawa.

> ...few war correspondents have experienced the horror which Gil Bundy, the artist, went through on his first assignment. He got into a landing boat with some of the regimental command on D Day. Bundy's boat received a direct hit about seventy-five yards from shore, probably from a Jap 90-mm. mortar. All others in it were killed or blown out of the boat, but Bundy miraculously was unharmed. That was only the beginning of his troubles. He jumped from his disabled boat, intending to swim to another boat. But a swift current carried him several hundred yards out

to sea. Finally, he managed to pull up panting to another disabled boat. Several dead men were in it, but by then it was dark and Bundy had no choice but to spend the night with the dead Marines. Early on the morning of the second day a boat which was returning from the beach stopped by Bundy's morgue. Captain Harry Lawrence of Albany, Georgia, the officer in charge of the amphtrack company, almost shot Bundy for a Jap - during the night Japs had swum out and manned some of the amphtracks. Bundy, rescued, was taken back to a transport. Until today we had assumed that Bundy had been killed. His identification papers had been found in his original boat, and several Marines had reported having seen his lifeless body, as men in battle often report things they are ninety percent certain of.[178]

Bundy survived the war, but upon return to peacetime life, his family and friends felt that his prior joy for life and his art were never the same. In 1955, on the anniversary of his experience with the Marines in the landing craft off Tarawa, he committed suicide.

***

The *Tennessee* left Pearl Harbor on 15 December, and arrived in San Francisco on the twenty-first. As usual, Baumrucker filled his liberty time with friends and dates in what could be described fairly as a whirlwind of activity. He

Betio airfield.

Betio airfield following the bombardment. Casual examination reveals a small area studded with shell craters. Closer examination reveals a damaged plane revetment and a few scattered vehicles. [Photograph from Baumrucker's album.]

Betio: This post bombardment aerial photograph shows damaged plane revetments and a few vehicles at the top of the image, and a collection of buildings in the lower right hand corner. Shell craters are evident. [Photograph from Baumrucker's album.]

Betio: This post bombardment aerial photograph shows destruction of trees, shell craters, and a few vehicles on the side of the airstrip. Robert Sherrod wrote, "What I saw on Betio was, I am certain, one of the greatest works of destruction wrought by man. Words are inadequate to describe what I saw on this island of less than a square mile. So are pictures – you can't smell pictures." [Photograph from Baumrucker's album.]

saw Ginger at La Fiesta, and then Billie at the Copacabana; he called Roberta Maas and set up a date that got canceled due to the death of her mother. Learning that Lynn and her husband were in San Francisco, he called her to make a date with them for his next liberty day. He discovered that his friend, Charlie Steele, was in San Francisco, and he joined him for dining and nightclubbing. On 27 December, he saw Steele at the Bohemian Club, an exclusive men's club that had been founded originally as a gathering place for journalists, musicians, and artists, but later expanded to include businessmen. Afterwards, he capped off the evening by attending the Ice Follies with Bob Chambers. His rolling from one diversion to another was interrupted on the twenty-ninth as the ship got underway for Long Beach.

January 1944 began with short cruises off Long Beach, with firing practices and repeated rangefinder calibrations. When at liberty, he continued to see Virginia, whose favorite dating places were the Riviera Club and the Hilton. A dinner date with Mary at the Brown Derby was followed with entertainment at the Earl Carroll Theatre on Sunset Boulevard in Hollywood. Above the entrance to this theatre were found the words, "Through these portals pass the most beautiful girls in the world." On his way back to the ship from this night on the town, he located Bobbie and made a date with her for the Trocadero the next evening. "No sleep, but a wonderful evening."[179] He met Bobbie early on the twelfth and made a big impression on her when he was able to get tickets to a Frank Sinatra broadcast. He secured these tickets from the local office of his old advertising firm, McCann-Erickson.[180] He followed this up with dinner at Har Omar's Armenian restaurant and, later, they went to the Palladium. Thus ended this run of shore leave as he returned to the sea.

On 13 January, the *Tennessee* formed up with fifty-three other ships and got underway for Hawaii. As they set sail, their next mission was not yet known. One day out, Baumrucker got the first word that he would be receiving orders for transfer to the *West Virginia*, then at Bremerton, Washington. His orders arrived on the twentieth, but the Captain informed him that he would stay aboard the *Tennessee* for the next operation.

CHAPTER 7
Kwajalein

Kwajalein Atoll: This aerial photograph shows the two small islands, Namur and Roi, on the northern end of the atoll. Roi (top right) was the site of the Japanese airstrips while Namur (center) held barracks and support structures. The two small islands were connected by a causeway (shown). Following the naval bombardment, Namur emanated dense black smoke and was essentially destroyed. [Photograph from Baumrucker's album.]

The *Tennessee* was anchored in the Lahaina Roads, a channel in the Hawaiian Islands, off Maui, on 21 January 1944, with Admiral Chester Nimitz and Undersecretary James Forrestal aboard. Their next operation was going to be the conquest of Kwajalein Atoll, and Forrestal had come aboard to observe it from the decks of the *Tennessee*. This atoll is comprised of ninety-seven small islands. The largest, and southern-most, of these is Kwajalein Island. The northern-most were the islands of Roi and Namur, which were connected by a long causeway. Roi was the site of the Japanese airstrips while Namur contained barracks, radar installations, and gun emplacements.

As was often the case, Baumrucker found time to fish over the side of the ship before it got underway. His love of fishing was never in doubt, but the times that he chose to fish could seem a bit odd to the casual observer – before, during, and after naval bombardments, if he was not on duty. One could speculate that he used fishing as a means of maintaining a state of inner calm when much else about him was quite frenetic, and even uncertain. On 22 January, the ship went to General Quarters as they prepared to get underway for Kwajalein. Baumrucker looked on as Forrestal came up from his Admiral's quarters in khakis, but without a regulation cap. A Marine sergeant gave him "a good chewing out before he [knew] who he was talking to, but Forrestal quietly said, 'Oh, must I wear a cap?' and went below to get one."[181]

During the journey to Kwajalein, Baumrucker continued to work on his fishing gear whenever he was not on duty. On the twenty-fourth, he told his diary, "Was relieved two hours late on the 2000 – 2400 watch, by the same friend who didn't relieve me to hear the colonel's talk on Tarawa"[182] and, four days later, "Got stuck with another 2000 – 2400 watch, by the same character."[183] A week into their journey en route to Kwajalein, they found themselves surrounded by ships. Reconnaissance photographs of aerial bombardments were dropped aboard ship, and they learned that the Tennessee's assignment was to be the bombardment of Roi and Namur Islands. On 31 January, they went to General Quarters early as they opened their bombardment in support of the landings. In a near disaster moment, the battleship U.S.S. Colorado (BB-45) put a 16" shell between the Tennessee's masts from the opposite side of the island. It speaks well for the people in charge of fire control on these battleships that friendly fire disasters – even near disasters – did not happen more than they did, especially when these small islands were being bombarded from both sides by big guns that had tremendous range.

On 1 February 1944, the Tennessee's big guns hit some ammunition dumps "for some spectacular explosions,"[184] and landings were made on a well prepared Roi and Namur. On the third, having seen enough, Forrestal was flown off the ship. The next day was spent "standing by" while the islands were secured. With a sense of professional pride, Baumrucker noted, "A considerably better job of preparation was made here than at Tarawa."[185] On 5 February, Baumrucker was told to stand by on half hour's notice to leave the ship by whaleboat to board a transport for the States. "Packed my gear, then located the negatives of the bombardment photos made by our spotting planes and got the photographer's mate to make me a set of prints."[186] The next day, he "was helping finish the prints and waiting for them to dry when word was passed that my boat was alongside and I was to leave the ship. It took so long for them to dry that the exec - my old buddy - passed the word personally twice more, and I finally went down so fast that I left my topcoat in my room. Told the exec I'd been saying good-bye to the captain and had a very wet ride over to the transport Calvert."[187] The U.S.S. Calvert (APA-32) was an attack ship that had taken troops ashore on Kwajalein on 1 February as part of the invasion force. She had to wait for the warships to steam out of the lagoon at Kwajalein before she could get underway. She finally got out to sea en route to Hawaii on 8 February. This was another low-key journey in that it involved "no watches or duties" for Baumrucker and he spent the day topside reading "McSorley's Wonderful Saloon," written by the American journalist, Joseph Mitchell. This was a fairly recent release with a

This post-bombardment photograph shows the degree of destruction on Namur. Baumrucker recorded, "The radar center, lower left of center, required special treatment, as it was heavily cased in concrete." The damaged causeway connecting Namur to Roi is shown projecting to the left side of the island in this image and landing craft are seen on the shoreline in the lower right corner. [Photograph from Baumrucker's album.]

publication date in 1943, but the subject matter represented a pleasant departure from technical manuals.

Mitchell wrote about street characters that he referred to as "visionaries, obsessives, imposters, fanatics, lost souls, the end-is-near street preachers, old Gypsy kings and old Gypsy queens, and out-and-out freak-show freaks." During his trek on the *Calvert*, Baumrucker was quartered "in a sweat box with 20 Marine officers who had been ashore and who had appreciated our bombardments."[188] He traded some of his spotting plane photographs for some of theirs, and other miscellaneous souvenirs. In the coming days, he began to write a story while alternately reading a book on fishing. A little house cleaning along the way included tearing up a lot of old letters, "especially some explicit ones from an old friend in Maine."[189] When he learned that the *Calvert* was headed for San Francisco, he decided to change to a ship that would make Long Beach. He left the ship in Pearl Harbor, went to the Bachelor Officers' Quarters and, unwilling to miss any social opportunity, made a date to visit his friend, Don Stewart. His diary entry for 17 February claims that he had received orders to the transport, *U.S.S. Moravia*. He had to be mistaken as to the name of this ship, or, perhaps, made a typographical error in transcription. It is believed that the ship to which he referred was the *U.S.S. Monrovia* (PAP-31). The *Monrovia* was another attack transport that had participated in the amphibious assault on Kwajalein, and then returned to Pearl Harbor carrying casualties and prisoners of war. On the eighteenth, he was underway for San Diego and experiencing some seasickness because of the unfamiliar roll of the ship. It took a couple of days to recover from this. He finally made San Diego on the twenty-fourth, whereupon he reported in for further orders, and telephoned Bobbie before hopping a bus for Los Angeles, where he checked into the Ambassador Hotel. He worked in a visit from Mary the next day, and took Bobbie to the Cocoanut Grove the following night. He was about to go home on expected leave and to fly by military transport. In anticipation of the flight, he had Mary drive him down to Long Beach in search of a parachute for the flight. On the ride back to Los Angeles, he decided there "wasn't the future for us that she wanted at this time."[190] On the twenty-eighth he picked up a parachute in San Diego and saw Virginia in Long Beach on the way back. She finally explained all her tall tales. "The elder 'friends' we had visited were her parents, and she didn't live in the apartment where I took her 'home,' and Captain Musick still had no children."[191]

Namur: Presumed munitions dump that was struck by naval bombardment. Baumrucker claimed, "Spectacular hits were lucky shots. This one blew a couple of our planes out of the air." [Photograph from Baumrucker's album.]

Regardless of his naval wartime experience to date, he still had to deal with practical problems. In late February, he went to the Los Angeles offices of McCann, his advertising firm, to try to cash a check. The manager, Cochrane, was not in and no one else would cash it for him, even though he was posted on their service Honor Roll. He found Cochrane in at McCann's the next day, but he would not cash any check or endorse Baumrucker at the bank. If he received any explanation for this behavior toward him, he did not mention it in his diary. He went to the Mocambo that evening with Bobbie. A couple of days later, he prevailed upon Mary to help him get the check cashed, and made another farewell, before having dinner with Bobbie.

On 4 March, he received his orders to report to the *U.S.S. West Virginia*, still at Bremerton, with thirty days leave. The battleship, *U.S.S. West Virginia* (BB-48), was to be Baumrucker's last ship assignment of the war. The *West Virginia* would carry him on a most remarkable wartime journey, and it would be from the *West Virginia* that he would make his greatest contributions to the war. All that had gone before this was mere preparation for what lay ahead.

CHAPTER 8
The West Virginia

After his assignment to the U. S. S. West Virgina, Baumrucker obtained this file photograph for his album. It shows the West Virginia in flames outboard of the Tennessee at the time of the attack on Pearl Harbor. He noted that the man being pulled from the water by the crew of the whaleboat was Snuffy Smith. Smith was blown off the West Virginia but later became a shipmate of Baumrucker's aboard the Tennessee. [Photograph from Baumrucker's album.]

On 5 March 1944, Baumrucker was en route to Chicago at 13,000 feet with parachute but without supplemental oxygen for the altitude. His flight took him over San Francisco, Albuquerque, Oklahoma, Kansas City, and then on to Chicago, where it was ten degrees below zero and "my topcoat on the Tennessee out in the Pacific."[192] Back home in River Forest on the sixth, he caught his parents up on the situation with his Navy tour, and, later, saw Louise Givens. Her husband, Sam, was serving as Judge Advocate on Admiral Halsey's staff. He spent his evenings catching up with as many old friends as he could locate, including Louise and Sammy Givens, Jr., Barbara Frey, Jays McFarland, Virginia Driscoll, "Bernie the Beautiful Bookkeeper" from Hays MacFarland's office, Khaki McNulty, and Bob Boswell. As if this were not enough visiting while on leave, he took a train to Cleveland to have a few drinks, and spend the night, with Al Sommer. From there, he was off to Boston to see his "old friend from

This is a file photograph of the fantail of the West Virginia after she was bombed and torpedoed during the attack on Pearl Harbor. Baumrucker's label read, "Fantail of the Wee Vee. We flew this flag again in to Leyte Gulf and Surigao." [Photograph from Baumrucker's album.]

Maine" whose intimate letters he had shredded. His journey continued to Stamford, Connecticut to see his brother and sister-in-law, then on to New York by train to visit his brother, Bill. From New York, he went to Washington, D.C. to see his sister and brother-in-law. En route to D. C., he read Robert Sherrod's book on Tarawa.[xx] The trek continued to Alexandria, Virginia to visit sister Florence and John, and lunch with Sayre Bradshaw. On the twenty-fourth, he flew back to Chicago and then returned to River Forest. He stayed on the move spending as much time as he could with as many acquaintances as he could locate, until, on 31 March, he concluded, "Not much doing around here so I say a few goodbyes and decide to go back to the coast for a few days with Bobbie in LA before Bremerton."[193]

Off to war again, his second journey from River Forest to meet up with a ship was not without complications. On 1 April, he was bumped from his plane at Kansas City and was up until 3:00 a.m. trying to make new connections. He decided that the easiest way to complete his journey would be to take Naval Air Transport. He caught a bus to the station at Olathe, Kansas where he was offered a flight the next day. He boarded "a comfortable transport for LA,"[194] but, after one stop at Albuquerque, the plane turned north and landed in Oakland. He just missed connecting with the Maas', failed to locate Janet, and ended up making "the rounds" with Staples. He finally caught a flight to Los Angeles where he took Bobbie on a date to the Pirate's Den. The next day, the two of

---

xx Sherrod's book saw quick publication with the first edition dated 1944.

them spent some time together at the Ambassador Hotel before going back to her apartment.[195] He was on yet another flight the next day, this time for Seattle, where he checked into the Sand Point Bachelor Officers' Quarters. A reunion with Dave Jarvis led to Baumrucker discovering that Mary had married "her old and intended boyfriend"[196] in Virginia. With Lynn's husband at sea aboard his submarine, Baumrucker included her in social activities with his group of friends. On 8 April, he took a ferry to Bremerton and reported in for duty only to find the "Wee Vee" still in drydock. Unhesitatingly, he returned to the bachelor officers' quarters, took in a movie, and socialized at the Officers' Club with his old friends, Lois and Doris. He returned to the ship the next day where he met Thomas Lombardi for the first time. They took a tour of the ship with a group of officers, and Baumrucker received his first duty assignment with the *West Virginia*. He was assigned to the fourth section, second in rank, in the Fire Control Division. Aware that the ship needed more time in drydock for repairs, he arranged a series of ski trips. Snoqualmie Pass in King County, Washington became a favorite ski destination. When not standing routine duty watches or studying fire control manuals, Baumrucker maintained a highly active social life, dating a number of young women in the Bremerton area. In late April, he decided that the ship's repairs would keep him in the area long enough that he would purchase a car - a 1940 Ford Coupe. This purchase provided him additional freedom and mobility during his off duty days. When conditions were right, he continued to pursue skiing and trout fishing.

The *U.S.S. West Virginia* had departed Pearl Harbor on 7 May 1943, headed for Puget Sound Navy Yard, where she required fourteen months for repairs, refitting, and modernization. As she neared the end of this construction, increasing numbers of officers and crew joined her in preparation for her return to sea. Among the crew that joined her late in her repairs was Charlie Loving. Loving was born and raised in the very rural setting of Roseland, Virginia, in Nelson County. He was working there as a farm hand when he enlisted in the Navy in 1944. In one sense, the *West Virginia* had been born just four years prior to Loving. April 20, 1920 marked the birth of the battleship as her hull was being laid at Newport News Shipbuilding and Dry Dock Company of Newport News, Virginia, about one hundred sixty miles, and less than three hours drive, from Loving's birthplace. When Loving met the *West Virginia*, he was nineteen years old, and his journey to the ship required more than three hours' travel time, taking him to the opposite coast of the country. He was sent to Great Lakes, Illinois for basic Navy training. From there, his first assignment was as a deck hand on the *West Virginia*. En route to the ship, he had a one-week layover in San Francisco before going directly to Bremerton. His first impressions on seeing the ship were powerful. He "had never seen a boat that big. The only boats [he] had ever seen were row boats or canoes on the tiny lakes in Nelson County - and they were few."[197] He had immediate concerns as to whether "a ship that big that was made of metal could float."[198] His second concern resulted from the large number of men he saw going aboard her. He wondered where all those men could be put on such a ship and he was anxious, wondering what life would be like aboard the ship. Many of his concerns melted away as the Navy got him, and his shipmates, busy. They were assigned the duty of cleaning up from all the repair work, and readying the ship for getting to sea. Loving had many days when he was "home sick" and just wanted to be back in Nelson County. As he got to know other young men with similar feelings from varied backgrounds, he realized that he was not alone. Friendships formed quickly and, in very short order, everyone began to feel at home.

Robert Wilson, born and raised in South Bend, Indiana, attended both the University of Chicago and Northwestern University. He enlisted in the Navy and, as a young ensign, he was trained to serve on "small craft." At the time, the largest ship to be designated as a "small craft" was a destroyer escort (DE). By the time he completed his training, there were no small craft in need of his services. He was then trained as a Communications Officer, becoming proficient in the use of semaphore flags and light signals transmitted visually in Morse code by signal lamps. He was assigned to the *West Virginia* and joined up with her during her last couple of months at Bremerton. In the coming months, he would serve as the ship's signal officer and would develop a very close working relationship with Captain Wiley. A close working relationship was necessary, as Wilson would interact with the Captain on the bridge, the signal bridge, CIC, or even in the Captain's quarters. He took messages to be transmitted directly from the Captain and had them transmitted by the signalmen under him. He came to know the Captain well and eventually proclaimed him to be "a great man."[199] Wilson came to know both Lombardi and Baumrucker while at Bremerton, though not well. He liked them both very much.

The *West Virginia* got underway for a trial run on 4 July 1944 with a "nice moon that evening, cruising up Puget Sound."[200] On return from this short cruise, Loving gave a sigh of relief as he thought, "Thank Goodness, it can float!"[201] Training while underway in Puget Sound intensified as they conducted engine trials and gunnery drills. Baumrucker was tasked with helping to break in the crew, "15 hundred of which had never seen salt water before."[202] It was not unexpected that training the new crew would be a difficult task as he recorded "many fouled up drills."[203] He continued to drill himself in the performance of his individual duties as he rehearsed bore sighting of the 16" guns, range finding, and figuring "ballistics for the computer." In mid-July, they got underway for a shake down cruise to Long Beach, California. They continued to rehearse and refine their skills along the way, including responding to General Quarters. Cruising off Long Beach, the planned live firing was delayed a couple of days because of poor visibility due to fog. Finally, on 26 July, they fired their first salvo from the main battery. "We could do with a little more drill."[204] The following day was punctuated by an uncommon occurrence. They had to "Muster of all divisions to sight all men because a man had been reported overboard."[205] The happy result was that all members of the crew were present.

Ashore at Long Beach, Baumrucker wrote that

"made probably the biggest tactical error of my Navy career. A group of our officers and from my former ship, the Mississippi, were waiting at the door of the Riviera for our various contacts to arrive. A low 25 foot long Jaguar with a right-hand drive pulled up with a spectacular redhead at the wheel who calmly looked the crowd over, smiled, and then drove to the parking lot. Then it occurred to me - that was my date! She came into the lobby where we laughed at it, drove to Laguna Beach and came back to the ship for dinner aboard with a few other guests including Ginny Simms."[206]

August of 1944 began with five days of cruising off Long Beach. The main battery fired at towed targets, while the anti-aircraft guns targeted small drones that were released from, and controlled by, patrol torpedo boats. On 14 August, they fired the first eight gun salvoes from the main battery with full service loads. Baumrucker made note of an inconvenience. He lost his "good inboard room" to a "slightly higher ranking trade school officer"[207] and was relocated to the blister.[xxi] The inconvenience resulted from the fact that the room in the blister was always locked when the ship was at General Quarters and under air attack. On 23 August, Baumrucker reported a very successful shore bombardment of Catalina, but the following day did not go so well. This was due possibly to "a very rainy stormy mid watch on the bridge, with knee deep water sloshing back and forth from inadequate drains and wind velocities up to 50 knots."[208]

Back ashore at Long Beach, Baumrucker and Lombardi got to know each other better as they socialized with their dates and group of common friends composed of officers from the *West Virginia* that included Sines and Fruechtl. They hit the Tropics, the Trocadero, the Beverly Hills Hotel at Serge, the Mocambo, the Pirate's Den, and a cocktail party at Laurette Rubinstein's. All of this was compressed into four days! On 8 September, the *West Virginia* received orders to proceed to Pearl Harbor escorted by two destroyers. Baumrucker used the time to make examination questions for rangefinder men "to break in a junior officer who was now in charge."[209] They made Koko Head on the fourteenth. The aircraft carrier, *U.S.S. Hancock* (CV-19) was entering Pearl Harbor ahead of the *West Virginia* with Baumrucker's friend, Bennie Kirk aboard. The *Hancock* would depart Pearl Harbor on 24 September to join Admiral Halsey's Third Fleet at Ulithi. The *West Virginia* tied up at Ford Island at the same spot where she had been sunk on 7 December 1941.

The day after the *West Virginia* arrived at Pearl Harbor, Baumrucker invited Sam Givens aboard ship for dinner. Givens was one of his best friends from home and they enjoyed this brief reunion. The next evening, he and Givens shared dinner on shore, where he also ran into Ed Grant, a classmate from Dartmouth. As Baumrucker made good use of every moment of liberty time ashore, the *West Virginia* was a very busy place, as she took on ammunition and made other preparations to get underway for destinations south. Lynn's husband's submarine was in port and Baumrucker took the opportunity to visit him at the submarine base to thank him for the company of his wife. Baumrucker described his friend, Sam Givens, as a "long-time reservist who wanted to go to sea."[210] Consequently, he made arrangements for Givens to go out with the *West Virginia* for a four-day shoot. With four days' leave from Halsey's staff, Givens got to sea as the *West Virginia* took final firing practice. Their long-range battery bombarded Kahoolawe as they fired all day and well into the night. Anti-aircraft gun drills consisted of firing at drones, both in daylight and under nighttime conditions. Givens and Baumrucker stood together on the bridge as the *West Virginia* made her way back into Pearl Harbor. While the ship took on more ammunition and supplies, Baumrucker got to spend two hours ashore with Givens. After the war, as Baumrucker was making a typewritten transcription of his diary, he added a note to the entry for

---

xxi The "blister" was an outward bulge of the ship's hull, designed to offer protection from torpedo strikes.

23 September 1944: "...two hours with Sam ashore... the last time I ever saw him. He was lost on a routine flight to Kwajalein some time later."[211]

Provisioned with large stores of ammunition, food, clothing, a well-trained crew, and everything needed to sustain a ship at sea, the *West Virginia* was ready to join the fighting war. She had emerged from the Puget Sound Navy Yard as a ship that had been transformed remarkably. Her silhouette and skin were changed. She now bore a new camouflage pattern. She had a displacement of 33,590 tons and was 624 feet long. Her beam had been increased from 97.3 feet to 114 feet. Her original beam, being less than 108 feet, meant that she could traverse the Panama Canal, if necessary, but the excessive new beam meant that she was relegated to the war in the Pacific. She had a draft of 30.5 feet. The ship could make speeds of 21 knots (24 miles/hour) and her usual crew complement was 1,407 officers and men. Her reconstruction plan also called for improvements in her armaments. She now carried eight 16" guns, sixteen 5" guns, forty Bofors 40mm guns, and fifty Oerlikon 20mm cannons. Depending on the type of rounds being used, the shells for the big 16"guns weighed around 2,000 pounds or a little more. The ship was well equipped to wage war and to protect herself.

As her repairs and modernization were being completed, the Navy produced a booklet titled, "BB-48 BOOKLET OF GENERAL PLANS." This twelve-page booklet measured approximately 9 ¾ by 4 inches. In the bottom right corner of the cover was the designation, "BU. SHIPS NO. BB-48-S0103-193296." This book was generally distributed to the officers of the *West Virginia* and it contained the design of every deck and architectural feature of the ship, including dimensions, crew complement, and fire plugs. The following crew complement was listed:

Captain	1
Commanders	4
Lt. Commanders	5
Lieutenants	17
Lts. – Junior Grade	17
Ensigns	44
Warrant Officers	13
Marine Officers	3
Total	104
Chief Petty Officers	67
Seaman Branch	1198
Artificer Branch	99
" " E. R. Force	406
Special Branch	98
Commissary	39
Messmen	48
Marines	74
1st Serg.-Marines	1
Aviation	17
Total	1965
Total Ships Force	2069[212]

Also listed were two 26' Motor Whaleboats, each with a capacity of 24 men.

***

As a war machine, she was a powerful weapons platform, but in another sense, she was home to the men who breathed life into her. She was a small, self-contained city, floating in the ocean. As such, life aboard ship was analogous to life in a small town. No place on the *West Virginia* was "off limits." The men were free to move about the ship at will. The battleship was so large, and housed so many men, that the only people an officer or crewman got to know well were those with whom they worked or bunked.[213] Except on the calmest of waters, the men spent most of their time inside the ship. The open decks were dangerous in rolling seas that made footing difficult, or in storms that made the decks wet and relatively slippery. In good weather, men would venture topside to smoke cigarettes in the open air. Opportunities to venture topside were often limited by one's duty station.

Russell Umbenhour was a junior ensign from Canton, Ohio who served in engineering. Because his duty station was well below decks, he got to make his way to topside only occasionally for some fresh air or to watch a sunset.[214] Frontis Winford was another junior ensign, from Sikeston, Missouri, who was assigned to an antiaircraft division. He helped man a 5"/38 caliber antiaircraft gun on the port side. When at sea, he and others like him were on watch for four hours followed by four hours off duty. As soon as their watch ended, they headed to their bunks to sleep for the better part of four hours.[215] Loving spent as much time as he could on the decks. Having been raised on a farm, he liked the open spaces and the views that being on deck afforded. He was convinced that the hemorrhoids that he developed while in the Navy were the result of his spending long hours on deck, sitting on steel structures while smoking.[216] He never smoked below deck. Both exterior and interior surfaces of the ship were painted. Below deck, regardless of the actual color of the walls, there was always a change in the shade of the paint when moving from "crew territory" to "officer territory." While these were not hard lines drawn in the metaphorical sand, they were gentle reminders to the crew to be on best behavior in officer territory. Captain Wiley allowed the men free access to the bridge, and to the Combat Information Center (CIC) as long as they observed the rule of relative quiet, so that they would not disturb the work of those assigned to those stations. The concept of a CIC did not exist when the *West Virginia* was first constructed and, therefore, no space was designated for it in her original plans. The location of the CIC varied from ship to ship and could change within a given ship, according to circumstances. Early on, the *West Virginia's* CIC contained a large circle that showed the path of incoming enemy aircraft. The information was recorded and updated by hand using a grease pencil. Things changed with the advent of radar. The CIC room had to be large enough to contain the radar equipment, plot, and the men to operate it.[217] Radar equipment evolved during the war, as did the experience to make optimum use of it. During her reconstruction, the *West Virginia* was outfitted with the best radar then available to the Navy.

The only sound to be heard inside the ship was the constant low-pitched hum of the ship's blowers. These blowers circulated air throughout the ship, and helped keep engines and electronic equipment from overheating. Walking about the ship, one did not hear much of human voices, due largely to the steel

The U. S. S. West Virginia off the Puget Sound Navy Yard following her repairs and extensive modernization. She displays her modern camouflage pattern as she was about to rejoin the war. [Photograph from Baumrucker's album.]

decks and bulkheads, and the resulting compartmentalization of the ship.[218] Throughout the living quarters of the ship, there was no particular odor but for the faint smell of steel. Whether at anchor, sailing calm seas, bombarding enemy islands, or repelling enemy aerial attacks, the kitchens were constantly cooking. Aided by the blowers circulating air, the upper areas of the ship, including the bridge, CIC, wardroom, and upper living quarters were permeated by the pleasant smell of soup cooking. "There was always soup cooking. At night, the smell of soup cooking was replaced by the smell of bread baking. They always did the baking at night."[219] The "smoking lamp" was always off at night and the interior of the ship was never completely dark.[220] The crew slept on hammocks that had thin mattresses. The hammocks were stacked six high, and the men slept in a head to feet orientation. When not in use, the hammocks folded up against the bulkhead. The junior officers' bunks were in the furthest compartment of the ship aft, and, as a result of this, these men got bounced around quite a bit in rough seas.[221] Laundry was done once a week. Each man put his soiled uniforms into a mesh bag, cinched it up, affixed a metal tag that identified it as his clothing, and dropped it off in the laundry to be washed. The crew was not required to press its uniforms, only to wear clean ones, and the Navy saw to it that each man had an ample number of uniforms to satisfy this need. Ironing was available to any man who chose to press his uniforms, but it was not commonplace to do so.

Meals were served "family style." The food was served onto compartmentalized metal trays. The men walked through the mess line, had their food served into the various compartments of the tray, and then found a seat at any of the numerous tables. After eating, the trays were emptied of uneaten food and stacked in the appropriate place to be washed before the next serving. While the kitchen had a permanent staff, other crewmen rotated through mess duty as assigned. The food was good and there was always plenty of it.[222] A battleship was large and could store huge quantities of supplies. While there was never a shortage of food, there were rare occasions when long intervals between resupply occurred. During these times, the food was still plentiful, but the menu did not vary as much.[223] Loving's first assignment aboard ship was to the Chief Petty Officers' Mess. "They had the best pick of food and [I] got to enjoy it. [I] had fresh milk when the rest of the crew was out of it."[224] Loving liked this duty assignment so much that, after his scheduled six weeks there, he talked his way into another six-week rotation, but got reassigned to other duty after that.

A standard workday was eight hours, but this did not include time spent standing watch. The crew spent leisure time - i.e., off duty time - with a number of pursuits while on ship. Common activities included reading, talking with buddies, smoking on deck, or grabbing extra sleep. The crew was told that gambling on board was not allowed, but many men ignored the warning and gambled regularly at poker, black jack, or dice. The anchor locker was a popular place for the men to escape the scrutiny of officers while they played poker. Officers were aware that the men were gambling but, as long as order was maintained, they turned a blind eye to it. After all, these were very young men, captive on a ship at sea, with few options for entertainment. Occasionally, the crew was treated to boxing matches that were organized between crewmembers or to a band concert held on the ship's fantail. When anchored off some Pacific Islands, it was commonplace for the Captain to allow "swimming over the side" of the ship. The splashing about in the water of so many men could attract the attention of sharks, and it was customary to post sailors with rifles to be on shark alert. At times, men could get to the ship's machine shop to pursue wood or metalworking.

"Standing watch" has been a sacred duty in the Navy that dates to ancient times. When a sailor was told to stand a watch, he was posted at a specific location within or on the ship for the duration of his watch. During the period of his watch, he was relieved of all other duties. For centuries, the duration of a watch has been four hours. In former times, prior to the advent of mechanical or electrical chronometers, time aboard ship was kept with a sand-containing hourglass. Formerly, the hourglass contained sufficient sand for only thirty minutes. A sailor designated to attend the hourglass would ring one bell when the sand ran out of the top, then invert it for another thirty minutes, whereupon he would ring two bells. Thus, a four-hour watch consisted of eight bells, completing eight thirty-minute periods. It was customary for a sailor who was being relieved from his watch to announce to the man coming onto watch, "Eight bells and all's well." This indicated that the four hours of his watch had ended and that everything in his area of responsibility was in order. From that moment, the responsibility for the watch station belonged to the new man. Each day was broken into the following watches:

0000 (midnight) – 0400 (Mid watch)
0400 – 0800 Morning watch
0800 – 1200 Noon or Forenoon watch
1200 – 1600 Afternoon watch
1600 – 1800 First Dog watch
1800 – 2000 Second Dog watch
2000 – 0000 First Watch

Abandoning a post prior to completing a watch and being properly relieved, sleeping on watch, or being inattentive on watch were punishable offenses.

From the time that men first set out to sail the oceans, *discipline* has been of paramount importance to ship's captains. A lack of discipline compromises both the ship's mission and its safety. Discipline is needed also to maintain harmonious and effective working relationships among the officers and crew. On the *West Virginia*, offenses were dealt with on a number of levels. By far, the most common form of discipline was "non-commissioned officer" (NCO) justice. The NCOs had a close working relationship with the enlisted men and were aware almost immediately of any behavior or actions that could endanger the ship or its personnel or disrupt the smooth operation of the ship. NCO justice was smooth, immediate, and effective. An NCO could reprimand or punish a member of the crew for a wide range of minor infractions. Under the aegis of maintaining safety and effectiveness of the ship, a crewman could receive punishment for things that were not written down in any official document. Common causes for NCO justice were 'shirking' duty, performing tasks improperly, minor misconduct on watch, minor insubordination, tardiness, or improper dress.

Punishments handed out by the NCOs typically included extra work details, longer work shifts, or extra watches. NCO punishment was usually effective because of its immediacy, and because no record was kept of the offense or the punishment. A crewman had nothing to lose by accepting the punishment handed out by an NCO. However, if a sailor wished to challenge the claim of an NCO, or the fairness of the punishment that was awarded, he had the right to insist on having his case heard at Captain's Mast. This carried with it the risk that the punishment might be worse than that given by the NCO, and the incident would appear on the sailor's record.

Offenses that were serious enough to be handled at a level higher than routine NCO justice were taken to a Captain's Mast. Captain's Mast was held as frequently as needed, based on the number of men being charged, but it would not convene while combat operations were being conducted. The Captain himself could be the convening authority for these proceedings, but it was more common for a lower ranking officer to be appointed to represent the Captain. On the *West Virginia*, a Captain's Mast would consist of the Convening Authority and the accused crewman. The crewman's Petty Officer and Senior Petty Officer would be present to help represent him. The charges would be presented to the crewman and he would have the opportunity to refute the charges or to defend himself. The Convening Authority served as judge in the matter. He could declare the crewman guilty or not, or, after hearing the charges and evidence,

Captain Herbert Victor Wiley at his desk aboard the U. S. S. West Virginia. This was the photograph that he selected to be included in the "Shellback Book." He served as Captain of the West Virginia from 14 January 1944 until 2 May 1945. [Photograph from Baumrucker's album.]

he could refer the matter to the next higher level of consideration, which was a military Court Martial.

As a form of "non-judicial punishment," a Captain's Mast was not considered to be a trial and, when punishment was given, it did not constitute a conviction. Similarly, if no punishment was given it did not constitute an acquittal. If a crewman elected to bypass NCO justice in favor of having his case heard before a Captain's Mast, he did so with the understanding that the judgment of the Convening Authority was final with no further appeal open to him. Consequently, he had to accept whatever punishment was handed down to him. In the majority of cases, it was far wiser for a sailor to accept the punishment given by his NCO, keep it off any official record, and amend his behavior in order to avoid further episodes. The results of Captain's Masts and Courts Martial, with the attendant punishments, were recorded in the ship's daily Deck Log. A common punishment resulting from a Captain's Mast was "confinement," or "solitary confinement," "on bread and water" for a specified number of days. The ship's brig was small and could not contain everyone on the ship who was sentenced to confinement. Such overflow men were designated "Prisoners At Large," or "PAL," in daily jargon. They still moved about the ship and carried out duties. They were, after all, still "confined" by virtue of being on a ship at sea.

A review of the *U.S.S. West Virginia's* Deck Logs for the six months from 1 January 1945 to 30 June 1945 reveal that Captain's Mast was held thirty-seven times, Deck Court or Court Martial sat thirteen times, and nine men were made "prisoners at large" while awaiting further action. Common offenses leading to Captain's Mast were: shirking duty, neglect of duty, failure to follow orders, insolence to superior officers, disobedience, fighting, theft, and the curious offense of "throwing bottles over the side [of the ship] without breaking them." The implication is that an unbroken bottle could float, be recovered by the enemy, and provide some form of "intelligence." Common punishments included: a "warning;" confinement on bread and water for three to five days; extra days or hours of duty; solitary confinement; or, reduction of rating. Reading while on watch led to a Captain's Mast, but sleeping on watch was always a Court Martial offense. The seriousness of this offense was reflected in the higher complexity of punishments that were awarded. As an example, one sailor accused of sleeping on watch pled guilty at his Court Martial hearing and received the following punishment: he had to perform extra police duties for a period of two weeks; he was placed in solitary confinement on bread and water for a period of fifteen days with a full ration every third day; and he lost thirty-three dollars of pay per month for a period of six months. On further review, the loss of pay was remitted on condition that the sailor maintain a record satisfactory to his Commanding Officer during a period of six months, otherwise that part of the sentence would be executed. A second sailor who pled guilty to the charge of sleeping while on watch was sentenced to loss of pay amounting to twenty-seven dollars per month for a period of six months and to be discharged from the United States Naval Service with a bad conduct discharge. On review, the loss of pay was reduced to twenty dollars per month for a period of three months, and the bad conduct discharge was remitted on condition that the sailor maintain a record satisfactory to his Commanding Officer for a period of six months, otherwise the bad conduct discharge would stand. It was customary for the punishments resulting from Captains' Masts and Courts Martial to be reviewed by a higher authority and, if indicated, to be altered. This was done to prevent any draconian practices, and to ensure that punishments for given offenses were handed out fairly and evenly among the offending crewmembers. Charlie Loving, and a fellow shipmate, went, nervously, before Captain's Mast on a single occasion. While ashore on Hawaii in uniform, they were harassed by a civilian who persisted in insulting them and the Navy. Loving and his friend responded by pushing the man around a little while punching him on his arms. The incident was witnessed by Shore Patrol who put them on report for fighting with a civilian. When they told their story at Captain's Mast, the convening authority smiled slightly and said, "Don't do it again."[225] It was customary for reason and fairness to prevail.

***

The ship's chaplain wore a number of hats and performed any number of duties, including the expected task of conducting religious services, presiding over burials at sea, and serving as personal advisor to the men who needed him in that capacity. The chaplain on the *West Virginia* took on another role. Loving recalled that, when the ship was bombarding an island or fighting off aerial attacks, the chaplain got on the ship's PA system to keep the crew informed of what was happening. Loving also recalled his being summoned on one occasion over the PA system to report to the chaplain's office. He remembered vividly that the chaplain was "very nice" as he gave him the news that his mother had "passed away" on September 15. For the rest of his life, Loving was deeply impressed with the kindness of that chaplain. While the name of the chaplain was lost in memory, the deed was not.[226]

As ombudsman for the crew, the Chaplain's role was complex. While he was a member of the clergy, he was also an officer in the U.S. Navy. He had to conduct himself before the men with kindness and compassion, but also with a well-calculated military presence. A Chaplain could be presented with problems of sufficient complexity that there were no official roadmaps for solving them. Such was the case of young Joseph V. Variot, Seaman 1/c, who manned one of the ship's 5"/38 guns. It was his job to set the fuses on the rounds they were firing. Variot was born in Detroit, Michigan and enlisted in the Navy, underage. He was fifteen years old when he enlisted. "I enlisted under false pretenses."[227] He had tried to enlist at the age of fourteen years, using his brother's birth certificate but he "got caught." Not to be deterred, he saw a second opportunity to enlist. He had a friend who was about to turn eighteen years old. His friend knew that he would be drafted, but he did not want to go into the service. Variot used his friend's birth certificate and succeeded in enlisting in the Navy under his friend's name. When he was seventeen years old, and after having served in two major conflicts, he decided to try to make things right but for an unusual reason. He had a ten thousand dollar life insurance policy that was payable to someone he did not even know – named by the friend whose identity he had 'borrowed.' He wanted to change the name of the beneficiary on that policy to someone in his own family. Not knowing how to correct this situation, he took it to the Chaplain. He told the Chaplain that he had a "confession" to make.

> I told him what I had done and why I was there – I wanted to straighten out the insurance problem. And he said, 'Well, you've committed a general court martial offense. You've gone into the military in wartime under false pretenses. And I don't know if I can do anything for you or not.'...I told him I wanted to stay in the Navy. And he said he'd see what he could do for me...At that point he more or less chewed me out in the manner of a Chaplain.

About two months later, the Chaplain got back to Variot with the word that he could stay in the Navy because he was now seventeen years old, and the Chaplain had gotten his parents' permission. "But they put me on a subsistence allowance and I got six dollars per month for the next six months for living expenses...but we needed nothing anyway – we were in the South Pacific so I didn't miss anything." Variot was gratified by the Chaplain's handling of his case – he solved the problem while also serving as a disciplinarian. Like many of the other crewmembers, Variot appreciated the role the Chaplain played in keeping the crew informed of what was happening around them. He "was on the loud speaker system and he was like our reporter. He would give us a blow-by-blow description of what was going on. Whenever we were under fire or whatever we were accomplishing, he would let us know on the loudspeaker system. So, we knew exactly what was happening all the time."

***

On 24 September, the *West Virginia* got underway for Manus, in the Admiralty Islands, with a single destroyer as escort. En route, Baumrucker corrected the examination papers for fire controlmen rates, and the ship continued firing practices. Still en route to Manus in late September, the

Shellbacks and Pollywogs began plans for the crossing-the-equator ceremony. The ceremony associated with the crossing of the Equator has been observed by the navies of numerous nations, taking place both in peace and in war. It is referred to as the "Shellback Initiation." Shellbacks are sailors who have already crossed the Equator. They are regarded as "Sons of Neptune." Those who have not crossed the Equator previously are referred to as "Pollywogs." At the appointed hour and day, the Pollywogs are paraded on deck in humiliating attire and required to perform otherwise disgusting acts as part of the initiation. On successful completion of the initiation, each sailor is issued an official "Shellback card." Baumrucker was a Shellback. He crossed the Equator aboard the *U.S.S. Tennessee* en route to the New Hebrides in 1943. Although no Shellback initiation ceremony was observed on that occasion, he was issued his official Shellback card upon which was inscribed:

IMPERIUM NEPTUNI REGIS –
To All Sailors Wherever Ye May Be and to all Whales, Mermaids,
Seas Serpents, Porpoises, Sharks, Dolphins, Eels, Skates, Suckers, Crabs,
Lobsters and All Other Living Things of the Sea.
GREETINGS: Know ye, that on this 26th day of October 1943 in Latitude 00000 and Longitude Sunset,[xxii] there appeared within our Royal Domain the U.S.S. Tennessee bound Sunset for the Equator and for the destruction of all the armed forces of the Japanese.
BE IT REMEMBERED
That said vessels, officers and crew thereof have been inspected and passed on by Ourself and Our Royal Staff AND BE IT KNOWN by all ye Sailors, Marines, Landlubbers and others who may be honored by his presence that Lt. Robert Owen Baumrucker, U.S.N.R. having been found worthy to be numbered as one of our trusty Shellbacks he has been duly initiated into the SOLEMN MYSTERIES OF THE ANCIENT ORDER OF THE DEEP. Be it further understood that by virtue of the power invested in me I do hereby command all my subjects to show due honor and respect him wherever he may be. Disobey this order under penalty of Our Royal Displeasure. Given under our hand and seal this 26 OCT 1943.
  Davey Jones   *Neptunus Rex*
  His Majesty's Scribe   *Ruler of the Raging Main*

On 4 October 1944, Baumrucker had the 0800 to 1200 watch. From the bridge, he witnessed the wild initiation of eighteen hundred Pollywogs on the deck below him as an enemy plane circled the ship but out of range of gunfire. The Captain sent a signal to the destroyer escort to come in closer to the ship to observe the ceremonies.

Manus was the largest of the Admiralty Islands, and the fifth largest island in Papua New Guinea. The Japanese had established a military base there in 1942. The U.S. attacked it as part of the Admiralty Island Campaign of February - March 1944, and established a naval base there. The *West Virginia* arrived at Manus on 5 October 1944 to find about two hundred fifty ships at anchor,

---

xxii Because the ship was at war at the time of the crossing, the exact longitude was omitted and replaced with the word "Sunset."

including most of the battleships. The fleet was forming up for the next campaign, and the ships were anchored inside submarine nets. Baumrucker noted, "Fortunately, I'm not on the bridge as we get tangled up in the nets and a have hell of a time with The Whole Fleet watching."[228] The *U.S.S. Tennessee* was with the fleet in the harbor and Baumrucker seized the opportunity to visit a lot of old friends who were aboard her. His land tour of Manus was restricted due to the fact that there were Japanese soldiers who were surviving in the hills and who were still conducting raids.

Before the fleet left Manus, Baumrucker was informed that his duties were being expanded. In addition to his duties within the Fire Control Division, he would have collateral duties as the ship's Intelligence Officer and as the Public Relations Officer. He quickly embraced the role of Intelligence Officer because it placed him in the unique position of having immediate access to plans for the ship as well as to classified material. The title also carried with it permission to keep and use a camera, which he gladly took into his battle station in the main battery director. As Public Relations Officer he was expected to be responsible for newspaper releases related to the ship's actions, and he was expected to interact with any media personnel who came aboard. On 12 October it was learned that their next destination was to be Leyte Gulf, for the invasion of the Philippines. Planning for the bombardment of Leyte began the next day as they got underway. Two days later, Baumrucker noted "a glow on the starboard beam....as we pass some Jap island evidently getting a going over."[229]

CHAPTER 9
Leyte Gulf

On 19 October 1944, the West Virginia's main battery opened up on Leyte. The blurred appearance of the gun barrels undoubtedly resulted from the vibration they caused for the photographer. [Photograph from Baumrucker's album.]

On 15 October 1944, en route to Leyte, "we get a final briefing on the invasion plans. The day before we are to enter the Gulf, the two islands outside are to be taken over, then we move in."[230] On this same day, amidst all the battle planning, Baumrucker recalled that, while serving on the U.S.S. *Mississippi*, his friend, Bill Hasler, had shown him a book titled *USS West Virginia Crosses the Equator*. This book was written and published in peacetime. Baumrucker got the idea to write another similar book titled *USS West Virginia Crosses the Equator Again* with a story about the initiation ceremony supported by pictures of the crew organized by divisions. He intended for this to be a souvenir book "for this hard-working bunch and we start taking photographs of the crew as we cruise back across the line to our first engagement."[231] The next day, he stood "a-watch-in-three on the bridge," meaning that he was on one watch and off two in sequence. The seventeenth found them cruising around a "minor typhoon" as the "two outer islands are taken."[232] Presumably, his diary was making reference to Suluan and Dinagat islands. Omitting their names may have been an intentional act to avoid placing official intelligence into his diary. Rangers defeated a small force of Japanese defenders on Suluan and destroyed an enemy radio station. As fortune had it, Dinagat was unoccupied.

On the eighteenth, the battle line formed off Leyte Island, and they steamed into the Gulf as the crew of the *West Virginia* used small arms fire to detonate a large floating mine just off their starboard bow. This was a noteworthy day because it was the first time that Baumrucker witnessed daylight air attacks by the Japanese. "It seems funny to realize those are real enemy planes up there, and not just a movie."[233] While this was certainly not to be his last encounter with enemy air attacks, this first encounter had to make a lasting impression. They began preliminary bombing of the main landing beaches on the nineteenth. Baumrucker watched from the bridge and Spot I as the underwater demolition teams went in and he "[saw] blood in the water."[234] On 20 October, Sixth Army forces landed on their assigned beaches in the morning and the *West Virginia* moved the deepest of any battleship into the Gulf to cover the landings, and later took wounded soldiers aboard. Although the enemy air attacks were letting up to some extent, the *U.S.S. Honolulu* (CL-48) was torpedoed that afternoon by a Japanese torpedo plane, but managed to make it back to Manus for temporary repairs. A large amount of anti-aircraft fire illuminated the sky that night.

The twenty-first of October was both an odd and a momentous day. Baumrucker was fishing from the quarterdeck amid the debris of battle while watching the fighting ashore. "At dusk, while in Spot I in the midst of a fairly good air attack, a Jap plane skims over my head and makes a spectacular crash on the Aussie cruiser Shropshire, just ahead of us."[235] *H.M.S. Shropshire* was a London-class cruiser that, in October 1944, had been allocated to Task Group TG 7.2, and she was in the battle line ahead of *West Virginia* at the time of this incident. Commenting on this event, Baumrucker recorded, "We thought it was an accident, but this was the first kamikaze."[236] One cannot be certain of Baumrucker's conclusion here. The *Shropshire* was definitely hit by a Japanese plane, but it is generally accepted that the first kamikaze attacks occurred on 25 October 1944, four days following this incident. Certainly, Leyte Gulf is regarded as the first battle in which the Japanese carried out *organized* kamikaze attacks.

With the number of air raids increasing by the twenty-second of October, Captain Wiley "knocks off sightseeing while off watch."[237] Men had made a habit of going topside to watch the dramatic events taking place in the sky above the ship, as Japanese planes bore down on American ships, firing machine guns and dropping bombs, and anti-aircraft fire rose into the sky from the ships. It was fairly common for pieces of hot metal, large enough to seriously wound or kill a man, to fall on the deck of the ship from unidentifiable sources. For reasons of safety, the Captain minimized the number of men topside during air attacks. The *West Virginia* was also coping with a separate mechanical problem. Just the day before, at daybreak on 21 October, the ship had gotten underway to proceed to its assigned Fire Support Area and, while turning to port, she touched the bottom, damaging number 1, 2, and 3 propellers:

> Later investigation by divers showed the blade tips of these 3 propellers to be turned between 45 and 60 degrees. This occurrence has, because of

vibration, limited the ship's speed to 16 knots, and to 18 knots in emergencies.[238]

Any thoughts of repair had to be delayed due to the present situation.

Baumrucker's diary entry for 24 October began: "Leyte. Heavy air raids all day. We get word that the Jap fleet is on its way in the late afternoon and I take my crew to the director to tune up the radar and check out procedures."[239] Baumrucker knew only that the Japanese fleet was coming, but he had no way of knowing their plan. Later, he would learn that the Japanese fleet had been divided into three separate forces that were designated the "Northern Force," the "Center Force," and the "Southern Force." The Japanese strategy was to use the Northern Force as bait to lure the U.S. covering forces away from Leyte. Once this happened, the other two forces would move on Leyte from the west. The Southern Force, under Vice Admirals Nishimura and Shima, was to attack the landing area by way of Surigao Strait. The most powerful of the three forces, the Center Force under Vice Admiral Kurita, was to pass through San Bernadino Strait into the Philippine Sea, and turn south to join the attack on the landing area. Nishimura's force consisted of the battleships *Yamashiro* and *Fuso*, the heavy cruiser, *Mogami*, and four destroyers. On 22 October, Kurita moved eastward into the Sulu Sea, and then northeast past Negros Island into the Mindanao Sea. Nishimura proceeded northeast past Mindanao Island into the southern entrance of Surigao Strait with the intent to exit the north end of the strait into Leyte Gulf, where he would join Kurita's force.

This photograph shows the 5" secondary battery firing at Leyte. They are firing at short range as evidenced by the low angle of the barrels. [Photograph from Baumrucker's album.]

The *West Virginia's* War Diary entry for 24 October contained the following account of an expected encounter between the American and Japanese navies:

> Returned to logistic area south of Mariquitdaquit Island, and 10 miles east of Leyte coast, where we operated during a morning of air attacks by small groups of Japanese aircraft. At 1408 [hour] went alongside U.S.S. Chepatchet (AO78) and fueled from her until 1630 [hour], when we cleared tanker and stood down to the south end of Leyte Gulf in company with Task Group 77.2.
>
> During the previous two days, many reports of sightings of Japanese men-of-war had been made by our submarines and aircraft. These reports crystallized together to show two heavy concentrations of vessels proceeding toward us - one coming through Surigao Straits. These forces could arrive during this night of 24 - 25 October. CTG[xxiii] 77.2 therefore, during the afternoon, issued instructions for this task group to prepare for night action. AT 2000 [hour] the Battle Line composed of the WEST VIRGINIA, MARYLAND, MISSISSIPPI (CBD 3 ComBatLine), TENNESSEE, CALIFORNIA, and PENNSYLVANIA, in column, were on course East about the Latitude of Hingtungan Point, Leyte, and proceeded on Easterly and Westerly courses across the Northern end of Surigao Straits, awaiting expected action.[240][xxiv]

The American fleet of battleships was traversing patiently back and forth in its battle line, awaiting the Japanese fleet that would come straight on, so that

This photograph, dated 20 October 1944, shows "tracers in the night as the Japs initiate their kamikaze attacks" (Baumrucker). [Photograph from Baumrucker's album.]

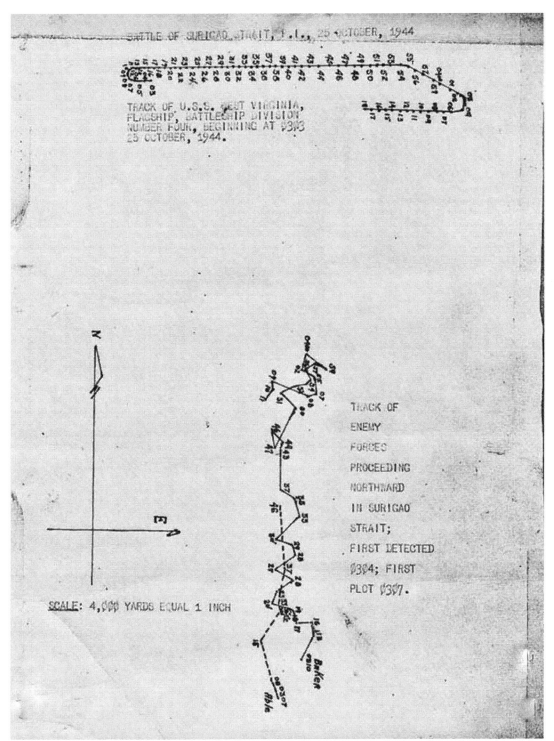

Shown is one of two plots found in the West Virginia's war records that show the paths of the American and Japanese fleets in Surigao Strait. It is illustrative of the tactic of "crossing the T." The American battle line is shown at the top with the Japanese fleet approaching vertically from bottom to top. [Courtesy of the National Archives, College Park, Maryland.]

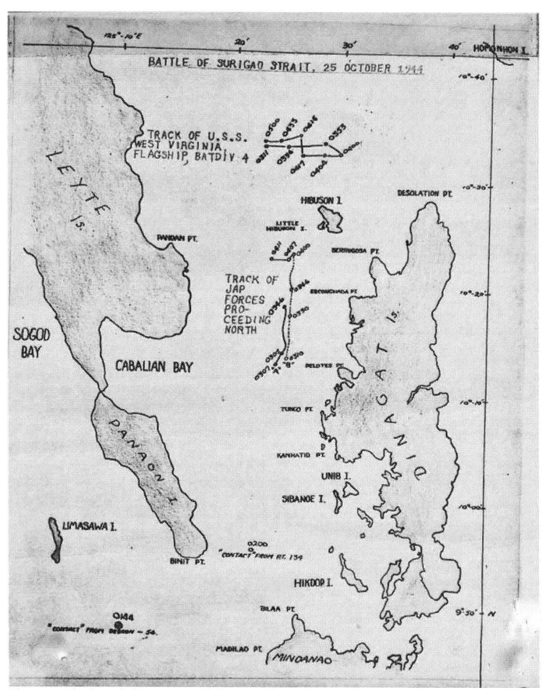

The second plot of the course of the two fleets during the battle of Surigao Strait was superimposed on a crude map. [Courtesy of the National Archives, College Park, Maryland.]

the Americans could execute the ancient tactic of "crossing the T" - the Japanese fleet representing the stick of the "T" and the American fleet the top of the "T." A major consideration for placing the *West Virginia* at the head of the battle line was the superior radar that was installed on her during repairs at the Puget Sound Navy Yard. Of course, the battleships were not the only American ships in the strait. There were thirty-nine PT (Patrol Torpedo or Motor Torpedo) boats, four heavy cruisers, four light cruisers, and three destroyer squadrons. Lacking nighttime aerial reconnaissance with radar, the PT boats and destroyers became the "eyes" of the fleet. The three destroyer squadrons were DesRon 54, DesRon 24, and DesRon 56.

* * *

The War Diary entry for the next day contained a summary of the events leading to and including the battle for which they had been waiting. The Action Report for the *West Virginia* was written on 1 November 1944 under the title, "ACTION IN BATTLE OF SURIGAO STRAITS 25 OCTOBER 1944 USS WEST VIRGINIA - REPORT OF. COVERS NIGHT ACTION IN LOWER LEYTE GULF FOLLOWING INITIAL LANDINGS ON 20 OCTOBER 1944, IN TASK GROUP 77.1. REPORT COVERS 24-25 OCTOBER 1944."[241] This Action Report contained a "CHRONOLOGICAL ACCOUNT OF ACTION" that represents the time line of events that describes how this naval battle unfolded.

The atmosphere about the ship must have been a mixture of anxious tension and excitement as they awaited the approaching Japanese navy in the dark of night. Because the encounter occurred at night, neither navy had the availability of air cover or aerial surveillance. Until the Japanese came within radar range, the Americans had to rely on radio reports of visual sightings that were transmitted to the battle line from smaller vessels in the Strait that were the first to encounter the enemy. These messages were not broadcast to the entire ship over its PA system. Most of the officers involved on the bridge, CIC, radar, plot, and fire control, received the radio messages through their earphones in real time. Many of the officers immediately repeated the messages for other officers and NCOs who were standing about, and updates spread quickly throughout the ship by word of mouth. The time of receipt of each message was recorded. (Times are listed in the left hand column.)

25 October 1944.

0001   *On course 090 in battle disposition, this vessel leading the battle line.*

0026   *Received report from MTB[xxv] 127[xxvi] that 3 enemy DD's[xxvii] plus 2 large ships were ten miles off the southeast tip of Bobol heading north. That position is 200° 89 miles from us. Search radars were focused on southern part of straits with negative results.*

0041   *Received contact report ten miles 310° from Camiguin Island which is 85 miles away.*

0108   *Flares of starshells were reported by MTB 53 18 miles SW of Panoan Island.*

0130   *Saw three starshells to NW of us, perhaps over land and fired in connection with troops operation. Wished they would stop as light might silhouette us.*

0144   *DesRon 54 reported contact 10 miles SW of Panaon Island.*

0152   *Ships right to 270° True.*

0204   *MTB 134 reported contact abeam PANAON Island.*

---

xxv "Motor Torpedo Boat" (PT-boat).

xxvi PT-131 was the first vessel to make contact with the Japanese fleet.

xxvii "DD" denotes "destroyer."

0205   *Received report enemy large ships under attack by our PT boats –*
        results undetermined[182][xxviii]*. Saw a light over horizon to southwest.*

0206   *Saw starshells to southeast far distant.*

0208   *Gunfire sighted bearing 180° True.*

0209   *Same.*

0210   *PT boats report target they are attacking is trying to drive them off*
        with gunfire.

0232   *Went to General Quarters upon signal.*

0239   *Starshells to N. W. Probably same as 0130 note.*

0241   *Surface contact reported 184° True 18 miles.*

0246   *DD reported surface contacts 4 in column 184° distance 15 miles.*

0301   *DD's report they have fired torpedoes at enemy*[xxix]

0303   *Saw gunfire go south.*

0304   *Enemy appeared on scopes of SG-1 RPPI – 20 mile scale. The pip*
        was visible at extreme edges of the tube on bearing 164° range
        44,000 yards. Several groups of friendly pips appeared on the
        scopes as our DD's closed to attack from east and west. Two DD's
        patrolling to north of Dinagat and our cruisers a few thousand
        yards to the southwest were showing on the scopes. However, in
        the dark, and from CIC reports only it was difficult for the Captain
        to be certain just where our forces were.

0305   *Changed course to 090 by turn movement.*

0307   *Destroyers report two large and one small enemy. Enemy is*
        straddling them.

0310   *Main battery plot* [xxx]*reported Spot 2's Mark 8 radar had the target.*
        (It never lost it until after cease firing),

0311   *Saw gunfire to south.*

0313   *Surface contacts 2 large 2 small were in strait heading north speed*
        20.

0314   *DD reported 5 targets 2 may be hit slowing down and dropping*
        behind some.

0315   *CIC reported two groups about 39,000 yards, one of 3 small pips,*
        the other of a large and medium pip preceded by several smaller
        pips.

0322   *DD report enemy 2 BB*[xxxi] *2 cruisers and 1 DD.*

0330   *CIC reports 1 group 174° 36,000 other group a little closer by about*
        4000 yards.

0331   *Notified all stations of fighting light code.*

0332   *Received orders from Commander Battle Line to commence firing at*
        26,000 yards.

0333   *4000 yards to go. Gunnery officer reports range 30,000 and has*
        solution with a large target.[xxxii]

---

xxviii For over three and a half hours, the PT boats attacked the Japanese force, but they were not able to score any hits. They did send contact reports that made for valuable intelligence.

xxix At about this time, both the *Yamashiro* and the *Fuso* were hit by torpedoes from American destroyers.

xxx This is reference to Baumrucker in Spot 2.

xxxi "BB" denotes "Battleship."

xxxii This "large target" was the battleship, *Yamashiro*.

0345   Saw explosion in target area. Talked with gunnery officer to be sure our target was not among our own DD's. Fire control[xxxiii] stated he had been on target for some time. CIC stated our DD's were clear.

0349   Starshells in target area. Can't tell if our DD or enemy is firing them. Our range 24,000. Am hesitating to fire until certain target is enemy. ComBatDiv 4 directed open fire.

0351   Our cruisers on our right flank opened fire. Our gunnery officer[xxxiv] says he has had some big target for a long time and it is enemy. Commanding Officer ordered commence firing.

0352   Notified Commander Battle Line we were opening fire.

0352-10 First salvo 8 guns range 22,800 yards AP[xxxv] projectiles.

0353   Could hear gunnery officer chuckle and announce hit first salvo. Watched the second salvo through glasses and saw explosions when it landed.

0354   Salvos very regular about 40 seconds interval. Other BB's opened after our second or third salvo.

0356   See explosions in target.

0358   Gunnery officer reports target is stopped and pip is getting small.[xxxvi]

0402   BB turn 15 on signal. Ordered cease fire. Have to think about small amount of ammunition on board. (110 AP left). CIC reports targets turned left and reversed course.

0405   CIC reports target speed 0.

0411   Pip reported to "bloom"[xxxvii] and then fade.

0412   Target disappeared. Can see ships burning – one is a big fire.

At about 0354, the battleships, *U.S.S. Tennessee* and *U.S.S. California*, opened fire with their 14-inch guns. *Tennessee* fired sixty-nine rounds and *California* fired sixty-three rounds. The radar control of the American ships was superior to the fire control systems of the Japanese and allowed the American fleet to fire on the enemy at a range far greater than the Japanese could match. The other three American battleships had less advanced gunnery radar making it more difficult for them to arrive at firing solutions. The *Maryland* used the splashes from the rounds of the other ships to achieve visual ranging and she was able to fire forty-eight 16-inch rounds. Unable to find a target, the guns of the *Pennsylvania* remained silent. The *Mississippi* was able to fire a single salvo of twelve 14-inch shells. She fired her salvo just after the order to "cease fire" had been given. The *Yamashiro* sank at approximately 0420 with Admiral Nishimura aboard.

***

Nearly two decades later, the famous naval historian, Samuel Morison, offered an eloquent epitaph to this famous battle:

---

xxxiii This is another reference to Baumrucker.

xxxiv These continue to be reports from Baumrucker.

xxxv "AP" denotes "Armor Piercing" shells.

xxxvi This indicates that the target is being destroyed.

xxxvii "Bloom" denotes an explosion.

WORLD BATTLEFRONTS

bottom: two battleships, four carriers, nine cruisers, three flotilla leaders and six destroyers.

¶ Possibly sunk were a battleship, five cruisers and seven destroyers.

¶ Damaged when they left the Philippine Sea were six battleships, five cruisers and ten destroyers.

¶ Of 60 warships sent into action, only two escaped without hurt: the 34 that limped home, broken and smoking, would clog their repair yards for months while U.S. planes hammered at them to put them out of business for keeps.

Born of Necessity. While they were waiting to see where the U.S. blow on the island defenses would fall, the Japs had dispersed their fleet, at stations from the home islands to Singapore. When General MacArthur's men stormed ashore on Leyte with four assault divisions, the admirals set their prefabricated plans in operation.

They had lost the initiative long ago; now to get at Leyte Gulf and its cluster of soft-shelled U.S. transports, their warships must pass through narrow waters. Nothing south of the Philippines would do for the attack; Lieut. General Kenney's airmen based on Morotai had closed those routes. There were only two channels through the Philippines. The Japs bent their strategy to geographic necessity.

Their central thrust, with a force built around five battleships, would rush the narrow San Bernardino Strait and strike Vice Admiral Thomas Cassin Kinkaid's Seventh Fleet, guarding the Leyte beachhead, on its northern flank (*see map*). Although black-browed Tom Kinkaid had received divisions of escort carriers and at least five battleships to fill out the contours of his normally skinny fleet, the Japs knew he would be hard pressed to stave off this assault. To make doubly sure, their southernmost force would charge through Surigao Strait. Either or both of these forces would strive for a chance to pot sitting ducks—the helpless transports off Leyte.

Their third, northernmost force, which included four of their precious, dwindling stock of flattops, would send off planes to smear Admiral Mitscher's bare-decked carriers when the latter's planes were far away, giving Kinkaid support which the Japs were confident he would need and demand.

Oversight. On paper it was a fine complex plan. There were only two things against it: one was that Old Stagers Halsey, Mitscher and Kinkaid were combing the seas with planes and submarines looking for the attack; another was the overwhelming power of the U.S. force.

Two or three days before the battle, U.S. submarines in the South China Sea surfaced in darkness and radioed what they had seen: major Jap fleet units advancing northeast from Singapore. Then the subs went to work, sank two *Atago*-class heavy

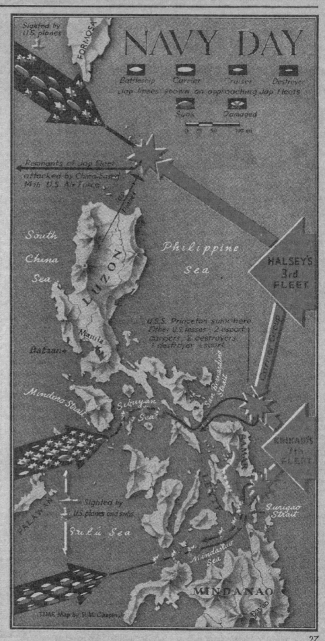

Map of the battle of Surigao Strait as depicted in Time vol. XLIV, No. 19, November 6, 1945. [Provided by Robert Wilson.]

Mississippi's one salvo, fired at *Yamashiro* just after Admiral Oldendorf ordered Cease Fire, concluded this major phase of the battle. Silence followed, as if to honor the passing of the tactics which had so long been foremost in naval warfare. The Battles of Lowestoft, Beachy Head, The Capes of the Chesapeake, Trafalgar, Santiago, Tsushima, Jutland, every major naval action of the past three centuries, had been fought by classic line-of-battle tactics. In the unearthly silence that followed the roar of Oldendorf's 14-inch and 16-inch guns in Surigao Strait, one could imagine the ghosts of all great admirals, from Raleigh and De Ruyter to Togo and Jellicoe, standing at attention to salute the passing of the kind of naval warfare that they all understood. For in those opening minutes of the morning of 25 October 1944, Battle Line became as obsolete as the row-galley tactics of Salamis and Syracuse.[242]

In his diary, Baumrucker made note that,

"the assistant gunnery officer in Spot I is unable to pick up the targets coming up Surigao Strait so control is switched to me in Spot II. Commenced firing at 0353 with a direct hit on the first salvo at the leading Jap battleship and many following hits are made. The admiral on board was pleased that we were the first battleship to open fire, but the man in plot was so excited he forgot to give the buzzer warning and both bridges were temporarily blinded by the initial flash."[243]

The Action Report for 25 October 1944 concluded,

This vessel fired 16 salvos at a vessel, reported to be a battleship, which finally sank. At 0413 ceased firing - the enemy remnants proceeding Southward, leaving behind several burning vessels. Our forces continued to patrol until daylight, and then return to the transport area for logistics purposes. ... No damage was sustained either by this ship nor by its personnel.[244]

The lack of aerial or surface film footage of this battle elevates the Action Report to a special level among historical documents. The detailed chronology of the events as they unfolded gives the non-participant of this action the best possible feeling for how the battle evolved. History labeled this officially as The Battle of Surigao Strait, and many boasted that the performance of the men of the *West Virginia* was the finest example of naval gunfire of the war. The assistant gunnery officer in Spot I referred to in the Action Report was Lt. Thomas Lombardi. When he was unable to get a radar fix on the Japanese fleet or offer a firing solution, fire control was transferred to Lt. Robert Baumrucker in Spot II. Baumrucker had readied himself for such an occasion. In addition to the formal training afforded him by the Navy, he spent many hours of independent, individual training with manuals, and he was constantly calibrating his equipment and drilling his men. When word reached him of the approaching Japanese fleet, his first response was to get himself and his men into Spot II, to ready them, and his equipment, for the impending battle. When control of gunfire was transferred to him, he was ready. He had been tracking the Japanese fleet for some time and already had a firing solution. He needed

Following the Battle of Surigao Strait, the West Virginia retired to Espiritu Santo to enter the floating dry dock (shown above) for repairs to her bent propellers. [Photograph from Baumrucker's album.]

only to await orders to fire and to wait for the enemy ships to get within range. *That night at Surigao* - as Baumrucker titled it - was the greatest moment of his life.

Baumrucker's record for 25 October appears to have been a combination diary and memoir:

> "On securing from General Quarters we learn there is a lot more enemy outside the Gulf, having fooled Halsey and come down from the north and we stand by to go out after them although we were not over supplied with armor piercing shells and would have thrown out some of our remaining bombardment shells. But another group on another assignment did Halsey's work for him and the main Jap fleet turned around."[245]

***

The day following the battle, while memory was fresh, Baumrucker wrote his account of the events of the battle under the title, "That Night at Surigao." It was censored heavily before being sent to newspapers. Baumrucker included the entire article in his "Shellback Book: USS WEST VIRGINIA CROSSES THE EQUATOR AGAIN."

The account of the battle in the Action Report was a precise, factual, unemotional, military record of events. For the public, however, Baumrucker - the former English major from Dartmouth with a penchant for writing - put a more literary spin on the story.

Chapter 10
That Night at Surigao

One could sense a surge of exhiliration run through the ship as the word was passed over the PA system late that afternoon, four days after the attack on Tacloban. The speakers blared:

'All hands to quarters for a special announcement!'

The invasion attack had been exciting enough, as it was the first action for many of the crew. At least it had provided a welcome stimulant after the grueling days of drill and the many uneventful days of steaming to our objective. And it had been an historical day for the West Virginia as she moved in to lead the attack, for she was flying the same colors she flew when she went to the bottom on December 7th.

But it lacked much of the excitement of Tarawa and Kwajalein; pre-invasion bombardments were almost down to a science by now. On D-plus-one day, with the beachhead firmly established but with intermittent bombardment still going on, the Wee Vee was lying offshore and we were fishing from the quarterdeck in the litter-strewn water of Leyte Gulf. We actually looked forward to the early morning and evening visits of Washing Machine Charlie as a few planes at a time would run the gauntlet of ships to the Gulf, drawing great pyramids of AA fire. They gave us something to look forward to, as we waited around wondering what our next move would be.

What! No Mail?
Mail call was still too vague to date in the future, and it was a little early yet for topside movies.

The planes reminded us of lone mudhens hjgh-tailing across a public shooting ground on the first day of the season, dodging shots of hundreds of gunners the best they could. Almost inevitably they wound up in a flaming mass, and the crew not on watch took station twice a day to see the performance. Bets were placed as to whether this one or that one would burst into flames in mid-air and disintegrate, or streak into the sea in a column of smoke, or crash in flames in the hills beyond.

But on the morning of D-plus-four day we noticed a change from these light attacks. More planes than usual came over for the dawn run, and our gunners were kept at work long after breakfast time. Then, just as chow was piped for the noon meal, they came again-fifty or sixty of them-and kept us at our guns until 3 o'clock before we could eat.

That Old Scuttlebutt
Rumors were running wild throughout the ship that the Jap fleet was out, on its way from Borneo and Manila and Formosa and even from Japan. Groups of battleships, large groups of heavy and light cruisers and masses of destroyers were escorting their largest carriers, and closing in from all directions. But these rumors were largely laughed at and classed

as the usual scuttlebutt-bum dope that helped keep us amused and pass the time of day.

But at quarters we got it straight. Four battleships, six cruisers, a couple of carriers and a large number of cans had been sighted, steaming through the Mindanao Sea on their way up to Surigao Strait, and we were going out to meet them! Now we were really going to do some business.

The evening meal was a substantial one, and welcome, for we'd been on lean rations for several days. We were issued K rations to keep on our battle stations, for no one knew when we'd get fed again. As dusk approached there were many little preparations in evidence-jugs of water and blankets were lugged to battle stations, and once in a while a can of fruit that had been 'big-dealed' from the commissary issuing room. Charlie didn't draw much of an audience that night, as we had bigger game in mind, and most of the crew was at battle stations long before General Quarters.

The Wee Vee in the Van

The battle line steamed out of Leyte Gulf through a gorgeous red and pink sunset. Our small observation planes were flown off the ship, as the expected gunfire would blast them to shreds on the fantail. They would be of little or no use in a night engagement.

The West Virginia was in the van again, leading more of the "victims of Pearl Harbor" and once more flying the colors she'd carried to the bottom. From the hatch in my battle station, in the main battery director on top of the mainmast, I looked down the column of this "scrap iron Navy," and out to the cruisers and destroyers escorting us.

That night came up black. The sea was smooth, with moderate ground swells. There was intermittent AA fire at various points on the horizon, and occasionally unidentified lights flared up on various bearings. Small lightning flashes lit up isolated portions of the sky.

I settled back inside the director and plugged in on the Captain's battle circuit to listen to the dope. My pointer and trainer and others of the crew lounged in the open doorway, laughing and chattering about some liberty back on the coast. I trained the director into the breeze to try to cool it off, for it had been soaking up hot sun all day.

Watchful Waiting

Back and forth we patrolled, east and west across the northern end of the Strait, waiting for the enemy to arrive. Then, about 2300, one of our PT boats in the south entrance to the Strait reported a large black shape had entered and turned north, and we went to General Quarters.

Then another report-a very large ship had passed through, but still out of range.

Some time later, the PT's were ordered to attack, and we wondered if they'd finish them off before we got a crack at the targets ourselves. The reports weren't clear-not all the word came over the circuit. But it seemed as if the PT's hadn't done too much damage, and soon we were tracking out three of our destroyers which were sent to investigate.

We trained the director out on the Strait, and I promised my operator the biggest gedunk I could wrangle out of the soda fountain if he picked up the targets before anyone else found them.

We were facing right down the Strait now, a strip of water about fifteen miles wide and fifty miles long, and we trained our eyes to be sure not to miss the faintest sign of the enemy's approach.

Here They Come!

Several very large vessels were now reported moving up through the murky blackness, and occasionally I'd look through my powerful spotting glasses or raise up through the hatch to scan the horizon through my binoculars. But all was solid blackness, and the faint glimmer of occasional lightning flashes still only lit up minor areas in the sky. Our destroyers were still moving out.

Suddenly-there they were!

'On target! On target! Commence tracking, plot!' We were trained on a large enemy ship, sneaking up on us through the black of night, hoping to catch us unawares-and here we had him right in the notch!

Soon other targets appeared, some of them large and others obviously the destroyer screen. Still out of range of our guns, they were coming straight at us at high speed. Their T was crossed! And by a lady who'd been rudely mussed up almost three years before, who was now out here for some satisfaction.

We picked up the largest closest target, trained out our guns, and waited for the order to commence firing.

Destroyers Go In First

We watched our three destroyers move in on the enemy's port beam, and checked and rechecked to be sure our range was not fouled by friendly ships. We got a little anxious about who was going to fire on whom first; our target was well within range now, but still no order came from the bridge.

Then things happened in a hurry. We saw the destroyers open up, and the enemy answer back-balls of fire loping across our line of sight-apparently at short range because of the flat trajectory. Then our cruisers commenced firing, and their first salvo was high in the sky and well on its way when - at 0353 - we got the word.

'Commence firing! Commence firing!'

'Fire one,' was the calm word from plot, and the Wee Vee rocked back on her side in a great cloud of flame as our first salvo was on its way. My eyes were glued on the spotting glass now, waiting for the signal that tells us when our shots will land – hoping to get a glimpse of the target so as to spot the next salvo on. At this range it was almost too much to hope for a hit or even a straddle on the first salvo. The buzzer sounded, and I saw our balls of fire arcing downward and WHAM!

Right On!

'Ya hit 'im! Ya hit 'im! No change, no change!' Out there on the horizon I saw a tremendous burst of flame. Only a heavily armored target would explode our 16 inch armor-piercing projectiles on impact, and almost immediately we fired again.

Salvo after salvo went out, and nearly all of them were right on. Part of the time I was halfway out of the director hatch, not even conscious of the concussion from the giants below, and part of the time my eyes were glued to the spotting glass to help guide them to their mark. Our cruisers had opened up in rapid fire now, and soon our next battleship in column was firing.

Sheets of flame were bursting from the targets. Sometimes I caught glimpses of a great hulk silhouetted in the flames – other times it looked like Niagra Falls out there from the splashes of the many salvoes. My pointer claims he saw the pagoda superstructure of a battleship. I was too busy on other details to confirm or deny.

Plot reported the target slowing in the water, then turning around – and the Captain ordered 'Cease Fire'.

Why Waste Bullets?

And then watched the great glowing masses on the horizon, as reports came in that only one of our destroyers had taken a hit,[xxxviii] and she was still under control. One PT had rammed an underwater obstruction, and the Strait was filled with Nips who had abandoned ship – or whose ships had abandoned them.

The destroyers were picking up survivors – those that would come aboard. A few small targets were escaping out of the southern end of the Strait, but we had word that our planes would be out there to work them over as soon as it was light enough.

Until dawn we watched the great fires burning on the horizon – enemy ships ablaze! The largest glow began to die down, when suddenly it loomed up brighter than ever, and we saw great clouds of fire shoot into the sky as the flames evidently reached the powder magazines and blew the remains to smithereens.

Bring On Some More!

By 0730 we had secured from General Quarters, and gathered in small groups on the quarterdecks to talk it over. We learned that our escort carriers were engaging another force to eastward, and that our fast carriers had been in action to the north. As this is written we have but fragmentary reports on the action – we don't even know just how large a fleet we'd taken on.

But it was something pretty big, and the 'scrap iron Navy' had really done a job. With no air support in our phase of the battle, we'd done more than send them back licking their wounds – we'd sent most of them to the bottom.

The Wee Vee was no longer a virgin – but she was still a lady as she proudly maneuvered with her sister ships awaiting further orders.

---

xxxviii Baumrucker did not mention the name of the one destroyer that was hit by the enemy. The name may have been omitted for security reasons. The damaged destroy was the *U.S.S. Albert W. Grant* (DD649). One of the last two Fletcher class destroyers to be built, she was operating at Surigao Strait as part of DesRon 56.

CHAPTER 11
Espiritu Santo

On 27 October, the kamikaze attacks increased, and several ships of the fleet were hit. While the *West Virginia* "splashed" several kamikaze planes close aboard, none actually hit the ship. Amidst the potentially lethal air attacks, Baumrucker enjoyed a brief, humorous episode that involved the Captain. He had taken a working party over to an ammunition ship for a large load on an LST.[xxxix] "Just as 150 shiny aluminum cases of main battery powder and a great number of shells are laid out on the open deck, two enemy planes are under fire directly overhead and voice radio says 'Flash red, control green.' The skipper turned to me and said, "What the hell does that mean – we keep hearing it all the time.' I'm sure he knew it meant, 'No friendly planes in the air – shoot at anything flying.'"[246] After loading the ammunition onto the ship, they received orders to proceed to the New Hebrides for repairs to the ship's propellers. En route to Espiritu Santo, Baumrucker returned to his pet project – writing up the Shellback initiation for the souvenir book. While standing a mid-watch on the bridge, he noted passing a darkened ship followed by one with running lights! He was amused momentarily as he recalled "our careful indoctrination [on running lights at sea] at Tower Hall."[247]

Some time shortly after October 31, 1944, a memorandum was issued to the entire ship's complement by the Executive Officer, Commander G. J. King:

B-U-L-L-E-T-I-N

(1) The Japanese have announced the formation of a Corps of especially trained suicide bombers whose mission is to crash an especially equipped plane on our ships. We have seen the work of some of their pilots. Twice they have damaged ships in this group even when they missed and crashed in the water near by.

(2) Out lookouts must find and our gunners must explode these planes before they reach us. In the old days just a hit on the plane to make it evident that the plane is going to crash was enough. Now it is different. These planes must be broken up in the air. They must be shot at until they explode or a wing comes off. <u>*This is a must.*</u> *It will require large expenditures of ammunition. It boils down to this, "Either we get them or they will get us."*

(3) All hands not on exposed gunnery stations <u>must</u> take cover when AIR DEFENSE is sounded. All hands must wear long trousers and long sleeves to avoid flash burns. A flash burn from a nearby explosion is a very serious and painful injury. Even the flimsiest body covering is of inestimable value.

All hands must wear life jackets for their own protection if knocked overboard.

All exposed men must wear helmets to protect them from fragments and shrapnel.

---

xxxix "LST" denotes "Landing Ship Tank."

_B-U-L-L-E-T-I-N_

Now it can be told, but you can't tell everything. Inasmuch it has been officially announced that the WEST VIRGINIA took part in one of the actions in the Philippines, it is permissible for personnel to mention the fact in their letters to their friends and relatives. However, they are still restricted as to just how much they can say. Personnel may not, repeat, may not, mention what action we were in. They may not mention the range at which the action took place, the method of fire control or the amount or the accuracy of the gunfire. No mention will be made of damage to our ships, small as it was. They may not mention what other ships were with us nor the time that the action took place, in fact, you can say practically nothing more than was mentioned in the press news distributed on board on 31 October 1944. To some people this may appear as an undue restriction. However, there is a good and sufficient military reason behind these restrictions. Operation orders and plans are drawn up based on knowledge of the location of or disposition of enemy forces, the strength of these forces, and their capabilities. Therefore, we cannot mention who was where, as this information will help the enemy in analyzing the action and enable him to learn from his own mistakes and assist him in planning his future courses of action. Be patient, the news will be eventually released in more detail and credit will be given where credit is due.

Censors will be governed by the above in censoring mail of personnel of this vessel.

G. J. King,
Commander
U.S. Navy,
Executive Officer.

The trip to Espiritu Santo provided Baumrucker time and opportunity to work on his "Shellback" book. As they sailed past the island of New Guinea, he began to check the names of two thousand two hundred crewmen against their photographs that were to appear in his book. On 8 November, the _West Virginia_ experienced its first two deaths since the bombing of Pearl Harbor. Robert Rocktashel, the pilot of one of the ship's 'Kingfisher' spotter planes, and Andrew Chup, his radioman, were killed when their plane crashed. One of the plane's wings fell off as it was coming in for a routine recovery. Baumrucker speculated briefly that the wing might have been weakened at Leyte Gulf in the storm, but he later recalled that the planes had been flown off the ship that night before the battle in Surigao Strait. Making Espiritu Santo on 9 November, they entered a small cove and went into a huge floating drydock.

While repairs were getting underway on the ship, a number of officers and men were able to get ashore to visit a small club for a few beers. From the men in the club, Baumrucker learned that lots of fish were being caught off the dry dock but he avoided the temptation to fish in favor of spending all of his spare time on the "Shellback" book. Seven days after arriving at Espiritu Santo, the ship's propellers had been hammered back into proper shape, and the _West Virginia_ set sail on a return course for Leyte Gulf. For the most part, the journey was uneventful. Never idle, Baumrucker spent some time in transit in the machine shop, making cigarette boxes out of 40 mm shell cases. While still en route, Thanksgiving Day arrived, but Baumrucker found it "so hot we don't have much of an appetite for turkey."[248] The greatest moment of anxiety during this trip was not attributable to the Japanese, but to himself. "Couldn't find some pictures that were supposed to be Top Secret and I was a little concerned who might find them."[249] They arrived at Leyte Gulf the next day and he "found the pictures just where I'd hidden them."[250] Returning to Leyte Gulf put them back on the doorstep of the fighting war. On 26 November, he made unsuccessful attempts at holding rangefinder calibrations as the number of enemy air attacks increased. Amidst all this activity, the industrious Baumrucker made preparations for a War Bond Drive. The twenty-seventh found them in a heavy air attack that produced another close call. They shot down an enemy plane that crashed close into the ship but did not hit her. The same day, while patrolling Leyte Gulf, the *West Virginia* tied up alongside the *U.S.S. Caribou* for refueling. After two hours of taking on fuel, they cast off from the *Caribou* and, within minutes, they were firing at incoming enemy planes. They were highly vulnerable to air attacks while in the process of refueling. The War Diary recorded that they shot down one plane that was attempting a suicide dive on the ship, and they assisted in shooting down several other planes.

Two days later, as they were getting underway for Palau, the enemy air activity fell very quiet, and Baumrucker seized yet another opportunity to turn his attention back to his Shellback project, and he started working through the San Francisco office of his advertising agency to locate a printer for the book.

CHAPTER 12
Mindoro

On 5 January 1945, en route to Lingayen, a kamikaze flew over the West Virginia from astern and crashed into the U. S. S. Ommaney Bay, an escort carrier just ahead of the West Virginia in the formation. This photograph was taken from the West Virginia. With ammunition exploding and fires raging out of control, the Ommaney Bay was abandoned. Baumrucker watched from the director of the West Virginia as torpedoes from the destroyer, U. S. S. Burns, sank the Ommaney Bay. [Photograph from Baumrucker's album.]

The *West Virginia* arrived at Palau on 1 December 1944 and anchored in Kossol Roads, a body of water that was enclosed by a reef. This geological feature served well as the site for a floating dry dock and a resupply base. The ship took on a large amount of mail, including a package of preserved fruit for Baumrucker and a letter from Mary John. The letter from Mary must have been of little consequence as he only mentioned its receipt but not its content. He turned his attention back to the War Bond Drive. The drive was actually the chaplain's assignment, but Baumrucker decided that it needed more promotion than it was getting. He prepared chits for free "gedunks"[xl] at the soda fountain

---

xl "Gedunk" is a term that originated in the Navy in 1931. It can be used to refer to the canteen or snack bar of a Navy ship, or it can refer to an edible treat that is obtained from such a snack bar. The "gedunks" are often ice cream or ice cream-based.

for all divisions that got one hundred percent participation in the drive. He posted a chart on a forward bulkhead as visible evidence of how the drive was progressing. The quietude of Palau allowed the crew to view movies on the fantail of the ship topside, and they enjoyed swimming "over the side" of the ship. Rested and resupplied, they got underway for Leyte Gulf on 10 December, arriving on the twelfth. The ship picked up a correspondent and they continued to steam down through Surigao Strait with other ships. As the Public Information Officer, it was Baumrucker's duty to interact with this correspondent. He commented that "there is always something doing when newspapermen come aboard."[251] Sailing through the Strait, Baumrucker noted "lots of Philippinos line the shore and watch us from their crowded sailing boats. They must have had a good look at the Jap fleet during the night of action at Surigao."[252]

The next day, enemy activity intensified, and the *West Virginia* survived a narrow miss. Just as Soderberg was relieving Baumrucker on the bridge at 0800, they sighted a Japanese "Zero" almost dead ahead of them, "skimming over the water and headed right for our bridge. [Soderberg] gave a hard right rudder to bring the guns to bear and we splashed it abeam of us just as it was about to crash a carrier on our port side."[253] They continued steaming up and down the area within range of numerous enemy airfields, coming under frequent air attacks. Cruising in the Sulu Sea the next morning, as Baumrucker was coming onto the bridge to relieve the 0800 watch, a large flight of enemy planes was reported to be approaching the ship. When the flight got close enough, Baumrucker followed standard procedure and called out the Captain. This resulted in another light moment in the face of a potential crisis. When Baumrucker called the Captain,

> he doesn't come and I begin to have a lot of excitement. Then he comes out laughing in a good and confident mood and said 'I was naked as a jaybird in the shower when you called.' A very fine man. We do another nice job on a plane about to crash that same carrier on our port beam and there is much activity all over the sky.[254]

They were entering a very active time. The ship's War Diary for 15 December recorded that, while steaming in the Sulu Sea this day, they came under air attacks several times. At dawn, amphibious troops landed on Mindoro Island and the ship commenced retirement. Mindoro Island had been seized from the Japanese in order to establish airfields there that would be within fighter range of Lingayen Gulf. The Japanese force defending Mindoro was small and the only significant resistance came from the kamikaze planes. Lingayen was to be the site of a major amphibious invasion of the Philippines. Baumrucker's diary entry for the fifteenth summarized the day from his perspective. While cruising in the Sulu Sea,

> Air Defense sounds again, just as I'm relieving the 1200 watch. At least, I had lunch. An emergency right turn is ordered by voice radio to avoid some active 'dog fighting' on our port beam but my signal officer didn't get the word and suddenly I see the formation headed directly for us or across our bow. I call for a hard right rudder again, but since it takes 35

seconds for the ship to start swinging there is a bit of confusion for a time but nobody gets rammed.[255]

It was the next day, while having a "bull session" with Davis, the correspondent, that Baumrucker and other officers learned that troops were landing on Mindoro. This was taking place just east of the *West Virginia* and out

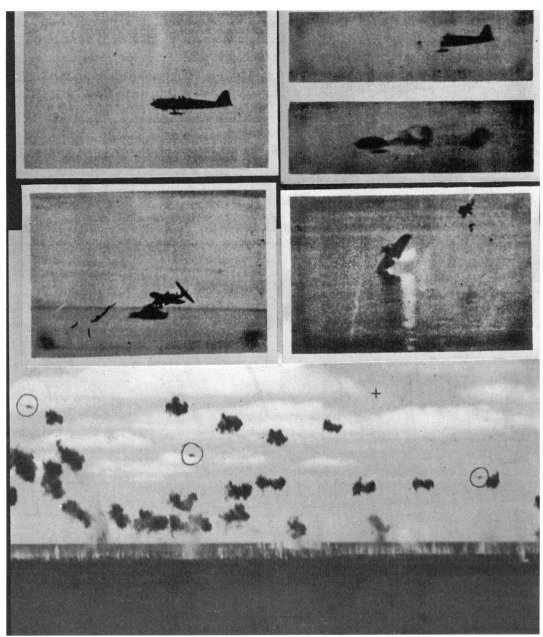

Mindoro: "December 12 – 16. More kamikazes than ever, and most of them on my watches on the bridge." (Baumrucker). Baumrucker circled three kamikaze planes that were headed directly for the West Virginia. None of them was successful in crashing into the ship. [Photograph from Baumrucker's album.]

of their sight. The *West Virginia* was then part of the force charged with covering against possible enemy surface interference.

> "We then get a report of a large enemy task force approaching our vicinity and we turn to meet it but discover that some nervous scout plane had sighted and reported <u>us</u>! We head around Negros Island on route to Leyte Gulf."[256]

On the way to Leyte Gulf, it did not escape Baumrucker's notice that they passed over the Japanese ships they had sunk at Surigao.

Having the correspondent aboard ship produced some tensions, and annoyance, for Baumrucker and there was immediate relief when he left. "The correspondent leaves us so we settle down for nothing but air attacks."[257] The War Bond Drive was a success with one hundred percent participation throughout the ship. A total of $51,450 worth of bonds was sold "for which the chaplain took the credit and later got a bronze star. Good for him, because I was too busy to help him on a later one and it flopped pretty badly."[258] They had returned to Kossol Roads by 23 December, where life was once again relatively quiet except for the usual daily fare of standing watches and enduring minor incidents that were unrelated to the enemy. On Christmas Eve, a huge amount of mail and parcels came aboard. Mail was still being sorted on Christmas day.

> "My Christmas packages are sent up to me while on the mid watch by a messenger who is enjoying some candy which spilled out of one package. Then I get a broken package with a little of that same candy remaining."[259]

While standing the dog watch on the twenty-sixth, he spotted a whaleboat – quick to note that it was not "ours" – that had caught fire in the harbor off the *West Virginia*'s starboard beam. He called out the fire and rescue party to extinguish it. When not on duty, he spent more time in the machine shop and fishing off the quarterdeck. The year ended with the *West Virginia* still at Palau. On the last day of the year, Baumrucker entertained Roger Baird, a neighbor from home, who came aboard ship for a visit and lunch. Later that afternoon, Baumrucker, Soderberg, and Doc Reiner got out on the water in a small rubber raft that was propelled by oars. They were able to get a few miles away from the ship. The scene painted by his diary entry leaves one with the feeling of nearly false serenity. The three officers were in a small rubber raft, fishing over a coral reef, while a nearby ship was having a "happy hour" band concert. The crew of another ship was "swimming over the side." Yet, in the distance, they could see American planes dive-bombing and strafing some Japanese left on one of the islands. By now accustomed to the sights and sounds of horrific destruction being wrought upon the enemy, his last diary entry for 1944 ended with the mundane thought, "Very good fishing, but fortunately there was no outgoing tide."[260]

CHAPTER 13
Lingayen Gulf

The *West Virginia* departed Palau on 1 January 1945 en route for Lingayen Gulf in the Philippines. With the realization that busier times were ahead, Baumrucker wound up his activities in the machine shop where he had entertained himself making ashtrays and other items from spent shell casings and parts from Japanese aircraft. He received assignment to Division Officer, F Division, in charge of aiming and firing all the ship's guns. By 3 January, the air attacks had begun to intensify again and, the following day, seventy-nine Japanese planes were shot down in the vicinity of the *West Virginia* during Baumrucker's watch. Most of these were shot down by the fleet's air cover. On 5 January, at 1712 hours, a lone kamikaze plane passed over the *West Virginia* from astern and crashed into the *U.S.S. Ommaney Bay* (CVE-79), an escort carrier that was ahead of *West Virginia* in the formation. The plane crashed into her amid ships on the starboard side while releasing two bombs. The damage was severe with exploding ammunition and fires that raged out of control, and the ship had to be abandoned. Baumrucker looked on from the director as the destroyer, *U.S.S. Burns* (DD-588), used her torpedoes to scuttle the dying ship. The *U.S.S. Twiggs* recovered the survivors and, later that evening, transferred them aboard the *West Virginia*. Baumrucker shared his room that night with one of the rescued pilots.

They arrived at Lingayen Gulf on 6 January with heavy seas that made for difficulty with the landings. The *West Virginia's* War Diary for that date recorded,

> Entered Lingayen Gulf with Task Group 77.2 to carry out scheduled shore bombardment on San Fernando Point. Formation was under frequent attack by suicide planes. During the late afternoon we penetrated about 20 miles into Lingayen Gulf where, prior to our retirement, the AUSTRALIA, CALIFORNIA, and NEW MEXICO were hit by suicide planes. The reason for this penetration, particularly at the slow speed of 5 knots, is not understood. Retired from Gulf at night.[261]

Baumrucker's diary went beyond the ship's War Diary to comment that none of the American ships was sunk and "I have a fine view of it all from my director 30 feet above our bridge."[262] The bombardment continued the next day while the air attacks slowed down a bit, but Baumrucker mentioned a separate threat to the *West Virginia*. She had moved close enough to shore to be within range of enemy land-based artillery. "We knock out several shore emplacements after they splash shells around us."[263] Very heavy shore bombardment continued the next day and on 9 January the troops began going ashore "in a very orderly fashion – the beach head easily secured."[264] Baumrucker held intelligence-gathering conferences with the ship's pilots who had been spotting targets on shore all that day. They continued to cover the landings with their shelling while a constant stream of supply ships entered the gulf. Baumrucker knew that his friend, John Rockwell, was on his destroyer as it passed close aboard the *West Virginia* on its starboard side, but they did not have an opportunity to communicate.

On 11 January, they came close enough to the Australian cruiser, *H.M.S. Australia*, to see how battered she was from kamikaze attacks. During the Leyte invasion, the *Australia* had been hit by a single kamikaze plane, and, during the Lingayen operation, she was struck by five kamikazes. Despite heavy damage from these attacks, she remained on her fire support station until she was needed no longer. The *Australia* was a sobering sight for the crews of the *West Virginia* and other nearby ships, and the War Diary entry for 11 January 1945 addressed it directly.

> After sunrise Task Group 77.2 divided into Task Units 77.2.1 and 77.2.2 who joined up with 77.4.1 and 77.4.2 respectively and patrolled with them....This unit is known as the Lingayen Defense Force and is charged with the responsibility of preventing the entry of Japanese Forces into Lingayen Gulf. Since about 30 ships of our force have been hit by suicide divers, there is considerable tension among exposed personnel. However, since this vessel is one of the few that has not been hit, the personnel are very alert to keep it so.[265]

There were numerous causes for rising tensions. The day after the troubling sight of the *Australia*, the ship received a report of an enemy submarine in their vicinity. This potential threat was made worse by the fact that an ammunition ship was close aboard the *West Virginia* at that time. Fortunately, this was one of many submarine threats that never developed further. The *West Virginia* remained in Lingayen Gulf, took on fuel and ammunition, and was the target of unsuccessful high altitude bombing by the Japanese. Baumrucker endured this relatively monotonous time by fishing off the quarterdeck, and he started playing "acey-ducey"[xli] with Soderberg, "a formidable opponent."[266] Baumrucker's life became a little more complicated as he took on a new battle. On 26 January, his diary ended, "Standard watches while shore fighting continues. Quit smoking."[267] Three days later, "Smoked one cigarette,"[268] followed the next day by, "Smoked three cigarettes."[269] Finally, on 31 January, he lost this short-lived battle. "Started smoking."[270]

By the end of January, tensions on the ship ran high due to frequent Japanese air attacks, word of an approaching Japanese fleet, and a severe lack of mail from home. Mail was crucial to the crew's morale and the Navy attempted to keep deliveries frequent, even in the midst of battle. *West Virginia*'s War Diary for 31 January 1945 recorded,

> Anchored as before. One air alert occur[r]ed this date at 2230 lasting about 20 minutes but enemy did not attack. No damage reported. We were placed on one hour's notice at 0745 by Task Group Commander in

---

xli "Acey-ducey," by a number of spellings, can refer to a very fast card game or to a fast version of Backgammon. Because Baumrucker made notations about designing and fabricating an acey-ducey board, and making "acey-ducey" pips from parts of a downed Japanese plane, this is certainly the form of the game to which he referred. This game was favored because it was fast to play and it could be interrupted quickly when circumstances demanded it.

Lt. Baumrucker observes the bombing of Luzon through the hatch in Spot I of the West Virginia. [Photograph from Baumrucker's album.]

furtherance of his assumptions that the Japanese fleet is in a position to make a fast strike against this area.

The lack of receipt of U.S. mail during this month has been a setback to morale. No mail has been received since 3 days prior to our departure from Manus on 27 December 1944.

During the period at anchor, this ship went to "Air Defense" Quarters each morning prior to sunrise and each evening at sunset. The few Japanese planes which approached the area made no attacks on vessels at anchor. However, the possibility of at least one large scale attack by Japanese planes, suicide or otherwise is a continuing threat.

H. V. Wiley [Captain][271]

On 5 February, they finally left Lingayen Gulf en route to Leyte Gulf. Baumrucker once again began drilling his men in plot, but noted that things were "considerably fouled up."[272] This time he concluded that the men were "overtrained, no doubt."[273] Only three days later, the officers were rationing their few remaining postage stamps to the crew, but greatly needed relief came on 10 February when they reached Leyte Gulf and finally got some mail aboard. After the brief two-day stay at Leyte Gulf, they got underway for Ulithi, an atoll in the Caroline Islands in the western Pacific. At Ulithi, they took on more ammunition and stores. This was always a certain sign of "another obvious action coming up."[274]

Orders arrived from CINCPAC[xlii] on 16 February to make all possible haste in preparing the *West Virginia* for departure, and she was given the highest priority for refueling and provisioning. The provisions came aboard faster than they could be taken below and they were simply stacked on the quarterdeck. Among their loads were a welcomed seventy bags of parcel post. At 0230 hours on 17 February 1945, they received orders to take to sea as soon as ready with the destroyers, *U.S.S. Izard* (DD-589) and *U.S.S. McCall* (DD-400), as escorts. They were to proceed to Iwo Jima to report to CTF 51 for duty.

---

xlii CINCPAC = Commander in Chief of the Pacific

CHAPTER 14
Iwo Jima

A pre-invasion aerial photograph of Iwo Jima with a clear view of Mt. Suribachi. [Photograph from Baumrucker's album.]

AT 0400 on 17 February 1945, the *West Virginia* completed the loading of three hundred tons of provisions and got underway for Iwo Jima at 0730.

It was routine procedure aboard the *West Virginia* for "Orders of the Day" to be issued in written format each day. These were usually terse, one page documents that outlined the order of the day's activities. The Orders of the Day for 19 February 1945 read:

U.S.S. WEST VIRGINIA
ORDERS OF THE DAY
Monday, 19 February 1945
DUTY DIVISION: 10TH Division relieves the 9th Division.
FOLLOW THE DAILY SEA ROUTINE EXCEPT:
0600 REVEILLE.
0645 MESS GEAR
0700 Sunrise, light ship.
0800 Turn to.
0830 MUSTER ON STATIONS.

1145 MESS GEAR.
1200 DINNER.
1315 Turn to.
1645 MESS GEAR.
1700 SUPPER.
*1831 Sunset, darken ship. Smoking lamp is out on all weather decks from
        sunset to sunrise.*
*NOTE: We should arrive at the invasion area at about 1000 to the usual
run of red alerts and occasional raids. ALL HANDS on their toes, keep their
eyes open, be alert every minute on watch and saw them up in the air.
Numerous friendly forces will be present. Be prepared to give counter
battery and call fire any time after arrival. It is believed we will be too late
for the pre-landing bombardment.*

> G. J. King,
> Commander, U.S. Navy
> Executive Officer

They sighted Iwo Jima at 0907 hours on 19 February. Baumrucker recorded seeing his "first view of an actual Japanese island, Minami Iwo"[275] on his watch. *Minami Iwo Jima* – meaning "South Sulfur Island" – was the southern most of the Volcano Islands group of the Ogasawara Islands. As they approached, they saw various units of the fleet bombarding the island from all sides, and the initial landing was already taking place. They arrived in their designated area at about 1045 hours, reported to CTF 51 for duty, and requested operation plans. The War Diary recorded, "We made the 900 mile run in about fifty (50) hours at an average speed of 18 knots, which speaks well for the Engineering Department."[276] The War Diary entry for 19 February continued:

At 1125 CTF 54 Operation Plan No. 1-45 arrived aboard via dispatch boat and at 1145 we proceeded to fire support station as directed. Prior to this time, we had aboard only Commander Fifth Fleet's Basic Operation Plan for the assault and occupation of Iwo Jima. Grid charts, fire support areas, cruising formations, and the masses of information which are usually received in time for at least a brief period of study prior to an operation were not aboard. As a result, we arrived on the scene with no specific knowledge of what was going on. The fact that the ship had been conducting bombardments recently was of immeasurable assistance to us in quickly sizing up the problem which confronted us.

They commenced bombardment of their assigned targets at 1249 hours with their main and secondary batteries, and 40 MM fire. Their targets were at ranges from two thousand five hundred to four thousand five hundred yards and included gun positions, revetments, trenches, artillery, and various other enemy installations. They silenced five enemy guns. During the time of this bombardment, they were free from enemy air attacks. The *West Virginia* was very close to shore. Baumrucker noted seeing "many interesting sights ashore; we are close in."[277] On the twentieth, they continued their bombardments of gun emplacements, blockhouses, tanks, assorted vehicles, a supply dump, caves, and a variety of other installations. They covered their targets with great proficiency, silencing one enemy gun, destroying a blockhouse, and hitting a

With a large amount of smoke rising from the island, this photograph shows the first waves of landing craft going ashore at Iwo Jima. [Photograph from Baumrucker's album.]

tank. Amidst this deadly business, a lighter episode occurred when "toward evening we thought we saw a sniper on a reef and laid him low with the 40 mm's but it turned out to be a navigational blinker our people had put there with some difficulty."[278] More vital targets were bombarded on the twenty-first and, as a result, Baumrucker noted, "the Japs were being moved toward the wooded end of the island to the east and our planes were dive bombing them with napalm which exploded in great balls of fire."[279]

The Orders of the Day for 22 February 1945 offered the crew some feedback on their handiwork of the previous day:

U.S.S. WEST VIRGINIA
ORDERS OF THE DAY
Thursday, 22 February 1945.
DUTY DIVISION: 2nd Division relieves the 1st Division.
FOLLOW THE DAILY SEA ROUTINE EXCEPT:
0515 REVEILLE.
0530 MESS GEAR.
0545 BREAKFAST.
0704 Sunrise, light ship.
1145 MESS GEAR.
1200 DINNER.
1645 MESS GEAR.
1700 SUPPER.
1833 Sunset, darken Ship. Smoking lamp is out on all weather decks from sunset to sunrise.
NOTE: The following dispatch has been received, addressed
To ALL HANDS of the Pacific Ocean Area:
The officers and men of the First Carrier Task

Force of the Pacific Fleet have dealt the enemy a crushing blow which will long be remembered. The same courage, skill, and teamwork which enabled our carrier pilots to destroy the enemy in bad weather over Tokyo are now being displayed by the forces which are taking Iwo Island, only 660 miles from Tokyo. They will also bring success when our troops land in Japan itself covered and supported by the ever increasing power of our air forces and the guns of the fleet.

To these brave officers and men who have been and are in combat and also to those whose support and assistance in rear areas are essential for these successes: WELL DONE.

> *G. J. KING,*
> *Commander, U.S. Navy,*
> *Executive Officer*

Commander King added a short, boxed comment to these Orders of the Day that read: "We did some good shooting yesterday. The gunners certainly laid them where our Marines wanted them. Let's keep up the good work."

***

The next day, they provided intermittent fire support as they moved around the island "frequently close enough to use 20 and 40 mm's. Volcanic steam arising from various points on the island."[280] Each day became similar to the one before it – bringing on more vital targets for the ship to destroy – yet the officers and crew of the *West Virginia* maintained their high standards of performance. The Orders of the Day for Sunday, 25 February 1945 closed with two "NOTES:"

NOTE: (1) The Gunners were up to there usual high standard yesterday which brought forth a remark from a carrier spotting plane to the effect that our shooting was the most accurate he has ever seen in this operation. During one phase of the firing he called it pin-point accuracy; keep up the good work. You certainly cleared the way for the Marines yesterday. (2) LOST: One (1) Dogma, anti-magnetic, Swiss movement wrist watch in the forward head between the hours of 0740 and 0745. Anyone finding same turn in to M.A.A. Office. A Reward of $50.00 will be given to finder.

Praise for the performance of the men of the *West Virginia* came directly from CINCPAC:

U.S.S. WEST VIRGINIA (BB48)
c/o Fleet Post Office
San Francisco, California
<u>*CAPTAIN'S MEMORANDUM TO THE CREW*</u>

The following message was received this morning:
From: Commander in Chief, Pacific Fleet.
To: U.S.S. WEST VIRGINIA.

<u>*"WELL DONE"*</u>

This unusual citation is to the credit of every department of the ship and man in the crew. It was not alone for our quick preparations in Ulithi, for that was due to our previous good work.

It was for the Engineers who turned up 36,000 miles the first six months in commission and kept us ready for full power at all times and enabled us always to report "ready for any mission now".

It was for the Gunnery Department which has been always ready and alert so that in battles we could pitch big league every time.

It was for the C&R Department which has kept our gear in repair and enabled us to answer all calls. It was for the Supply Department which has delivered the goods and kept us supplied with everything we needed, and for the Communicators who kept us at the peak with orders and information. The Medical Department guarded our health so that we were physically tip-top. The Chaplain guided our mental attitude and thinking.

This "WELL DONE" was therefore for a rapid shakedown, the ability quickly to take our place on the firing line, our accomplishments such as doing a 48 hour replenishment job in one night at Espirito Santo; the performances in Leyte Gulf, Surigao Straits, Sulu Sea and Lingayen.

In other words it was a "WELL DONE" for every man in the crew whose cheerful cooperation and hard work contributes to the demonstration that the WEST VIRGINIA is a smart ship and always ready for any mission.

> H. V. Wiley,
> Captain, U.S. Navy,
> Commanding, U.S.S. WEST VIRGINIA.

***

On 27 February, as the *West Virginia* arrived in its fire support area at 1032 hours, they spotted an enemy battery firing on the *U.S.S. Bryant* (DD-665) which was about five miles from the shore. The *West Virginia* closed its range to about 6,000 yards and opened fire with its secondary battery. "The gun was silenced with many direct hits."[281] That afternoon, American planes searched for targets of opportunity, but no enemy activity was noted in the *West Virginia's* assigned area. Conveying an element of satisfaction, Baumrucker's diary for 27 February made note that "our first plane took off from a captured landing field."[282] The War Diary entry for 28 February 1945, over the name of Captain H. V. Wiley, ended,

> While furnishing fire support at Iwo Jima on D-Day and thereafter, this vessel observed many more near misses from 'friendly overs' and 'friendly ricochets' than from enemy counter battery.[283]

On 1 March, the ship got underway for Ulithi, arriving on the fourth. En route, Baumrucker amused himself by polishing three cigarette boxes that he had made from 40 mm shell cases. They were at Ulithi, among other reasons, for rest and recreation. An important development in the Navy life of Robert O. Baumrucker occurred there. The War Diary entry for 5 March included the notation that at 1030 hours, Commander George J. King, U. S. N., was relieved by Commander John E. Fitzgibbon, U. S. N., as Executive Officer of the *West*

Virginia.[xliii] King was appointed to the rank of Captain for temporary service aboard another ship. The promotion of Fitzgibbon to Executive Officer, the second highest-ranking officer aboard ship, heralded another phase of life for Baumrucker with many unpleasant sequellae.

The same diary entry included the account of the number one motor whaleboat having sunk about one hundred yards off the ship's port bow. There were no injuries to the fifteen passengers, but the boat was not recovered.

> A Board of Investigation will be ordered by the Commanding Officer to determine the cause, and place responsibility, for the loss of the boat. The position where the boat sank was marked by a buoy, but all efforts to recover the boat were unsuccessful.[284]

A recreation party of approximately thirty-five officers and two hundred fifty men went to Mog Mog Island for recreation and beer. While at Ulithi, Baumrucker had a pleasant reunion with his old friend, Charlie Steele. Steele was serving as Admiral Mitscher's Flag Secretary in the Fast Carrier Task Force. The two had not seen each other since 27 December 1943, when they were in San Francisco. Steele came aboard the *West Virginia* by way of the Admiral's barge and "the ship nearly went to full dress as the flag approached."[285] Baumrucker thought that his friend "looked rather thin, from a lot more work than we'd been catching though their battleships had it relatively easy."[286] In a supplemental note to his diary entry, added during transcription, Baumrucker stated, "On this next May 11, [Steele] was killed in a kamikaze attack on the Bunker Hill."[287] The aircraft carrier, *U.S.S. Bunker Hill* (CV-17), was supporting the invasion of Okinawa on 11 May 1945 when she was hit by two kamikaze planes. Charlie Steele was among the three hundred forty-six men killed in the attack. The ship survived.

Following several days of relaxation on Mog Mog, swimming from good beaches, and enjoying some beer, things suddenly got busier on 8 March as the ship once again took on large amounts of stores. This was also the day that tensions developed between Lt. Robert Baumrucker and Commander John Fitzgibbon. Baumrucker documented the episode in his diary:

> A very busy and hectic 0800 – 1200 watch as supplies were coming in wholesale on both quarters. As one working party finished and went through the break in the deck The Spider, our thoroughly disrespected new exec – at least, in comparison with our previous exec – came up to me out of the shadows of the awning and asked if these men had been fed. When I told him I didn't know, he took time from the work to lecture thoroughly and to say 'Take care of your men and they'll take care of you!' (I think that was another phrase he had learned at Tower Hall). I was too busy to tell him chow had been <u>saved</u> for these men, but it was immaterial to me whether or not this particular group had eaten ashore. Thus began a new romance.[288]

Fitzgibbon had been appointed Executive Officer just three days prior to this incident. This was the first documented confrontation between the two men, but

---

xliii Changes in personnel were not decided on the ship. These changes came from the Navy's Bureau of Personnel.

Baumrucker's good friend, Charlie Steele, was one of three hundred forty-six men killed in kamikaze attacks against the aircraft carrier, U. S. S. Bunker Hill on 11 May 1945. [Photograph from Baumrucker's album.]

Fitzgibbon's troublesome attitude toward Baumrucker would continue, and the consequences would haunt Baumrucker forever. The following day, as he was returning from a ball game ashore, Baumrucker received the first news of the death of his friend, Sam Givens, who died in a plane crash while en route to Kwajalein to carry out an errand for Admiral Halsey: "I last saw him those four days out of Pearl when he had that happy time observing our firing last September 18 – 22."[289]

Subsequent days were occupied with routine ship duties alternating with recreation ashore. Baumrucker got off the last batch of copy for his Shellback book. On 11 March, a big officers' picnic was held ashore, and:

> that evening, while all ships present were showing movies topside, two Jap planes slipped in. One crashed an island, the other hit the carrier Randolph and set it afire. Totally, embarrassingly surprised, the ships blacked out and went to General Quarters, but that was all. Where did they come from, Yap?[290]

Yap was a western Pacific island in the Caroline group that was held by the Japanese but was passed over during the "island-hopping" campaign. Baumrucker speculated that the enemy plane that crashed into the island had mistaken its silhouette for an American ship. The plane that crashed into the aircraft carrier, *U.S.S. Randolph* (CV-15), was a Yokosuka P1B1 "Frances" kamikaze airplane. It struck the *Randolph* on her starboard side aft, but the ship was repaired while at Ulithi, and she returned to service. These two planes were the only enemy aircraft sighted that night. The following day, Baumrucker received the first batch of proofs for the Shellback book and he was very pleased with them. He mimeographed a batch of V-mail letters[xliv] to send to former members of the crew to notify them of the Shellback book. "Everyone to get one copy free, additional copies $1."[xlv] He met with Captain Wiley personally to learn which portrait he wanted of himself to be entered into this book.

On 15 March, Lombardi returned to the *West Virginia* from the Command Ship to which he had been transferred, and "Where a [lieutenant-commander] rates about as high as an ensign elsewhere."[291] On 21 March, with rest and recreation ashore ended and large quantities of stores having been brought aboard, the *West Virginia* got underway for Okinawa.

---

xliv V-mail stood for "Victory Mail". This method of mailing was devised in an effort to speed up the delivery time of letters from servicemen to home. It also diminished the physical volume of mail to be moved. Once a letter had been written by the service man and censored, it was photographed and shipped home in reels of similarly photographed letters. In the States, the letters were printed on photograph paper and delivered to their destinations.
xlv In 2010, this author paid $100 for a poor quality photocopy of the Shellback book. Fortunately, he later came into possession of Baumrucker's own copy.

CHAPTER 15
Okinawa

This pre-invasion aerial photograph of Yontan airfield on Okinawa reveals revetments, support structures, and a number of planes situated off the airstrip. [Photograph from Baumrucker's album.]

The *West Virginia* got underway at 0805 hours on 21 March 1945 as part of Task Force 54 bound for Okinawa. The battle line included, from vanguard to rear, the *U.S.S. Estes, U.S.S. Tennessee, U.S.S. Idaho, U.S.S. New Mexico, U.S.S. Nevada, U.S.S. West Virginia, U.S.S. Colorado, U.S.S. Maryland, U.S.S. Texas* and *U.S.S. Arkansas*. En route, the line of ships conducted anti-aircraft practice by firing at drones and sleeves. Baumrucker's diary entry stated simply, "AA practices, and for good cause."[292] Everyone expected the Japanese aerial attack effort, including kamikazes, to intensify as the fleet drew closer to the homeland. They arrived at Kerama Rhetto, one of the small Kerama Islands located to the west of the main island of Okinawa, and began their bombardment of the island immediately, and in the presence of heavy air opposition. They continued their bombardment for the next three days, during which time the *West Virginia* was the target of an unsuccessful attack by an enemy submarine. After Kerama Rhetto was captured by American forces on 26 March, it was used as a staging area for the invasion of Okinawa. This group of small islands near Okinawa served not only as a staging area, but also as a haven for the Navy's ships each night as they retired there for safe anchorage. On the same day that Kerama Rhetto was captured, Baumrucker had a change of duty:

> Transferred from my duty in the Spot I main battery director over the bridge, where I'd been aiming the battery and having a fine view of operations since Leyte Gulf, to take charge of the main battery plotting room where you see nothing but instruments and especially no kamikazes.[293]

The twenty-sixth of March was a very busy day as the West Virginia picked up a number of enemy aircraft on its own radar and received numerous radio reports of approaching "bogies." The destroyer-minesweeper, U.S.S. Robert H. Smith (DM-23), was destroyed by enemy aircraft, but the closest bogies to the West Virginia's formation were twenty-two miles out. The U.S.S. Wichita, six miles off the West Virginia, reported sighting a torpedo wake. Destroyers reported sound contacts[xlvi] between the Nevada and the Wichita, and attacked the spot by dropping depth charges. The Wichita later reported another torpedo wake running across her bow. For most of the morning, the sounds of destroyers dropping depth charges were heard, but no enemy submarine was produced. A lookout on the West Virginia reported seeing a gun flash on the beach, followed by a splash in the water about five thousand yards off her port bow. Further activity from shore was silenced by gunfire from West Virginia's main battery, but turret two was manned throughout that afternoon, standing by for counter battery fire. On the twenty-seventh, Baumrucker recorded in his diary that a minesweeper had been "torpedoed, upended and sank"[294] but this turned out to be more "fog of war" fare. The ship's War Diary stated definitively that the minesweeper, U.S.S. Skylark (AM-63), hit a mine about three thousand yards off West Virginia's port bow and sank. "Torpedo wakes, periscopes, and sound contacts were reported continuously throughout the morning by various ships in the vicinity."[295]

By 30 March, the smaller islands had been secured and preparations were made for the landings on Okinawa proper. Early that morning, the West Virginia left the formation and headed for its designated fire support station on the western side of Okinawa. A single spotter plane was launched from the ship as the West Virginia was called upon to provide fire support for underwater demolition teams and a general bombardment of the ship's area of responsibility on land. The task was complicated by intermittent rain over the island that resulted in very poor visibility. The pilot of the spotter plane also had difficulty locating targets due to the rain but they were able to begin their bombardments at 0835. Their targets were blockhouses, pillboxes, and enemy batteries. In spite of the poor visibility, the pilot was able to confirm that the fire mission was a success. By early afternoon, the boats of the underwater demolition teams were seen close to the beach, in spite of heavy smoke over the beach. Because the ship was close to shore, within reach of enemy land-based artillery, one gun turret was manned and standing by to provide counter battery fire if needed. At 1524 hours, the West Virginia received an order from the Commander of Task Force 52 to close the beach to within one thousand yards and to knock at least

---

xlvi Suspected submarines.

Okinawa. "D-Day. Easter, April 1, 1945. Three bullets in the air." The battleship is so close to land that its 16" guns are nearly parallel to the water. This photograph captured three projectiles in the air. Baumrucker used a pen to highlight them and then drew small arrows pointing to each. [Photograph from Baumrucker's album.]

three good holes in the sea wall along the shore line with gunfire. Using both main and secondary batteries, the ship demolished the wall.

On 31 March, reports reached the *West Virginia* that the *U.S.S. Indianapolis*, just two miles away, had been hit by a kamikaze plane. A "Zeke"[xlvii] was seen crashing into the water about twelve miles from the *West Virginia* and another "Zeke" was shot down just astern of the *U.S.S. New Mexico*. All the while, the *West Virginia* continued to use both main and secondary batteries to support underwater demolition teams and to hit designated enemy targets ashore. The War Diary entry for 31 March 1945 ended,

> We operated very close to Okinawa during the night as additional support for the transport groups arriving in the area during the night. Tomorrow is the day our troops go ashore on Okinawa! Easter.
> H. V. Wiley [Captain][296]

On 1 April 1945, the worst fears of the men of the *West Virginia* were realized. Baumrucker recorded,

> April 1 – Okinawa. The attack on the main island begins. We have a near miss by a kamikaze and his exploding bomb jolts us pretty good. At dusk, while Soderberg and I were playing acey-ducey under the fan-tail, a kamikaze got through on our port side of the foremast.[297]

---

xlvii "Zeke" was the Navy's reporting name for a Mitsubishi A6M Zero-Sen fighter plane.

The Japanese plane crashed into the O2 deck on the port side. Ensign Winford was in the director of his 5"/38 caliber antiaircraft gun when the plane crashed into the ship just ahead of him. There was so much activity in the air around the ship – antiaircraft fire, tracers, and enemy planes – that he was not certain when he first picked up the plane visually before it hit the O2 deck.[298] Difficulty spotting enemy aircraft and following tracer rounds would be addressed in an official report later. Fortunately, the bomb the plane carried did not explode.

Baumrucker and Soderberg headed for the crash site, but they were not the first to arrive there. An unknown number of crewmen had gotten to the crash ahead of them. Members of the crew removed a number of items from the wreckage of the plane for souvenirs. Among them was Seaman Charlie Loving. Loving and a shipmate were at their battle stations manning a fire hose near an aft gun turret when the kamikaze plane crashed into the ship. He and his friend were both nineteen years old at the time and, according to Loving, "afraid of nothing."

They ran to the crash site immediately. They found the body of the dead Japanese pilot still in the broken cockpit of the plane. Knowing that officers would be on the scene shortly, they quickly foraged for souvenirs. Loving's friend took the pilot's sidearm and Loving removed the pilot's Japanese body flag. They retreated from the scene quickly and concealed their treasures from curious officers before returning to assist with the clean up. Loving and his friend were the only two people to see the body flag. Loving kept it concealed until the end of the war. After the war, he kept the flag in a safe deposit box in his bank in downtown Lynchburg, Virginia.

The flag contained a number of inscriptions obviously written by different hands. Fellow pilots had signed this pilot's flag with inscriptions intended to wish him success in what was to be his final mission. The translations included: "Never lose!!!" Arima [a family name]; "God Wind;" "The earth is big!;" "Now, just before we go to the frontier of war, I feel complicated sadness." Akita [a family name]; "I wish good luck for the fight." [Fukuda Tosinori [a name]; "Devote life for your justice." Tsuchishiro [a name]; "Hope our soul will last forever;" "Beat enemy." Maeda [name]; "Good luck and bad luck." Husae [name]. This flag remains in the private collection of Charles Loving. The location of the pilot's pistol is unknown. Baumrucker's account continued,

> "Soderberg, as a former damage control officer, and I with collateral duty as Intelligence Officer, unofficially made our way through sealed compartments for the 400 feet to see where the bomb had hit the armor deck and broken in half – with yellowish powder scattered around. Had it gone off, it would have cleaned out the whole mast, bridge and much of the ship. As it was, it loused up part of the signal bridge and the crew's galley. Just then I was paged to report to the bridge to begin checking out the pilot, etc. As I arrived, The Spider [Fitzgibbon] was reporting to the captain that no one was killed but I had to report that I had passed four dead and many wounded on my way up. Should I have let him lie to the captain? I was then up the rest of the night going through the wreckage."[299]

The official account of this incident is contained in the *West Virginia's* War Diary for 1 April 1945. It recorded:

The U.S.S. WEST VIRGINIA is and has been engaged in the current operations at Okinawa Retto. We are furnishing fire support preparatory to the landing of our ground forces on Okinawa Shima. "H" Hour has been set tentatively as 0830 this morning. We have been bombarding the west coast of Okinawa from Fire Support Area Six.....Between 0100 and 0230, bogies were reported in close to Okinawa, and the Combat Air Patrol reported splashing two "ZEKES". At 0400, we were steaming on various courses at various speeds proceeding independently to Fire Support Area Six. At 0455, back all engines full to avoid collision with unknown destroyer crossing our bow... A Japanese plane – believed to be a "NATE"[xlviii] sighted off our port quarter about fifteen miles distant. Commenced firing our anti-aircraft batteries, shooting him down about two hundred yards off our port quarter. Four more enemy planes were sighted to port at 0617, and we again opened fire. One "NATE" was observed to crash into the sea. Commenced shore bombardment at 0630. Landing craft dot the ocean as far as we can see, awaiting for "H" Hour. "H" Hour has been confirmed as 0830. We have lost communications with one of our spotting planes, and have obtained the services of Wake Island plane 115. The landing craft are moving in toward shore. An L. C. I., in toward the beach, apparently hit a mine and disintegrated. At 0830, the first wave appears to be about three hundred yards off the beach. At 0842, our troops can be seen going ashore. Hoisted in one of our planes at 0900, refueled it, repaired its radio, and launched it again at 1257. Continued firing bombardment throughout the day, alert for counterbattery fire, our troops appeared to be moving rapidly inland, meeting very little resistance....We are lying to in Fire Support Area Six awaiting instructions for night deployment. Sounded air defense for evening alert at 1845. 1850 Flash "red", control "yellow". Set material condition modified zebra throughout the ship at 1903. Three enemy planes sighted a few miles dead ahead of us. Opened fire with our anti-aircraft batteries at these planes. They crossed to our port side, and then one of them looped over and crash dived into the ship. He hit the ship at 1913. The plane hit the O2 Deck on the port side just forward and inboard of secondary battery, Director No. 2. Four men were killed on one of the 20 MM groups, and several men were injured. The bomb carried by the plane broke loose and penetrated to the second deck compartment B-502-L. It did not explode, and was rendered harmless by our bomb disposal officer. The bomb was disposed of over the ship's side. Damage was slight; the Galley and Laundry being the hardest hit. The First Lieutenant reported that the ship's force can repair most of the damage done, and have both the Galley and Laundry in operating order very shortly...[300]

The *West Virginia's* Deck Log entry for 1 April 1945 included a page titled, "ADDITIONAL REMARKS BY THE NAVIGATOR." These remarks included the

---

xlviii "Nate" was the Navy's reporting name for a Nakajima Ki-27 (Type 97) fighter.

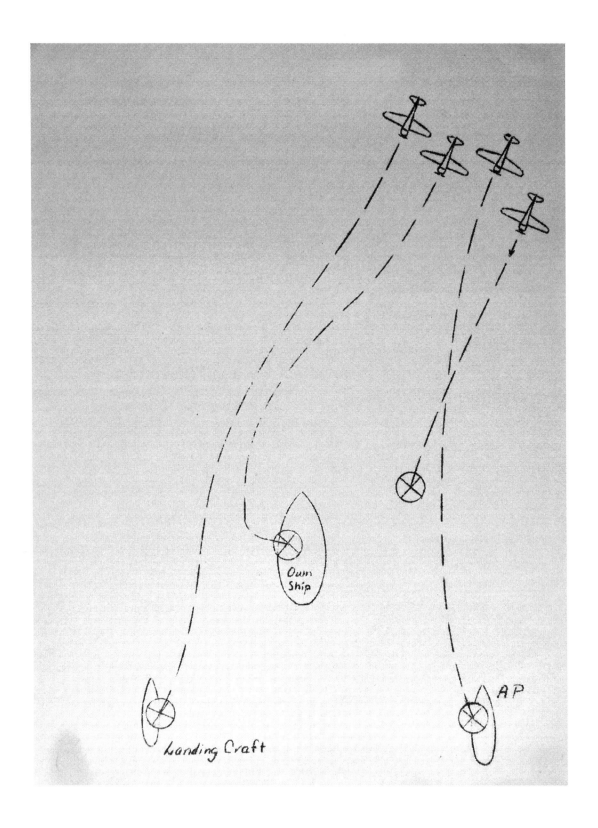

names of the four Navy Enlisted Men who were killed by the kamikaze plane. They were:

PETERS, William Frank   S. 1c, V-6, U.S.N.R., 554 26 37
POSEY, Clarence Yukon   S. 1c, U.S.N., 837 77 67
PRANIN, Stanley Harold   S. 1c, V-6, U.S.N.R., 565 39 51
REVEL, Nathan Delbert   Cox (T) V-6, U.S.N.R.,624 43 06

The diagnosis, prognosis, and disposition were listed the same for each of the four men:

Diagnosis   Injuries, Multiple, Extreme
Prognosis   Fatal
Disposition   Buried at sea[301]

The Deck Log also included the names of twenty-three enlisted men "casualties." Only one of these carried a prognosis of "serious." Seventeen of the men were returned to duty after receiving initial treatment.

Unknown to each other, Enisgn Russell Umbenhour and Seaman Charlie Loving witnessed the burial at sea of the four American sailors. This was the first time they had witnessed such a ceremony and they were moved deeply. For the remainder of their lives, they never forgot the scene or the emotions associated with it.

Regarding the drawing on the left:

Dated 1 April 1945, this drawing was extracted from the "REVISED FORM FOR REPORTING A. A. ACTION BY SURFACE SHIPS." These forms contained narrative descriptions of enemy air attacks supplemented by illustrations such as the one above. "Own Ship" is the U. S. S. West Virginia.

"At approximately 1907, four unidentified Japanese planes, possibly "Oscars" were sighted by lookouts at 020o relative bearing, range about 3000 yards, altitude 2,000 feet, flying directly toward the ship. Fire was opened at the leading plane at 010o relative at which time the group split, two planes flying aft on the starboard side, and two planes crossing the bow to port.

The two planes flying aft on the starboard side were fired on by the starboard 40MM and 20MM batteries and one was observed to crash in flames off the starboard bow. The second plane continued down the starboard side and crashed into a transport bearing about 165o relative, distant about 2,500 yards. It is believed that 20MM and 40MM fire from this ship was instrumental in the destruction of the plane shot down.

The two planes passing down the port side were taken under fire by the port 40MM and 20MM batteries. One plane flew aft on the port side and crashed into a landing craft on the port quarter. This plane was taken under fire by a few guns only. The second plane was taken under fire by the majority of the port 40MM and 20MM batteries. This plane, carrying a 250kg bomb made a tight left turn at about 270o relative, dived vertically on the ship and crashed in 20MM Group #6 just forward of 5" director #2 between frames 67 and 70." This narrative was followed by an analysis of why the ship failed to destroy the kamikaze before it crashed into her. [Courtesy of the National Archives, College Park, Maryland.]

As the Intelligence Officer for the West Virginia, Baumrucker was ordered to examine the kamikaze crash site and its pilot. This photograph shows a combination of destroyed ship parts and the wreckage of the plane. The two photographs were removed from the pilot's personal possessions. There were no labels to indicate the identity of the Japanese women. Seaman Charlie Loving removed the pilot's body flag before Baumrucker and Soderberg got to the crash site. [Photographs from Baumrucker's album.]

The following day, Baumrucker continued to handle the firing from main battery plot and, in his spare time, made detailed examinations of the kamikaze crash site looking for intelligence. He discovered a chart in the pilot's boot that indicated the he had come from Kyushu and had a retirement course to Formosa. The pilot was an officer. This led Baumrucker to speculate that he might not have been on a kamikaze mission. Baumrucker was maximally busy between his duties in main battery plot and collateral duty as Intelligence Officer.

On top of <u>this</u>, The Spider called me aside and told me to retrieve the pilot's pistol, wrist watch, parachute, body flag, etc. (which members of the crew had salvaged on the first bounce of the plane and hidden in the anchor chain locker and elsewhere) for him personally.[302]

Neither Baumrucker nor the Spider ever saw the pistol or body flag.

While Baumrucker speculated that this might not have been a kamikaze attack, history recorded it as one, and the records from the incident are confirmatory. His assessment of the situation was hindered by the fact that he did not witness the plane in its flight path as it crashed into the ship. The "Revised Form For Reporting [Anti-aircraft] Action By Surface Ships" dated 1 April 1945 contained narrative and diagrammatic details of the flight of the Japanese plane.

"The second plane was taken under fire by the majority of the port 40MM and 20MM batteries. This plane, carrying a 250 kg bomb made a right turn at about 270° relative, dived vertically on the ship and crashed in 20MM Group #6 just forward of 5" director #2 between frames 67 and70."[303]

This narrative was followed by an analysis of the problem shooting down the suicide plane.

"It is considered that the poor visibility of evening twilight combined with the volume of tracers blinded the 20MM gunners and 40MM sight operators so tha[t] they experienced great difficulty in staying on targets and in some cases lost targets completely.

This was especially noticeable when firing at the plane that crashed the ship to port. In view of this it is recommended that 40MM self destructive ammunition with a dim tracer feature be supplied ships in sufficient quantity to provide for more effective night firing against suicide planes."[304]

The intensity of kamikaze activity in early April 1945 is evidenced by several of the anti-aircraft action reports from the *West Virginia*, in addition to the report of the plane that struck her.

On 27 April 1945, the official Battle Damage Report of the kamikaze crash into the *West Virginia* was completed and forwarded to The Chief of the Bureau of Ships. The Japanese plane was labeled officially as an "Oscar"[xlix] in this

---

xlix "Oscar" was the Navy's reporting name for a Nakajima Ki-43 Hayabusa (Type 1) fighter.

report. The report gave a brief narrative of the action that resulted in the damage. The times given were approximate.

1845 - Air Defense sounded.
1855 – Modified Condition Zebra set.
1907 – Three (3) enemy planes sighted. Open fire. Condition Zebra ordered set from Central. Planes lost from sight, obscured by smoke and darkness.
1908 – One (1) plane sighted dead ahead, 60° position angle diving toward ship. Plane was under heavy fire by automatic weapons. Plane struck ship on port side of superstructure, gun platform (O3) level frame 69.
1909 – Fire on port side of O2 deck. All fire pumps ordered to boost pressure to 100 pounds. Small caliber ammunition exploding.
1910 – Fire reported in laundry…, galley…, and tailor shop.
1912 – Fire in crew's space.
1914 – Condition Zebra set with exception of doors and hatches in vicinity of plane crash.
1920 – Unexploded bomb discovered…
1930 – All fires out and bomb reported 'safe'.
2010 – Bomb body disposed of overside. The ship had weigh on.
2025 – Condition Yoke set with the exception of damaged areas.
2026 – Secured from Air Defense.
2043 – Anchored."[305]

In the damage assessment, it was believed that the bomb had detached itself as it struck the 20 MM gun pit or, perhaps, had been released a few seconds earlier. The plane itself passed through the O2 deck and came to rest against a bulkhead in the laundry. The bomb was identified as a 250 kg type 92, Japanese Army G. P. H. E. bomb, 11 ¾ inches in diameter and fused for detonation following a short delay. The bomb's initial impact was on the 20 MM gun platform on the O3 level where it made a neat, circular hole twelve inches in diameter and followed a path inboard and aft at an angle of 58° from horizontal. It traveled inboard a distance of nine feet and aft a distance of eleven feet through three thicknesses of ten pound steel and one high tensile steel plate of the main deck. "The second deck defeated the bomb. The bomb burst open on contact with the armored second deck and scattered a very toxic dust throughout the compartment….There was no explosion."[306]

With regard to all of the official reports surrounding the kamikaze plane crash, there is a curious element that was omitted from the War Diary record of the event – the ultimate fate of the dead Japanese pilot. Seaman Charlie Loving assisted some other crewmembers in lifting the pilot's body from the cockpit and placing it in a "wooden orange crate" that had been brought from the mess area. The pilot's head was placed on top and the crate was "taken below." None of these crewmen knew *where below* the body was taken. Decades later, veteran crewmen speculated that the body was dumped over the side of the ship. While a number of histories have dealt with the incident of the kamikaze attack, none addressed the issue of disposal of the pilot's body.

A lengthy search for a witness led ultimately to James O'Neil, a veteran crewmember who had first hand knowledge of the final journey of the dead pilot.

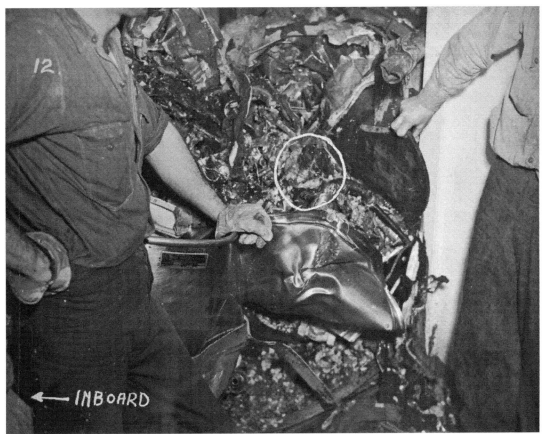

This photograph was taken from the damage report of the kamikaze crash into the West Virginia. The mangled metal represents a mixture of ship's parts and the crashed kamikaze plane. A white circle was drawn in the middle of the photograph to indicate the pilot's head. [Previously unpublished photograph; courtesy of the National Archives, College Park, Maryland.]

As the opening phase of the battle of Okinawa was raging, O'Neil was serving as a "volunteer stretcher bearer." His memory was lucid as he recalled that the pilot's body was taken below in the wooden crate to a shower room that was used as a collecting area for dead bodies. From there, the remains of the dead were processed. After the acuteness of the episode was over, O'Neil was called on to serve as a pallbearer for the pilot. The body of the Japanese pilot was placed into a canvas sack and weighted with an artillery shell in a manner identical to that used for dead American sailors. He and three shipmates placed the wrapped and weighted body onto a piece of plywood board with hand holds cut around the sides. They took it to the quarterdeck, balanced the board with the body momentarily, and then let the body slide into the sea. He recalled, "It was done with dignity but no fanfare." O'Neil served as pallbearer for the burial at sea of the four sailors who were killed by the kamikaze crash. The Ship's War Diary for 2 April 1945 stated simply, "At 0000, conducted burial services for the men killed in the suicide plane hit."

By 4 April, Baumrucker had finished searching through the wreckage of the kamikaze plane and left it for the crew to salvage any souvenirs they might find. For himself, Baumrucker made some acey-ducey pips from the plane's rubber gasoline tank. In the days that followed, the attack on Okinawa continued from both sides. On 6 April,

> The air attacks get heavier than probably ever before. The Spider calls me into his cabin, to show me <u>he</u> was able to get the parachute, now hanging from the overhead: 'But now I don't know what to do with it.' I said 'I have a suggestion, sir. Why not give the crew a break and cut it into 2000 pieces for souvenirs.' I can still hear his reply: 'What! Those ghouls?! Those body-robbers??!! Give <u>them</u> a break? I think I'll have it made into a wedding dress for my daughter.' Take care of your men, etc., indeed![307]

The following day, "Almost caught another kamikaze as he just about got to the ship before we got him."[308] The same day, a "Betty"[l] crashed close astern of the *U.S.S. Birmingham*, and the *U.S.S. Idaho* downed a "Val."[li] The *West Virginia* opened fire on a low-flying "Val" with its 40 MM batteries just before it crashed into the *U.S.S. Maryland*, but the *Maryland* reported her condition to be "excellent." That night the ships patrolled north and south about three miles west of Okinawa ready to intercept and engage a Japanese surface force believed to be heading their way. The enemy force never reached them as Task Force 58 reported sinking most of the ships in that fleet, including the battleship *Yamato*.

The bombardment of Okinawa, threats from enemy surface forces, and heavy air attacks did not prevent tensions from intrigue aboard ship. On 9 April, Baumrucker had another encounter with Fitzgibbon.

> The material for the Shellback book has finally been cleared by the Fleet Chief Censor, when The Spider tells me we must now eliminate all identification by divisions, leave out a number of names and group pictures and fudge up other sections 'So that it will not divulge our ship's complement to the enemy.' Either this, or abandon the project altogether. I was given to understand that if <u>his</u> picture were included the whole thing could stand, as cleared by the proper authorities, but since he was not aboard at any time the events took place that were covered in the book I saw no reason to make it confusing. The captain and exec, as included were extremely popular and respected.[309]

By the twelfth, Baumrucker admitted in his diary that the men were getting pretty tired from the prolonged shelling of the island. Adding to his fatigue was the fact that he had to leave his room in the blister whenever the ship went to air defense because it had to be secured as a watertight compartment. He tried to compensate for this loss of sleep in his room by catching naps in the wardroom and in the plotting room. Japanese air attacks on the ships remained heavy and, on this date, the *West Virginia* shot down one "Val" and one "Kate."[lii] The "Kate" had been sighted closing in on the *West Virginia's* starboard bow. The five inch and 40 MM batteries opened fire at a range of seven thousand eight hundred yards. The plane was hit at a range of three thousand four hundred yards and finally crashed into the sea about one thousand yards from

---

l "Betty" was the Navy's reporting name for a Mitsubishi G4M bomber.
li "Val" was the Navy's reporting name for an Aichi D3A attack aircraft.
lii "Kate" was the Navy's reporting name for a Nakajima B5N (Type 97) carrier attack bomber.

the ship. Less fortunate were the *Tennessee*, the *Salt Lake City*, the *Zellars*, and the *Stanley*, all of whom had been hit by enemy planes this day. The *West Virginia* continued to bombard Okinawa, hitting designated targets by day and, by night, answering called fire on targets, or putting out harassing and interdiction fire, often with illumination rounds. Apparently, their firing was highly effective. On 14 April, the ship's War Diary recorded some praise that was relayed to the ship by a spotter: "You're shooting perfectly, you could shoot no better, no change – no change" and "Check fire. Your shooting is strictly marvelous. I cannot express just how good it is." At 1730 hours, the ship held burial services for Lt. (jg) Wilbert Martin Gunther, 328169, U. S. N. R., who had died during the previous night. He was a patient who had been transferred to the *West Virginia* from the *Zellars*.

Baumrucker had been fortunate to avoid injury from the Japanese navy and from numerous kamikaze pilots who had had his ship in their sights, but he could not avoid wandering occasionally into the sights of certain superior officers. On 17 April, he recorded another uncomfortable incident in his diary:

> Another champion of the crew, the First Lieutenant, finds a lull in the battle to call me to the bridge in front of the captain and chew me out because my division has not been properly scrubbing down the area above the bridge. This is obvious because there is a distinct line on the mast structure where our territory is darker. I send my boats up the ladder to demonstrate, with a wet finger, that this isn't dirt but was caused by the First Lieutenant issuing a different color of paint for this area. Any more questions, sir?[310]

Later that evening, the *West Virginia* was with other vessels in a screening position to intercept any enemy surface vessels that might attempt to raid the American picket stations when a heavy underwater explosion was felt close aboard. One of the destroyers in the screen – the *U.S.S. Rooks* – reported that she believed that a buzz bomb had hit the water just astern of her. No damage was done.

By mid April, the *West Virginia's* mission at Okinawa had become routine – providing targeted fire on land targets by day and delivering harassing and illumination fire by night to support the infantry. "The bombardment continues, including our chance to break down Shuri Castle for which job every ship present takes credit."[311] Shuri Castle was a stone and wood structure that had been built in the fourteenth century. It had been designated as a national treasure by Japan before the war. During the war, however, the Japanese army used it for an underground headquarters. The castle was almost completely destroyed during the battle of Okinawa, but the *West Virginia* did not receive credit for the act.

On 24 April, the *West Virginia's* involvement in the bombardment came to an end. She returned to Kerama Rhetto and, the following day, got underway for Ulithi while under heavy air attack. She arrived at Ulithi four days later where a heavy list was placed on her so that men could work on the bottom of her hull. More mail and stores were taken aboard including more proofs of the Shellback book. As on the previous trip to Ulithi, men were sent ashore for recreation. Approximately fifty officers and five hundred enlisted men went ashore. On 30 April 1945, a momentous event took place for the *West Virginia*. At 1447 hours,

Photograph of the "body flag" that Seaman Charlie Loving removed from the body of the pilot who crashed his plane into the U. S. S. West Virginia on 1 April 1945. Loving managed to keep the flag concealed for the remainder of the war. After the war, he kept it in a safe deposit box in his local bank in Lynchburg, Virginia. The kamikaze pilot carried this flag into what was intended to be his last battle. The writings on the flag were from fellow pilots who wished him well on his last mission. Translations of these inscriptions include: "Never lose!", "God Wind," "The earth is big!", "Now, just before we go to the frontier of war, I feel complicated sadness," "I wish good luck for the fight," "Devote life for your justice," "Hope our soul will last forever," "Beat enemy," and "Good luck and bad luck." [This flag is the property of Mr. Charlie Loving who allowed the author to photograph it in support of this text.]

Captain R. W. Holsinger, U.S.N., reported aboard for duty as relief for Captain H. V. Wiley, U. S. N.

The first of May brought with it another unpleasant interaction between Baumrucker and the First Lieutenant.

I am instructed on relieving the watch, not to let any boats make the starboard ladder because it is fragile (it was the responsibility of the First Lieutenant to provide a proper ladder, but the US was then in a state of war). Nevertheless, in spite of all I could do short of firing my pistol at

Photograph of the West Virginia taken in Tokyo Bay with Mt. Fuji in the background. The photographer moved away from the ship in a small boat in order to capture this image. [Photography courtesy of Robert Wilson.]

him, a boat from another ship comes in and rams it...on a noon watch. Instantly, the First Lieutenant and The Spider are topside from the wardroom, outdoing each other in reviling me and threatening demotion to seaman second. Later I asked the Navigator, who is in charge of instruction for the deck watch what I could have done, but he sadly shook his head and said that was one item they hadn't taught <u>him</u> at the Naval Academy.[312]

A major event the following day did nothing to ease Baumrucker's growing sense of unhappiness with the ship's new leadership. On 2 May, "Our fine captain-since-Bremerton leaves the ship, and all hands are almost instantly dubious about his successor...especially in combination with The Spider."[313] The War Diary entry for that day was simple:

Anchored as before. At 1300 Captain R. W. Holsinger relieved Captain H. V. Wiley as Commanding Officer of this vessel. Captain Wiley then left the ship to report to the Commandant of the nearest U. S. Naval District.[314]

Robert Wilson had been communications officer on the *West Virginia* since she left Bremerton. He had worked very closely with Captain Wiley every day and had come to admire him greatly. This was a very sad day for Wilson as he observed his Captain from the communications bridge. The Captain was carried away from the ship in one of its twenty-six foot long motor whaleboats. Wilson stood, transfixed, as he watched the small boat pull away from the "WeeVee," with one sailor to pilot the boat, and its single occupant, Captain Wiley, sitting near the bow, looking backward, motionless, at the *West Virginia*. Very quickly, the small whaleboat was far enough from the ship that Wilson was unable to discern any emotion in the Captain's face. Wilson thought, "There goes the loneliest man in the world." This was an unhappy event for all of the officers and crewmen of the ship.

Baumrucker got some needed relaxation time, spending off-duty hours ashore and swimming from the beach. He borrowed a diving mask to observe tropical fish around a coral reef, and enjoyed it so much that he constructed his own makeshift mask from an old airplane inner tube and a piece of round glass from fire control spare parts. Three days later, he was about to go ashore with a liberty party to try out his diving mask when "a visiting public relations officer came aboard to shoot the breeze so I stayed aboard with him. Guess he wanted to learn about the war."[315] He finally got ashore to try his new mask two days later but, that same day, he also got "vague word from a Washington DC contact" that his orders to shore duty had been dispatched to the ship some time previously. "Don't they want me to go?"[316]

They got underway back to Okinawa on the thirteenth. En route, Baumrucker recommended that several of his chiefs be promoted to ensign, but "they prefer it where they are."[317] The return journey to Okinawa was uneventful. Arriving off Okinawa on the eighteenth, they resumed their role of bombardment and fire support on inland targets. Enemy air activity got heavier. At 0018 hours on 25 May, while at anchor, one of the last evening attackers passed over the *West Virginia* at two hundred feet and crashed into the *U.S.S. O'Neil* (DE 188) that was anchored one thousand eight hundred yards away. Numerous raids were reported coming from the north, but no others got closer than ten miles to the *West Virginia* that day. American and Japanese forces were heavily engaged on the twenty-fifth. American anti-aircraft fire from ships proved quite effective that day against the Japanese air attacks, and American fighter planes reported shooting down fifty-three of the enemy. The *O'Neil*, the *U.S.S. Barry* (APD 29), the *U.S.S. Cowell* (DD 547), the *U.S.S. William Cole* (DE 641), the *U.S.S. Stormes* (DD 780), and the *U.S.S. Butler* (DMS 29) were hit by enemy planes. Twelve casualties from the *Butler* were transferred to the *West Virginia*. Four of them died during the day and four more died that night. That night, they provided harassing and illumination fire for the 7th Army Division due to bad weather that prohibited spotting. The ninth casualty from the Butler died two days later.

While at Buckner Bay, a kamikaze plane skimmed in on the *West Virginia* below the radar's ability to pick it up, and

"the Steward's Mates open up on him with their 20mm's. The longer guns didn't even know he was there. They splash him so close that half the plane crashes up on the quarterdeck and I salvage part of the frame

"Star cut from the homeward bound pennant that was presented to Robert Wilson as he left the ship at the end of the war. [Courtesy of Robert Wilson.]

Commemorative stamped envelopes were produced with a drawing of the West Virginia in Tokyo Bay. [Courtesy of Robert Wilson.]

so the crew can make acey–ducey dice from it. An enlisted man says he got a wheel and it had a Goodyear tire on it."[318]

Bogey raids continued on the morning of the twenty-eighth as an enemy plane was sighted visually at five thousand yards and closing. Automatic weapons opened fire, knocking the plane down, and it hit the water twenty feet from the ship. Parts of the plane landed on the ship, but there were no personnel casualties and there was no damage to the ship. The weather continued to be intermittently bad, hindering bombardment and, at times, resulting in such poor visibility that the spotter planes could not be launched. Yet, the Japanese air attacks continued. Some of these were felt to be harassing attacks while others seemed very much in earnest. On 29 May, kamikazes crashed into both the *U.S.S. Shubrick* (DD 609) and the *U.S.S. Tatum* (DE 798). The *West Virginia* resumed night harassing and illumination fire on the thirtieth. The Shore Fire Control Party of the 7th Army Infantry Division sent the following message to the *West Virginia*: "I wish to thank you for your excellent illumination these past few days, you pulled us out of many a rough spot."[319]

Baumrucker's diary entry for the first of June stated simply, "Okinawa. Still shooting"[320] and "have another go at Shuri Castle with armor piercing shells."[321] The third of June brought him happy news as he received word that his Shellback book was in full production, and he noted that the crew was delighted with the sample page proofs that he posted in their quarters. He had ten thousand extra copies of the book ordered.

While the naval war in the Pacific was a mixture of boring inactivity and horrific life-ending combat, it also had its bizarre episodes. Such an incident occurred on 16 June when the *West Virginia* grazed a destroyer while making the port quarter on a delivery and "[took] her anchor aboard."[322] Baumrucker made a diary entry of the incident on the day it happened, but the War Diary did not comment until the twenty-seventh: "At 1500 [USS MANLOVE], coming alongside our port quarter, scraped our side for 30 frames, dented a 20MM gun tub and damaged one 20MM mount, leaving her anchor in a port chock. MANLOVE reported her own damage as minor."[323] While unusual, the anchor

Commemorative stamped, dated, envelope with U.S.S. West Virginia in the return address location and canceled stamps dated September 2, 1945. The cancelation mark displays the name of the ship and drawing of Mt. Fuji. (Courtesy of Robert Wilson.)

incident was probably the least significant event of the day. The spotting planes had been having difficulties for many days as a result of weather. Under the best of conditions, these tiny planes were launched from a catapult. When they returned from a mission, they landed on the surface of the ocean, came close to the ship, and were retrieved through the use of a hook and crane. The easiest landings took place on smooth seas but they could still land on waters that were moderately choppy using a clever technique that required close timing between the ship and the plane's pilot. When coming in for a landing on the water, the battleship would go to full speed and make a hard turn to port or starboard. The effect was similar to a wiper blade in that it momentarily created a small area of smooth water. When timed properly, the plane could land on the smooth patch of water before it disappeared. The maneuver required practice.

At other times, when the seas were too rough for such a maneuver, the planes were forced to find land. During this time, there were days when foul weather prevented launching, and days when visibility was so bad due to weather that the planes would have been of little or no value. On one occasion, a spotter plane had been launched but was unable to get back to the ship because of bad weather. It landed on the far side of Okinawa and was eventually taken aboard another vessel before conditions allowed it to return to the *West Virginia*. None of these things compared to an incident that occurred on 16 June. One of the spotting plane pilots – Lieutenant Walker – was shot down behind enemy lines and lost. The captain held up the *West Virginia's* firing in that area until he was certain they would not hit Walker. This arrested fire came in the face of pleas from the troops on the ground for fire support. Walker and his radioman had been seen going down by parachute and then running down a road to hide in some bushes, "but Soderberg lost sight of him then and thinks he was no doubt shot."[324] More details were found in the official War Diary report:

> AT 0640 received firing assignment from First Marine Division and went to General Quarters to fire main battery. Launched both planes, one to spot and the second to clear quarter deck....At 0943 spotting plane (No. 5311), was reported hit by AA fire and falling in flames; Pilot Lt. (jg) Donald Ray Walker, A-1, U.S.N.R. (351766) and LADSON, Melvin Eugene, AOM3c, U.S.N.R., V6, SV, 85 14 93 bailed out and were seen to land in enemy held territory by the pilot of second plane and by the pilot of one of the "VOF" spotting planes. Pilot was reported to have got up after landing, removed chute harness, and walked away, with a group of people. The gunner crawled into bushes with his chute on, and was later reported by the pilot of "VOF" plane to have disappeared with his chute.
>
> Later that day, "the pilot of 'VOF' believed our pilot and passenger were 'dug in' for day. The 'VOF' pilot intended returning at night, to search for signals..."[325]

No further comments were made in the War Diary related to this event but a handwritten addendum to Baumrucker's diary note indicated that both men were found on 30 June. Both had been shot in the back of the head. Ensign Umbenhour had gotten to know Walker quite well. They were in the same bunk area and often sat together at meals. Although they never spent any time together off the ship, they had become very good friends. Word of Walker's death by assassination spread quickly through the ship.[326]

The sixteenth of June turned out to be a day full of tragedies. The destroyer, *U.S.S. Twiggs* (DD 591), was on radar patrol off Okinawa. At approximately 2030 hour, a Japanese torpedo plane put a torpedo into the *Twiggs* port side, hitting her number 2 magazine. The plane then circled around and made a suicide crash into the aft of the ship. The exploding magazine and crash of the plane into the ship resulted in fires that engulfed the ship in flames in very short order. The ship sank within about thirty minutes of the plane's crash taking one hundred fifty-two crewmen to their deaths. Also counted among her dead was the Captain, Commander George Philip.

On the twenty-first of June, "The crew has been enjoying our entrance into Kerama Rhetto by getting up on the bridge and enjoying the comedy as the new skipper and The Spider, together, bulldoze their way into an anchorage, terrorizing the 'spit kits' (destroyers and lesser craft) who otherwise have the right of way but now must dodge this monster blundering into their water."[327] With Baumrucker's description of this episode, coming on the heels of the "anchor incident," he is demonstrating a growing dislike or distrust of the new captain, especially when he and the executive officer combine efforts that result in poor nautical skills. While he had reason to dislike the executive officer, it does not seem that he had been exposed to the new captain long enough to formulate a fair opinion. Captain Wiley had been so loved by his officers and crew that it is likely that, whoever was his replacement, he would have a hard time measuring up to Wiley. Baumrucker finished off his version of the incident with the *Manlove's* anchor in his diary entry for 27 June: "We have been carrying that destroyer's anchor on our port quarter for 11 days, apparently trying to decide what to do with it but confusing the rest of the fleet as to what the hell it's doing there. We finally unloaded it by lifting it off with one of the guns in turret 4."[328] The War Diary finished the anchor story with its entry of 30 June: "Tug came alongside for MANLOVE'S anchor." What unifies the two versions of this story is the idea that the gun was used to lift the anchor off the deck and transfer it to the tug.

On 1 July 1945, the *West Virginia* got underway once again for Leyte Gulf, arriving on the fourth. Following a couple of days' rest ashore, Baumrucker finally got his orders back to the States for shore duty. His part in the war had now come to an end. He got liberty at Samar where he had time to enjoy a new Officers' Club and "a swell Happy Hour show by the crew on the quarterdeck."[329] Little time was wasted once his orders finally arrived. He left the *West Virginia* for a transport on 9 July. He arrived in San Francisco on V-J Day and with thirty days' leave by way of Santa Barbara, Los Angeles, and home. This landfall in San Francisco seems to have been very different from all of his past stops there. He left no written evidence that he contacted any of his old friends, male or female, on this trip. Perhaps it was a case of saying 'goodbye' to that part of his life as he was saying 'goodbye' to the war. At the end of his thirty days' leave, he reported in for duty in the Public Relations Office at the First Naval District where he worked out his "points"[liii] and was separated from military service with the rank of Lieutenant Commander.

---

liii The "Adjusted Service Rating Score" was referred to widely as the "Point System." The system was used to help decide which service men got to go home first and it rewarded length of service, time overseas, and combat experience. Points were awarded as follows: one point for each month of service, one point for each month of service overseas, one point for each medal, one point for each campaign or combat star, and twelve points for each child under the age of eighteen years (with a maximum of three children). This system went into use after the victory in Europe at which time a serviceman or woman needed at least eighty-five points to be discharged. After the victory over Japan, the number of required points was decreased to eighty. Prior to victory, each person enlisting or drafted into the service had to serve "for the duration" – i.e., until the war ended plus one year. The exigencies of the service could override the point system at times.

Baumrucker had learned of the war's end as he was arriving in San Francisco, but the manner in which the *West Virginia* got word was recorded in the ship's War Diary for 10 August 1945:

Anchored as before. At 2115 we received a gargled radio report that the Japanese Government had agreed to surrender under the terms set forth by the Potsdam conference provided they could keep the Emperor as ruler. At 2125 we went to Air Defense on receipt of "Flash Red, Control Yellow." There were no bogeys, but indiscriminate use of AA fire by the Army and Marines on the island and ships in the harbor, celebrating the so called surrender news, was endangering friendly planes. At 2135 we secured from Air Defense.

One of the "Phoenix ships" of Pearl Harbor, the *U.S.S. West Virginia* would be present in Tokyo Bay for the formal signing of the surrender document. On 31 August, she made course for Tokyo Bay. At 0949 hours, the *U.S.S. Calahan* (DD 658) came alongside the *West Virginia* and transferred aboard a Japanese Pilot – Lieutenant H. Normura, I. J. N. – to assist with navigating the ship into the harbor. They "reached the end of the line" at 1252 hour and anchored in Berth A-71, Tokyo Bay, Japan. Five musicians were transferred from the *West Virginia* on temporary duty aboard the *U.S.S. Missouri* to augment their band, as it was to play at the Surrender Ceremony on 2 September. The following day *West Virginia* stood by to provide fire support for the landings of Army and Marine personnel ashore in the Tokyo area, but the War Diary recorded, "Landings by allied occupation troops in the Atsugi and Tokyo areas have been, as far as we have been concerned, entirely without incident. The ship is not darkened, movies are shown topside at night."

Ensign Winford led a reconnaissance detail of sailors and Marines ashore at the Yokosuka Naval Base. As he walked up the coast with about ten men, he encountered Japanese women, children, and old men, who all seemed to be afraid of the Americans. Occasionally, they offered cigarettes to the Japanese but no untoward incidents occurred.[79] An excerpt from the War Diary for 2 September 1945 read:

Anchored as before...The ceremony marking the formal surrender of the armed forces of the Japanese Empire commenced aboard U.S.S. MISSOURI at 0900. Allied Supreme Commander, General of the Army MacArthur and Fleet Admiral Nimitz signed the surrender paper for the Armed Forces of the United States. Rear Admiral Sowell, ComBatDiv FOUR, attended the ceremony from the WEST VIRGINIA.

Many veterans of the *West Virginia* believed forever that the surrender document should have been signed aboard her.

After the end of the war, the *West Virginia* continued to serve for a while in non-bellicose capacity, ferrying servicemen back home from the war in the Pacific. Eventually, however, she began her final journey home. Like all other ships in the Navy, she had flown her Commissioning Pennant from the moment she officially entered the Navy. In the U.S. Navy, this pennant was a long thin flag with a blue field containing seven stars at the hoist followed by a long red and white striped tail. Leaving the war for good, she flew a *Homewardbound Pennant*. This was a specially made pennant that U.S. Navy ships have flown traditionally on their homeward cruise following an extended time at sea – usually nine months or longer. The *West Virginia*, however, flew a specially made homeward bound pennant that contained one white star for every officer aboard and one foot of the red and white section for each crewman.

Communications Officer Robert Wilson had two of his signalmen spend months sewing together this special pennant "in anticipation of the great day when we headed home." When finished, the pennant was over two thousand feet long. Wilson recalled, "Of course when we did fly the monster, most of it dragged in the water although we picked a time when we had the best headwind." With a smile and slight chuckle he added, "Our initial attempt to 'fly' was to attach helium balloons every few feet, but that ended in disaster." At the end of the homeward journey, the pennant was cut so that each officer was given one of the white stars on blue field and each crewman was given a one-foot length of the red and white portion.

CHAPTER 16
Post Bellum

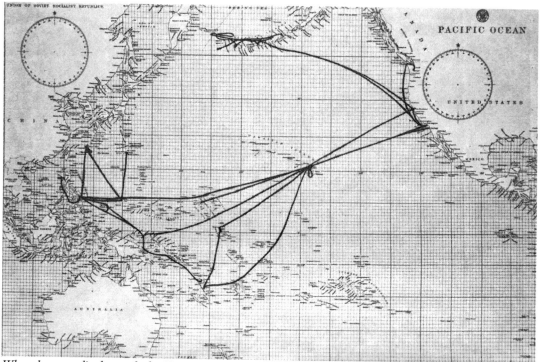

When he was discharged, the Navy presented Baumrucker with this map that contained a chart of the 134,820 nautical miles that he traveled during his service on three battleships. [Photograph from Baumrucker's album.]

Lt. Baumrucker was detached from the *West Virginia* on 6 July 1945, to slip slowly back into the relative anonymity of peacetime civilian life. He returned to the States for a brief period of shore duty in the Office of Public Information. This end to his service in the Navy followed his involvement in the campaigns of Kiska, Tarawa, Kwajalein, Leyte Gulf, the Second Battle of the Philippines, Mindoro, Lingayen Gulf, Iwo Jima, and Okinawa. In his service to the Navy, he traveled a total of one hundred thirty four thousand eight hundred twenty miles. He started his wartime diary on 22 July 1942, the same day that he was called out of reserve status to active service, leaving Chicago, Illinois to report for duty aboard the battleship, *U.S.S. Mississippi* (BB-41), then anchored in San Francisco. He made journal entries daily until his detachment from the *West Virginia*, as the war was coming to a close. His diary entries were necessarily brief due to the physical limitations of the journal in which he kept them. He made the decision to keep a diary knowing that doing so was against Navy regulations and that its discovery would lead to a court martial. The longest entries were related to social events, such as dating, skiing, and fishing. At times, he expended extra lines of text to describe the untoward behaviors of superior officers and the unpleasant interactions that resulted from them. He left a written trail of evidence that, from time to time, he had difficulties with his superior officers, and he left the impression that these occasions, singularly or in summation, may have interfered with his advancement in the service. The brevity of the journal entries is particularly curious when it is clear that Baumrucker was fond of writing. During major activity at sea, whether bombarding enemy-held islands or fighting off aerial attacks, he continued to write, and to collect photographs for, what he referred to as, "the Shellback book" (formally, *The USS West Virginia Crosses the Equator Again*) and he produced articles on fishing to be published in popular sporting magazines. It seems logical that this Dartmouth-educated English major with a penchant for writing would create lengthy diary entries with deeper insights into his experiences and observations, and with some elements of emotion. It may have been the case that the short entries represented a form of protective mechanism – a balancing act between having his diary discovered and having a diary discovered that contained too much information, either of a military nature or of a nature critical of superior officers. He made note of the horrific experience of artist Gilbert Bundy who tried to get ashore with the Marines at Tarawa, the horrible death of sailor Munson who was crushed by a ship's cannon, the deaths of sailors from the kamikaze attack on the *West Virginia*, and the deaths of some of his friends who were serving elsewhere in the Navy. It is difficult to believe that he became so inured to death that he was unaffected personally by these events. The diary is more of a timeline of events within his three-year tour with the Navy; yet there is sufficient information within this context to shed light on the daily life of a naval officer during the war. From the moment of his call to active duty, he encountered prolonged periods of inactivity, such as waiting for transport to the *Mississippi*, and waiting for repairs to the *West Virginia* at Bremerton, Washington. During these interludes, his zest for life and his energy did not allow him to be bored often or for very long. His dating life was very active whenever he was on liberty on the west coast, and he never missed an opportunity to ski or to find places to fish for trout. Of course, the events of his daily life became intimately intertwined with the routine and adventures of the ships on which he served. The details of his experiences are enhanced by matching the events in his diary with the diaries of these ships. These records included Deck Logs, War Diaries, Action Reports, and Damage Reports. When one examines the history of a battleship, the individuals who serve aboard her become invisible in the larger picture. When, however, the diaries of individuals are viewed as "diaries-within-a-diary," it is possible to synthesize a detailed picture of the wartime lives of the individuals as they contributed to the larger life of the ship.

While ashore in California and Washington, Baumrucker came to know a number of civilians with whom he dined, partied, traveled, or otherwise socialized, but there is no evidence that he maintained contact with any of these people after the war. There was no mention of the many women he dated – some more often than others – or of the families who extended generous hospitality to him. One is left with the impression that his time at war was a life unto itself – for him, a special time. The people that he knew, and with whom he served, were relegated to that part of his life. Certainly, he did not enjoy the idea, or the reality, of war, but he liked his role within that context. That his diary did not continue into civilian life suggests that he did not consider his peacetime life to be worthy of recording. Had he chosen to maintain a post-war journal, we would know if he maintained contact with any of his fellow officers from the *Mississippi*, the *Tennessee*, or the *West Virginia*, or with any of the civilians he was so fond of during the war. While on the *West Virginia*, he served and socialized with Lombardi and Soderberg, and it is reasonable to assume that they would have carried their relationships into postwar life. He returned to the advertising firm for which he worked before the war and he married, but too late to have children. He met his wife-to-be in San Francisco and they resided there for the remainder of his life.

According to his family, the war had defined Baumrucker. He was at his best during that time and, in spite of its inherent perils, he was comfortable with his life as an officer on a battleship at war. He was very good at his job, and his proficiency was demonstrated best during the nighttime Battle of Surigao Strait. The war ended, but Baumrucker was never far from it. He became an authority on certain aspects of the war – particularly those aspects with which he had first hand knowledge. His unauthorized diary played a significant part in this as it served as reminder and documentation of numerous events. His "Shellback Book" – originally intended to be a souvenir book for the crew of the *West Virginia* – became a coveted publication that was elevated to the status of source material for some historians. In 1975, he read *The Divine Wind* by Roger Pineau with Rikihei Inoguchi. On finishing it, he wrote a letter, dated 6 October 1975, to the United States Naval Institute in Annapolis, Maryland with his critiques. With attention to detail, he commented:

> I have just been doing some browsing in 'The Divine Wind,' and have a bit of trivia to contribute which may not have been called to your attention even at this late date.
>
> On page 48 (of the Bantam edition of September 1960) the footnote states that if Lt. (jg) Kuno <u>did</u> find a good target in Leyte Gulf it was not a U.S. warship.
>
> That is correct. That evening of October 21, 1944, I was in my battle station; main battery director Spot 1 of USS West Virginia. A plane flew overhead from stern to stem 'so close it nearly knocked my cap off.' It then crashed into HMAS Shropshire, anchored dead ahead of us, which continued to take a beating all the way up through Lingayen Gulf. We thought it was an accident, until the next day when we first learned of this new tactic.
>
> Again, on page 119, Capt. Inoguchi reports that 'all 11 (remaining) planes had dived at enemy targets. But since there were no escort planes to observe....' how does <u>he</u> know? Practically every sailor in the fleet then present at Ulithi knows - - for we were all showing movies topside! All we saw were <u>two</u> planes - - before we dove for cover and blacked out. One did hit the Randolph. The other crashed a small island that no doubt <u>looked</u> like a large ship in the darkness. We decided these planes must have slipped in from Yap; it seems incredible that they came the 1600 miles from Kanoya as the text reports.
>
> With collateral duty as Intelligence Officer, I checked the corpse of the pilot that hit USS West Virginia April 1 at Okinawa. His chart showed that he, too, came from Kanoya, but he had a retirement course to Formosa - - a mere 800 miles over all. Apparently the Azusa Special Attack Force didn't

intend to get back – to Kenoya, at least. But our visitor, three weeks later, hadn't committed himself to a one way trip.

To get back to Leyte Gulf: USS West Virginia went so close in she scraped a propeller so that – after the Surigao action – we had to go down to the floating dry dock in the New Hebrides. This provided enough leisure time to start production of a souvenir book for the crew: "USS West Virginia Crosses the Equator Again," incorporating my heavily censored account of the Surigao action as observed from my controlling director along with a detailed account of our shellback initiation and other memorabilia. Mail deliveries and censorship being what it was, the book was not delivered to the crew until 10 months later!

This is the only post-Pearl Harbor cruise book of USS West Virginia, according to Capt. Samuel G. Kelly, then Asst. Director of Naval History, when he requested a copy nine years later. I believe one of our Trade School officers gave a copy to the Academy library soon after it was published, and subsequent requests even came from as far as the British Imperial War Museum.

Does your offer of a free sample copy of 'Proceedings' still hold? And I would appreciate it if a copy of this letter could be forwarded to Mr. Roger Pineau. I didn't know where to address him since the death of Adm. Morison.

In the last paragraph of his letter, Baumrucker was making reference to Admiral Samuel Eliot Morison who wrote the fifteen-volume, <u>History of United States Naval Operations in World War II</u>. Because of his advanced age, Baumrucker had presumed that Morison was deceased. He was aware that Roger Pineau had been a valuable research assistant and contributing writer to Morison's naval history, and thought him to be the best contact for his letter. His letter did reach Pineau, who responded:

The Naval Institute kindly forwarded a copy of your good letter of 6 October. Last things first, I am delighted to let you know that any reports you may have heard of Admiral Morison's demise are like those of Samuel L. Clemens'. It was my pleasure to attend his eighty-eighth birthday party last July and we have been corresponding regularly since.

In any event, it was a pleasure to hear from you and have your observations about <u>The Divine Wind</u>. I have entered the hit on <u>Shropshire</u> in my file copy; also the Ulithi information.

If you check Appendix C, page 207, of <u>Divine Wind</u>, you'll see that, the hamikaze hitting <u>West Virginia</u> was properly listed as coming from Kanoya. Thanks for your corroboration.

Our Navy Library has just one copy of <u>USS West Virginia Crosses the Equator Again</u> which is guarded very carefully. If you come across any spare copies we would be grateful to acquire any and all.

Even at this late date, as you say, your 'trivia' is much appreciated. No one else had ever commented to me on the things you mention.

Thank you, and best wishes.

Sincerely,
Roger Pineau
Captain USNR

Director

Navy Memorial Museum

Pineau's letter to Baumrucker was dated 22 October 1975. Admiral Morison died seven months later on 15 May 1976. Baumrucker's letter to Roger Pineau did not end his efforts to provide historical accuracy when he could. After reading Herman Wouk's historical novel, *War and Remembrance*, he felt compelled to write to the Pulitzer Prize-winning author. In his 26 April 1979 letter to Wouk, Baumrucker stated:

> *Thank you for the superb analysis of the action at Leyte Gulf in War and Remembrance.*
>
> *However, I do feel it deserves a few lines to explain that, had Kurita steamed on into the Gulf, he would not have had clear sailing to the beaches.*
>
> *We of the old battleships and cruisers – the fighting, not the joy-riding, Navy – who so out-numbered the enemy in Surigao, still had enough shells of various types left to cause him lots of trouble, and we were prepared to use everything down to the last mess kit.*
>
> *I was Gunnery Fire Control Officer directing the main battery fire from a   director in the West Virginia – the first battleship to plot and open fire on the approaching Japanese ships. It has been reported that all eight shells of our opening salvo were direct hits on the Yamashiro.*
>
> *With collateral duty as Public Information Officer, I wrote an account of this action the same day, which was widely published in newspapers shortly afterwards, albeit mercilessly censored. A copy of this article is included in a crew's souvenir book titled "USS West Virginia Crosses the Equator Again", on file at the New York Public Library, the Washington Navy Yard Library, Imperial War Museum, etc."*

With gentlemanly respect, Wouk sent a reply to the above correspondence stating, "Letters like yours about WAR AND REMEMBRANCE are my finest reward for the many years work. Thank you for taking the time and trouble to write. Only one reader out of hundreds ever does, and I appreciate it. I agree with what you say about Kurita, but his mission was to try to get in there against all odds.

Cordially,

Herman Wouk

***

As late as 1981, Baumrucker read an article in the San Francisco Chronicle dated, Thursday, 15 January, to which he felt compelled to respond. The article was titled, "Sakurajima Talks of Kamikazes. The Ones Who Survived" by James Foley of Reuters.

> *Navy Ensign Ryosai Nagamine led a flight 36 years ago of 25 kamikaze pilots on a one-way mission against hundreds of U.S. Navy ships in the Mariana Islands south of Japan.*
>
> *Nagamine, who took off to attack American shipping at Ulithi Island in the Marianas, was one of a handful of kamikaze pilots who survived Japan's last desperate attempt to stem the approaching American tide.*

140

Mt. Sakurajima had a special meaning to the kamikaze (divine wind) pilots because in Japan it means the island of cherry blossoms, a symbol of Japan.

The pilots, many of them only 17 years old and barely capable of flying an aircraft, were seen by the Japanese as cherry blossoms falling into the sea in service of emperor, people and state.

About two dozen kamikaze pilots are known to have survived their missions, while another several dozen are believed to be alive but are too ashamed to identify themselves because they failed to die.

Those willing to talk are caught in a dilemma. They do not want to damage the memory of the 4500 pilots who died, yet at the same time they are critical of the admirals and generals who organized the kamikaze force.

The silver-haired Nagamine, now a fish wholesaler, said that while the kamikaze pilots had an important psychological impact on the Japanese, only 16 percent of the attacks were successful, according to postwar data.

In Nagamine's own case, he led a force of Ginga (Milky Way) bombers against 15 aircraft carriers and dozens of support ships at Ulithi.

More than half the planes developed engine trouble and failed to reach the target, but the rest did dive to their deaths.

The only hit was on the U.S. carrier Randolph.

Nagamine, an expert navigator who was to lead other kamikaze groups to their targets, landed on an atoll where he survived for two months until picked up by a Japanese submarine.

'I criticize the generals and the other top people who ordered the young people to go to their deaths,' he says today.

'I criticize the system whereby pilots were forced to fly missions. All pilots were lined up before officers and embarrassed into accepting missions.'

A pilot who was in kamikaze training at war's end, Toshio Konishi, said that some pilots made their final dives shouting over their radios that they were opposed to such tactics.

Despite their criticism of the kamikaze forces, the surviving pilots refuse to say that the young men died in vain.

'It would be cruel to say they died for nothing,' said Kenji Suzuki, 54, a local government official who survived a crash into a U.S. warship off Okinawa on April 17, 1945.

Flying from Izumi near here, he is the only known kamikaze pilot to have survived a hit. The other two crew members were killed and Suzuki woke up several days later in the sickbay of a U.S. aircraft carrier.

He does not know the name of the ship because he had already been severely injured in the face when his plane's canopy exploded from the fire of American fighter aircraft.

'All I remember is that we were bearing in under a wall of curtain fire from the fleet onto a reddish-brown ship. I was firing a 20mm machine gun along the decks,' he said.

Baumrucker responded to this newspaper article with a letter to the Reuters reporter who wrote it:

January 15, 1981

Dear Mr. Foley:

Thank you for your article on Sakurajima kamikazes in today's San Francisco CHRONICLE. I think you may be interested in this account of the Ulithi caper by Captain Rikhei Inoguchi in July, 1957 as told by Roger Pineau – who was Adm. Morison's primary assistant in writing the official 15 volume history of the US Navy in WWII.

Actually, only two of the planes got through to Ulithi; one hit the Randolph and the other hit a small island, no doubt thinking it was a darkened ship. Strange – because we were all lit up like Broadway with topside movies, assuming we were secure from Japanese airfields. But we blacked out pretty quickly after that, went to General Quarters but nothing else happened.

I hope I may see more of your coverage of this subject. Your column appeared today because the regular (local) columnist in this spot fell down a flight of stairs!

Cordially yours,

R. O. Baumrucker

It is not insignificant that Baumrucker would insist on historical accuracy when it came to events with which he was intimately familiar, but his greatest contribution to history, other than his "Shellback" book, might well be the assistance he gave to Dr. Myron J. Smith, Jr., who wrote histories of the *West Virginia*. A number of the photographs from Baumrucker's album were shared with Smith and appeared in his book, *Mountaineer Battlewagon. U.S.S. West Virginia (BB-48)*. In his "Acknowledgements" to that book, Smith stated, "Special thanks is due....especially [to] Robert O. Baumrucker, who has read every word I have ever written about this ship and whose 'Shellback' book has served as my inspiration." Thus, Robert Owen Baumrucker – Dartmouth College graduate, trout fisherman, ground-breaking competitive skier, and superb Navy officer – made a permanent and significant contribution to the history of the war from his personal involvement. While he was able to refine a number of details regarding the war in the Pacific – things that he knew from first-hand experience – there was one item of great importance to him personally that he was never able to change.

CHAPTER 17
Unfinished Business

At some point after the war, Baumrucker learned that his fellow officer and shipmate aboard the *West Virginia*, Thomas A. Lombardi, had been awarded the Bronze Star for his actions during the Battle of Surigao Strait. It is not known precisely when or how Baumrucker became aware of this, but he felt that an error had been made in the awarding of this medal, and he made written appeals to correct things for himself and for his men. He never indicated that he believed that Lombardi did not deserve recognition – he wanted the commendation to extend also to him and to his men in Spot II the night of that now famous battle.

The cover letter of his written appeal stated:

> *AN APEAL FOR CONGRESSIONAL ACTION to write the final chapter in the Wee Vee's Shellback Book.*
>
> *At 3 o'clock on the morning of Octobder 25, 1944, a portion of the Japanese fleet was approaching our landings at Leyte Gulf in the Philippines via Surigao Strait.*
>
> *USS WEST VIRGINIA was manned and ready to repel the attack, but LCDR Lombardi, in the Spot I Main Battery Director, could not pick up the target.*
>
> *Lt. Baumrucker and his crew in Spot II had a solution to the ballistics. Control was shifted to Spot II and the first salvo was a direct hit on the leading Japanese battleship at 11 miles. Otherwise, the West Virginia would not have been able to fire.*
>
> *Months - -almost years - - later, Mr. Lombardi received a citation and a Bronze Medal for 'distinguishing himself by meritorious achievement in Spot I at Surigao Strait etc.' Not even an kind word for Lt. Baumrucker and his crew.*
>
> *It was only a few years ago that I learned of this citation or any other to the West Virginia and I am now seeking relief.*
>
> *The first few following pages - - and the last - - cover the broad outline of this request. Fuller explanations are included in between.*
>
> Respectfully submitted
R. O. Baumrucker

Living in San Francisco after the war, Baumrucker appealed to the U.S. Senator from California, Alan Cranston, and received the following response. Under his official letterhead, "United States Senate, Washington, D.C. 20510" and dated 16 November 1982, Cranston replied:

> *Just a brief note to thank you for sending me your correspondence regarding the problems you're having with the Department of the Navy. I appreciate your keeping me advised. If it appears that you'll need my*

assistance, be sure to get back in touch with me at my San Francisco office.

Baumrucker kept copies of his correspondence in an album similar to his photograph album, and pasted his typed comments below them. Below the letter from Senator Cranston he wrote:

Senator Cranston and I have both received similar replies to our direct appeals to several Navy offices: 'Our hands are tied - - too much time has passed - - private legislation is the only possible recourse'. The Navy has, however, provided encouragement with ample documentation.

Following the entry, above, was a single typed paragraph, above which was written by hand, "From Fred Hammond, Gun Boss –."

As for your problems with Fitzgibbon, or was it Fitzgibbons, or again has my memory ducked out? I think most everyone had problems with the Spider. He was a most unattractive and unsavory character, to me the epitome of what could be the worst faults of the trade school boys. I had a few skirmishes with him, but kept out of his way for the most part, which was not too difficult, because he appeared to have little interest or expertise in gunnery and seemed more intent on the picayune administrative mole hills which he built into mountains. I think he could have served in some part as a model for Captain Queeg.

There were numerous letters and documents in his album that were part of his long appeal for "relief" in the matter of the commendation. Two things stand out from a review of these documents. First, his was not an entirely selfish request as he always sought credit for his crew as well as himself and, second, he repeatedly extolled the achievements of his beloved *U.S.S. West Virginia.* A careful review of his appeal letters leaves one with a sense of sadness, since his appeal is, in part, a desperate plea for formal recognition from his government for his service during the war.

His "appeal" album contained the following document, above which he had typed the label: "From: Ships Data Section, P10 Division, Office of Public Relations, Navy Department 'HISTORY OF THE USS WEST VIRGINIA.'" The document read:

OFFICERS AND MEN WHO HAVE RECEIVED AWARDS:
The following officers and men have received awards for outstanding action while serving aboard the USS WEST VIRGINIA:

Lieutenant Commander Robert R. Rodgers, former senior aviator on this vessel, whose wife lives at 2311 Forest Avenue, Dallas, Texas, was awarded the Distinguished Flying Cross. "For distinguishing himself by meritorious achievement while participating in aerial flight as pilot of an observation spotting plane during the assault and occupation of the Philippine Islands, Iwo Jima, and Okinawa.

Lieutenant (jg) Emil E. Kovachek, former aviator on this vessel, whose mother lives at 2148 South 18th Street, Milwaukee, Wisconsin, was awarded the Distinguished Flying Cross, "For distinguishing himself by meritorious achievement while participating in aerial flight as pilot of an observation spotting plane during the assault and occupation of the Philippine Islands, Iwo Jima, and Okinawa.

Lieutenant (jg) Richard P. Crossley, former officer on this vessel, whose wife lives at 726 South East 47ʰ Street, Portland, Oregon, was awarded the Silver Star Medal, "For conspicuous gallantry and intrepidity aboard a battleship during and following the action when a Japanese plane and its bomb struck the ship starting large fires which were accompanied by exploding ammunition on the night of 1 April 1945 off Okinawa.

Commander Robert Crawford, Jr., gunnery officer, whose wife lives at Rt. #2 Birchwood Road, Hinsdale, Illinois, was awarded the Bronze Star Medal, "For distinguishing himself by meritorious achievement as Combat Information Officer on a battleship in combat operations against the enemy during the Battle of Surigao Straits.

Lieutenant Commander Edward, J. Fruechtl, former officer on this vessel, whose father, A. A. Fruechtl, lives at 1532 Farmon Street, La Cross, Wisconsin, was awarded the Bronze Star Medal, "For distinguishing himself by meritorious achievement as Main Battery Plotting Room Officer of a battleship in combat operations against the enemy during the Battle of Surigao Straits, on 25 October 1944.

Lieutenant Commander Thomas A. Lombardi, former officer on this vessel whose wife lives at 15 Magnolia Avenue, Newton, Massachusetts, was awarded the Bronze Star Medal, "For distinguishing himself by meritorious achievement as Assistant Gunnery Officer and Spot I Officer of a battleship in combat operations against the enemy during the Battle of Surigao Strait on 25 October 1944.

Baumrucker's footnote to this document read: "This undated history of the ship was released several years after the ship had reverted to inactive status. (Mr. Crawford was still a LCDR[liv] on August 27, 1945, when his citation...was prepared, but is a full CDR[lv] here)."

It is evident immediately that Baumrucker felt that the citation and medal that was awarded Lombardi should have been bestowed upon him and his crew.

Even more clearly than in the original, Mr. Lombardi is credited with achieving exactly what <u>I</u> did in his behalf, when <u>he</u> couldn't pick up the target. I first saw this report only a few years ago; I had not previously realized that *any* citations had been made to our crew.

Dr. Smith gave proper credit to both Lombardi and Baumrucker in his history of the *West Virginia*. Following is the text of a letter from Lombardi to Smith in which he acknowledges without qualification Baumrucker's role at the battle of Surigao Strait. It is not known how Baumrucker came into possession of this letter but a copy was among his records. In Lombardi's letter to Smith, dated 25 July 1980, he stated:

---

livLCDR = Lieutenant Commander.

lvCDR = Commander.

Other than the article that appeared in the October 21, 1979 issue of the Charleston Gazette Mail, on the U.S.S. West Virginia's participation in the battle of Surigao Strait, I haven't seen any advance versions of your forthcoming book on the history of that ship.

Perhaps you have already covered the following two points in your book. If not, I wanted to make you aware of them at this time, so as to have the proper record.

First, the October 1944 book on "The U.S.S. West Virginia Crosses The Line Again"[lvi] is an outstanding book of it's kind. It was the handiwork of Lt. Bob Baumrucker, who authored it, wrote most of the copy, and had it published. It evidently was used as source material for the above mentioned newspaper article.

Secondly, with reference to the coverage of the section of the "Equator" book starting on page 66 on "That Night At Surigao", the primary Main Battery Control station developed a malfunction at a critical part of the action, and Lt. Baumrucker in charge of the standby control station took over. The graphic description of the battle in the above article, were the reactions of Lt. Baumrucker himself.

Because of the part he played in these instances, to keep the record straight, and in the event you don't already have the above data, I respectfully suggest that appropriate mention be accorded to Lt. Baumrucker in your coverage. I also hope this information will be in time to include in the publication of your book, which we all are looking forward to reading.

Sincerely,
T. A. Lombardi
Assistant Gunnery Officer
U.S.S. West Virginia at the
Time of the above matters.

Baumrucker made a notation below his copy of this letter that read,

Mr. Lombardi saw a newspaper account of this action at Surigao Strait on October 21, 1979, and wrote this letter to the author. The article was largely a reprint of my anonymous report of the action and Mr. Lombardi recognized it as such. The author, however, had no knowledge of who made this eyewitness report on which he based his article. The complete report 'That Night at Surigao' is included near the end of this presentation.

Smith received Lombardi's letter in time to include the accurate account in his history of the *West Virginia*. Indeed, Baumrucker received a fair amount of recognition in Smith's book. He was mentioned in the "Acknowledgements," was mentioned by name in the account of the battle of Surigao Strait, and he received name-recognition for a number of the photographs that were used from his album collection. Smith also included a photograph of Baumrucker seated in Spot I of the *West Virginia*.

Baumrucker was careful to note that he was not the only officer to be denied recognition for the Surigao Strait battle. He wondered why CDR Hardison, "the

---

[lvi]The correct title was, "USS West Virginia Crosses the Equator Again."

Gunnery Officer responsible for the total performance - - [was] not rewarded." As he built his paper case for "relief", he included the transition statement within his arguments, "Now it is time to explore why I was denied this citation [Bronze Star]. On the following pages is a copy of my fitness report after five enemy engagements, including Surigao Strait. The gun boss, CDR Hardison, evaluated my work, Executive Officer King confirmed them, and they could hardly be more favorable." His album contained the actual copy of the official Fitness Report.

Baumrucker felt strongly the he had been omitted from recognition because of ill will that had developed between him and Fitzgibbon – a rocky road that began just three days after Fitzgibbon's appointment as Executive Officer. He and Fitzgibbon – "The Spider" - had a number of unpleasant encounters and, for those reasons, Baumrucker suspected that Fitzgibbon had blocked his citation for the action at Surigao Strait. Fitzgibbon gave Baumrucker two unfavorable Fitness Report evaluations. These were against the backdrop of a highly favorable Fitness Report that had been signed by Captain H. V. Wiley. In the narrative portion of his review of Baumrucker (Fitness Report Period from 8 April 1944 to 28 February 1945) Captain Wiley noted:

> This officer carries out his duties in a conscientious manner. He is energetic. His work should improve as he gets the feel of the sea. Qualified for promotion when due. Conduct in battle has been of high standard. Personal character excellent. Military fair. Served with credit in Battle of Surigao Strait, Leyte Gulf, Lingayen, and Iwo Jima Campaigns.

Building his case that Fitzgibbon had blocked any recognition due him, Baumrucker wrote in his appeal package:

> On March 1 [1945], CDR King was replaced by CDR Fitzgibbon as Executive Officer. CDR Hardison forwarded his favorable recommendations for the following period, which were shown to me in the rough. But after CDR Fitzgibbon edited them, my marks wound up several columns to the left [i.e., worse rating].
>
> My fitness report is shown....with a new Captain but with CDR Fitzgibbon repeating his hatchet job.
>
> Following that report I commenced a short period of shore duty on V-J Day, with a new set of commanding officers. I am once more back in the 'win' column, and with a promotion to LCDR!

Fitzgibbon's second unfavorable Fitness Report on Baumrucker was completed and signed only after Baumrucker had been detached from the *West Virginia* and assigned to shore duty. In the narrative portion of the Report Fitzgibbon typed, "Not shown to officer as he had been detached." Depriving Baumrucker of the opportunity for a face-to-face encounter over the evaluation seems a cowardly act by someone so high ranking as Executive Officer. The Fitness Report reached Baumrucker at his new duty station in Boston. He wrote:

> *When a copy of my second unfavorable report from CDR Fitzgibbon reached me in Boston, I showed it to my superior officer who*

recommended and assisted me in preparing [a written] protest. I preferred not to detail my personal relationship with CDR Fitzgibbon out of consideration for his continuing Navy career. This letter was simply a matter of retaining my self respect as a soon-to-be civilian who had provided 3 ½ years of sea duty, with many others, in fleshing out Academy-trained personnel in the emergency. The war had been won and there was still no thought of any citations for what we had contributed.

In his letter of protest, he offered to give more details related to his personal problems with Fitzgibbon if they were requested of him, but they were not.

Continuing his thesis that Fitzgibbon was torpedoing him, his appeal documents included a photocopy of the cover of his "Shellback" book with the typed notation:

What reason did I have to feel CDR Fitzgibbon had singled me out for humiliation? The answer lies in this souvenir book that I prepared for the crew.

I got the idea during glimpses of the initiation, on watch from the bridge underway, and started preparations that afternoon.[lvii]

Since CDR Fitzgibbon has been dead for several years and the Naval Academy Alumni Association has lost track of his widow, if any, I feel I can at last recount the ridiculous origin of this persecution.

CDR Fitzgibbon replaced CDR King as Executive Officer five months after we crossed the Equator. With delays caused by infrequent mail exchanges and time consumed by the Fleet Chief Censor, it took another month to get page proofs out to the ship. When I showed them to CDR Fitzgibbon as a matter of courtesy, he insisted that his picture be inserted on this page 4 [to replace the photograph of CDR King]. I saw no way this could be done or justified. With that, he told me to scuttle the whole project, but the Captain [Wiley] over-ruled him and sustained my choice of portraits. CDR Fitzgibbon then gave me a direct order to delete, arbitrarily, a hundred or more names from the roster, eliminate a number of group pictures and to remove all Division identification, so that 'the enemy will not be informed of the ship's complement'.

He thus over-ruled the Fleet Chief Censor, who had passed all this material and caused great disappointment among many of the men who were not able to find themselves included with their shipmates. From that time on, my life aboard this vessel was one of continual harassment by this Executive Officer, who controlled far more than fitness reports. When he complained about me to the Gunnery Officer, Lt. Talley, who was present, told me CDR Hardison told him 'Lt. Baumrucker probably knows more about fire control than anyone on the ship'.

Thus I can only assume that CDR Fitzgibbon finally got his revenge by eliminating any recognition for my performance at Surigao Strait - - an event that took place over five months before he came aboard.

---

lvii As a minor note, this statement is contrary to his diary notation about the idea for this book. His diary indicated that, on 14 October 1944, he got the idea for the "Shellback" book after he was shown a copy of "The U. S. S. West Virginia Crosses the Equator" by his friend, Bill Hasler.

This unpleasantness followed the incident between Baumrucker and Fitzgibbon surrounding the kamikaze crash into the *West Virginia*, when Fitzgibbon had reported to the Captain that the crash had resulted in no casualties. Baumrucker had to inform the Captain that he had encountered four dead and a number of casualties. While Baumrucker felt that the issues surrounding the "Shellback" book were the driving forces behind Fitzgibbon's persecution of him, the harassment by Fitzgibbon had started much sooner than that. It began shortly after his promotion to Executive Officer. The origin of Fitzgibbon's dislike for Baumrucker is not clear, but apparently Baumrucker was not the only officer to be the object of unpleasant dealings with Fitzgibbon.

Baumrucker had appealed to Senator Alan Cranston of California for assistance, without result. He appealed also to Congresswoman Barbara Boxer of the 6th District of California. This may have been the final blow to his quest. A letter from Congresswoman Boxer, under her letterhead "Congress of the United States, House of Representatives, Washington, D.C. 20515," dated 21 May 1985, read:

Dear Mr. Baumrucker:

Thank you for contacting me regarding your service on board the USS West Virginia during World War II which you feel deserves Special recognition.

My staff made an inquiry with the proper Committee in Washington, D. C., to determine the possibilities of introducing a private bill on your behalf. The Committee informed us that it would be next to impossible for this type of legislation to be considered. The Department of the Navy has not supported this kind of legislation in the past and would not do so.

I would not like to give you false hopes by introducing a bill that I know it would not be considered in Congress.

I have assisted other servicemen in obtaining citations and commendation medals as you stated in your letter of May 7, 1985. However, in their cases, the commendations were awarded to them but there was a delay in obtaining the awards.

I am returning the file you sent for my consideration. I appreciate your service to this Country. Enclosed is a Congressional Award.

Thank you for contacting me regarding this matter.

In friendship,
Barbara Boxer
Member of Congress

The "Congressional Award" to which Congresswoman Boxer referred was a pre-printed certificate on very inexpensive paper that read:

CONGRESSIONAL AWARD
Presented to
Robert O. Baumrucker
FOR OUTSTANDING CONTRIBUTION
TO THE COMMUNITY, THE STATE,
AND THE NATION.

Barbara Boxer's signature was at the bottom of the certificate but, as testimony to the cheapness of the gesture, "Robert O. Baumrucker" was printed by hand on the line containing his name. There is no record of his response to this token gesture, but it would be reasonable for a naval warrior such as Baumrucker to be offended.

Perhaps it was the nature of Fitzgibbon to be a petty person when dealing with subordinates, but one must wonder what qualities his superiors saw in him that resulted in his rise to the position of Executive Officer on a battleship at war. One must wonder also what Thomas Lombardi thought when he received the Bronze Star for acts at Surigao Strait that he admitted to Prof. Smith were the work of Baumrucker. It may have been the case that Lombardi was unaware that Baumrucker and his men had been omitted from recognition. Indeed, just as Baumrucker was unaware of the commendations awarded to Lombardi and the others, they were probably unaware of the officers who were omitted from recognition. His letter to Myron Smith straightening out the course of events at Surigao was laudatory, but too late for Baumrucker to have gained any official commendation. Baumrucker never got the official government recognition that he sought for himself and his men.

John Tazewell – a U. S. Naval Academy Graduate – was the officer in charge of the 5" batteries on the *West Virginia* at the time of the Surigao Strait battle. He acknowledged that he had nothing to contribute in that battle – "it was a battle for the big guns [16" guns]." He knew both Baumucker and Lombardi, but not well. He admitted that he knew only who they were. Tazewell, at age 90, gave a very interesting and insightful oral history. He appeared physically much younger than his stated age, and he was intellectually intact with precise memory. He stated that he had received a Bronze Star at Lingayen Gulf, but he was never really certain why. He thought that the awarding of individual commendations and medals on a battleship at war made little sense. "It's all teamwork. Everything on a battleship is so complicated that everything has to be done by *teams* of people." Tazewell did not know Fitzgibbon personally and had no comment on his behavior. When he heard Baumrucker's story about the commendations for the Surigao actions, Tazewell thought the entire matter was of no significance, and he could not imagine why Baumrucker would pursue the matter so vigorously.

It may be the case that the necessity for brief diary entries prohibited Baumrucker from ever commenting on the war in Europe but it is curious that no mention was made of the final Allied victory in that theater. Tazewell recalled that the officers and crew of the *West Virginia* learned of VE Day from the daily news bulletins that were published on board. He believed these to have been copied from the Associated Press broadcasts. According to Tazewell, "It was sort of 'ho hum' news. We were pretty well focused on the Pacific."

There is evidence that Baumrucker intended to publish his diary. While his *diary* is labeled clearly as such, Curator for the *West Virginia*, Mike Mullins, came into possession of an interesting note. While attending the 2010 reunion of the *West Virginia* Association, he encountered a copy of Baumrucker's typed diary that had attached to it a note, typed and signed by Baumrucker, that read:

> *While I have the recent approval of the Naval Historical Center to publish this diary, I think it may avoid some possible future discussion if the contents are used without stating that they are from a diary.*
>
> *I had collateral duty as Public Information Officer and was thus permitted to keep track of events for publicity use which, actually, is what this still is.*

It might have been the case that he had been cautioned to avoid referring to his document as a *diary* because it would be an admission that he maintained one in defiance of Navy regulations. His intent to shift the focus from diary to "publicity" is unconvincing. Had the content of the diary been devoted to military matters, this idea might have been more tenable, but the diary contained much that was related to his private social life and comments about superior officers. These are matters that would not find their way into materials produced by a Public Information Officer for publicity purposes. The Baumrucker document was clearly a diary from the outset, and it is more valuable for historical reasons as such. As tedious as much of the diary is, it illustrates what life as a Navy Lieutenant was like during World War II. It was not filled constantly with the horrors of battle. Daily routine consisted of long periods of military inactivity and even boredom. Baumrucker seemed always to find ways to fill such times with interesting pursuits and people. These long spells of relative inactivity were interrupted by periods of intense military action, as he dealt with the shelling of Japanese held islands and kamikaze attacks.

***

This account of the World War II experiences of Robert Owen Baumrucker is in no way an attempt to elevate him, his skills, or his contributions, over those of his fellow officers. That his was the metaphorical 'finger on the trigger' at Surigao Strait was a matter of fate. Certainly, Lombardi and the men in Spot I on the *West Virginia* were as well trained and experienced as Baumrucker and his men in Spot II. It is most certain that, had Lombardi's radar not malfunctioned, he would have been successful in arriving at the firing solution that would have struck the Japanese fleet. The primary reason for telling Baumrucker's story is simply that it *can* be told. His diary – maintained in real time – and his photographs, represent a window in time that allows future generations to have an appreciation of what life was like for men serving on a battleship in the Pacific during World War II. It is history as seen through the eyes and mind of an individual, who could have known little more than what was immediately around him.

CHAPTER 18
Epilogue

The battleship *U.S.S. Mississippi* was decommissioned 17 September 1956. On 28 November 1956, she was sold to Bethlehem Steel Company for scrapping. The battleship *U.S.S. Tennessee* was decommissioned 14 February 1947. She was sold to Bethlehem Steel Company for scrapping on 10 July 1959. The battleship *U.S.S. West Virginia* was decommissioned 7 January 1947. She was sold to Union Minerals and Alloys Corporation of New York, New York for scrapping on 24 August 1959.

Wounded during the attack on Pearl Harbor, and still trying simultaneously to fight his ship and to save his crew, Captain Mervyn Bennion ordered his men to leave him on the *West Virginia* and to seek safety for themselves. He died aboard his ship. He received the Medal of Honor posthumously.

Herbert Victor Wiley, U.S.N., "Our fine Captain since Bremerton," was Captain of the battleship *U.S.S. West Virginia* from 14 January 1944 until 2 May 1945. He was awarded the Navy Cross for his role as commanding officer at the Battle of Surigao Strait. Following his detachment from the *West Virginia*, he became the Commanding Officer of the U. S. Naval Facility at Trinidad. While there, he suffered a heart attack, and retired from the Navy in 1947. Subsequently, he became Professor and Assistant Dean of engineering at the University of California at Berkeley. He died in May 1954 while on a lecture trip to the University of California at Los Angeles.

Robert Wilson never forgot the day that Captain Wiley left the *West Virginia*, looking "the loneliest man in the world", but that was not to be the last Wilson heard from Wiley. Wilson wanted to make certain that Captain Wiley had received a copy of the "Shellback Book" and he decided to send one to his former Captain. Wiley returned Wilson's kindness with a hand-written letter:

UNITED STATES ATLANTIC FLEET
TRAINING GROUP
FLEET OPERATIONAL TRAINING COMMAND
c/o Fleet Post Office
New York, N. Y,
Guantanamo Bay, Cuba
15 Sept 1945

Dear Wilson:
I was deeply touched at your thought of me when you entered Tokyo Bay. The letter arrived three of four days ago. I certainly wish I could have remained there four months longer and completed the Wee Vee mission of "on to Tokyo". I congratulate you on getting there and crowning a successful cruise in such a manner.
Today I received a copy of the Crossing The Line book and that made me homesick also. We had plenty of battles on the Wee Vee – and a little fun. You were right at my elbow in all the battles.

The load of shakedown ships has decreased from over 50 when I arrived to a daily average of about 20 now and will level off at about 15 near the end of next month. My staff of about 100 officers and 300 men is being reduced radically by discharges but the job will go along for many months yet. I don't relish being down here and isolated but will like it better when my family arrives next month. I fly my penant on an old DD but have nice quarters ashore.

Wish I could be in San Francisco or Bremerton when you arrive. I hope you are on your way by now.

I inspect from 3 to five ships a week. "Admirals" inspection at end of shakedown and I never fail to tell a poor "C" division that they should be the best on the ship like the Wee Vee.

All good luck to you and all the gang –
Well done –
Yours, Wiley

Thomas A. Lombardi was an acknowledged resource for Myron Smith's histories of the battleship *U.S.S. West Virginia*. Lombardi's memoir – written just days after the attack on Pearl Harbor – is a marvelous first-hand account of the actions and consequences of several of the *West Virginia's* officers and men during that action. While he acknowledged Baumrucker's role at Surigao Strait, the author has no evidence that Baumrucker and Lombardi maintained contact after the war. Mr. Richard Lombardi, son of Thomas Lombardi, posted a brief message on the official website for the *U. S. S. West Virginia* noting that his father died of cancer in 1990.

Little is known of John E. Fitzgibbon following the war. He rose to the rank of Rear Admiral. He died 23 November 1976 and is buried in Arlington National Cemetery. The website for the *U.S.S. West Virginia* contains the single line, "John E. Fitzgibbon served as Executive Officer of the USS West Virginia beginning shortly before the Okinawa campaign in 1945."

Robert Owen Baumrucker never received the official commendation that he sought from his government for his role in the battle of Surigao Strait.

Baumrucker married too late in life to produce children, but he was particularly close to his niece, Mrs. Judith Kroos of Boise, Idaho. Mrs. Kroos provided details of the final years of Baumrucker's life in her own words:

Bob suffered a massive stroke in mid-December 1996 and lived until April 24, 1999 in a state of greatly altered consciousness. He died in San Francisco, a city he loved and which had been his home since the end of the war. Wilma continued to live in their apartment for several years, but the big city is not kind to a rather confused and very elderly lady. Robert and Judith [Kroos] carried Bob's and Wilma's ashes back to Arapahoe, Nebraska, the small prairie town which had always held Wilma's heart, and which Bob came to think of as his chosen home. They lie between the graves of Frederick Edward Lallman and Mable Palmer Lallman, Judith's Grandparents, and the prairie wind, perhaps to the old sailor a following wind, will blow cold from the north and hot from the south across this small country cemetery sited in Township 4 North and Range 23 West of the 6th Meridian. Fly west out of Chicago with a destination of Denver, and look down where the wide Platte River creates a long, green valley. About fifty miles to the south is a lesser known but equally important river, the Republican. The citizens of Arapahoe know the value of water as did the Arapaho and Ogala Sioux, some braves of which left a scattering of arrow heads on several fields of land homesteaded by Judith's great grandparents. Bob loved to walk about the farm in the darkening hours of evening. While not a birth child of the prairie, he was certainly a heart child.

Night falls swiftly on the prairie.

Winds whisper through the tall grasses, and the sounds of the day are stilled.

Listen closely, and if you are very lucky, you will hear the wail of the coyote as he calls to the rising moon.

In truth, he is calling the children of the prairie home."

At ninety-five years of age, Robert G. Wilson reflected on his years of service aboard the *U.S.S. West Virginia* and concluded simply, "Sea duty on a battleship was the best duty one could have."

NOTES

[1] Smith, Myron J., Jr. *Mountaineer Battlewagon. U.S.S. West Virginia (BB-48)*. Pictoral Histories Publishing Company, Inc., Missoula, Montana, 1982.

[2] Smith, Myron J., Jr. *The Mountain State Battleship USS West Virginia*, 1981.

[3] Lombardi, Thomas. Memoir, 12 December 1941, page 6. Subsequent references to this document will be noted as "T.L." followed by the page number.

[4] Ibid.

[5] Ibid

[6] Ibid.

[7] Ibid.

[8] White, F.H., Lt. (jg). Statement of Japanese Attack on December 7, 1941. USS West Virginia; to the Navy Department, December 11, 1941.

[9] Ricketts, C.V., Lt., Statement of Japanese Attack on December 7, 1941. USS West Virginia; to the Navy Department, December 11, 1941.

[10] Ibid.

[11] Ibid.

[12] Ibid.

[13] Ibid.

[14] Porter, J.H. Oral History. September 14, 2009.

[15] Ibid.

[16] Ibid.

[17] Ibid.

[18] Ibid.

[19] Ibid.

[20] T.L., page 8.

[21] Ibid.

[22] Ibid.

[23] Ibid.

[24] Ibid.

[25] T. L., page 10.

[26] T. L., page 12.

[27] Ibid.

[28] Ibid.

[29] Ibid.

[30] Ibid.

[31] Ibid.

[32] Ibid.

[33] Ibid.

[34] T. L., page 14.

[35] Ibid.

[36] Ibid.

[37] Ibid.

[38] Ibid.

[39] Ibid.

[40] T.L., page 16.

[41] Ibid.

[42] Ibid.

[43] Ibid.

[44] Ibid.

[45] Ibid.

[46] T. L., page 18.

[47] Ibid.

[48] Ibid.

[49] Ibid.

[50] Ibid.

[51] Ibid.

[52] Ibid.

[53] Ibid.

[54] T. L., page 20.

[55] Ibid.

[56] Porter, J. H. Oral History. September 14, 2009.

[57] T. L., page 20.

[58] Ibid.

[59] Ibid.

[60] T. L., page 22.

[61] Ibid.

[62] Ibid.

[63] Ibid.

[64] T. L., page 26.

[65] Ibid.

[66] Ibid.

[67] Ricketts, C. V., Lt., Statement of Japanese Attack on December 7, 1941. USS West Virginia; to the Navy Department, December 11, 1941.

[68] Ibid.

[69] Ibid.

[70] T. L., page 26.

[71] White, F. H., Lt. (jg), Statement of Japanese Attack on December 7, 1941. USS West Virginia; to the Navy Department, December 11, 1941.

[72] T. L., page 30.

[73] Lund, Morten. Slalom Gets Its Start. While the FIS and the British feuded about the rules, a wet behind the ears Dartmouth undergrad won the world's first modern slalom. Ski. 8E. February 1984.

[74] Lund, Morten. The Strange Story of Slalom. Skiing Heritage, Vol. 8, No. 1, Winter 1996, pp. 35 – 37.

[75] Baumrucker's diary 23 July 1942. For the remainder of this manuscript, references to the Baumrucker diary will be denoted by "B. D." followed by the date of the entry.

[76] Ibid.

[77] B. D., 1 August 1942.

[78] B. D., 7 August 1942.

[79] Ibid.

[80] Ibid.

[81] B. D., 13 August 1942.

[82] B. D., 14 August 1942.

[83] B. D., 26 August 1942.

[84] B. D., 3 September 1942.

[85] Ibid.

[86] B. D., 5 September 1942.

[87] B. D., 6 September 1942.

[88] B. D., 7 September 1942.

[89] Ibid.

[90] B. D., 11 September 1942.

[91] B. D., 12 September 1942.

[92] B. D., 14 September 1942.

[93] Ibid.

[94] B. D., 15 September 1942.

[95] Ibid.

[96] A collage of these clipped articles appeared in Baumrucker's photograph album.

[97] Ibid.

[98] B. D., 5 October 1942.

[99] B. D., 9 October 1942.

[100] Ibid.

[101] B. D., 12 October 1942.
[102] B. D., 9 November 1942.
[103] B. D., 5 November 1942.
[104] Baumrucker, R. O., Lt. (jg), "Fair Weather Fishing", *The Southern Sportsman,* September 1943, page 14.
[105] B. D., 15 November 1942.
[106] B. D., 17 November 1942.
[107] Ibid.
[108] B. D., 29 November 1942.
[109] B. D., 30 November 1942.
[110] B. D., 1 December 1942.
[111] B. D., 2 December 1942.
[112] B. D., 3 December 1942.
[113] B. D., 4 December 1942.
[114] B. D., 5 December 1942.
[115] B. D., 12 December 1942.
[116] B. D., 14 December 1942.
[117] B. D., 24 December 1942.
[118] B. D., 4 January 1943.
[119] B. D., 21 February 1943.
[120] B. D., 23 March 1943.
[121] B. D., 8 April 1943.
[122] B. D., 4 May 1943.
[123] B. D., 19 April 1943.
[124] B. D., 22 April 1943.
[125] B. D., 6 May 1943.
[126] B. D., 8 May 1943.
[127] B. D., 9 May 1943.
[128] B. D., 10 May 1943.
[129] B. D., 25 May 1943.
[130] B. D., 30 May 1943.
[131] B. D., 1 June 1943.
[132] B. D., 2 June 1043.
[133] B. D., 8 June 1943.
[134] B. D., 13 June 1943.
[135] B. D., 14 June 1943.
[136] B. D., 16 June 1943.
[137] B. D., 21 June 1943.
[138] B. D., 23 June 1943.
[139] B. D., 26 June 1943.
[140] B. D., 9 July 1943.
[141] B. D., 12 July 1943.
[142] B. D., 18 July 1943.
[143] B. D., 19 July 1943.
[144] B. D., 21 July 1943.
[145] B. D., 29 July 1943.
[146] B. D., 25 July 1943.
[147] B. D., 2 August 1943.
[148] B. D., 4 August 1943.
[149] B. D., 7 August 1943.
[150] B. D., 15 August 1943.
[151] B. D., 16 August 1943.
[152] B. D., 18 August 1943.
[153] B. D., 24 August 1943.
[154] B. D., 17 September 1943.
[155] B. D., 19 September 1943.
[156] B. D., 30 September 1943.
[157] B. D., 5 October 1943.

[158] B. D., 7 October 1943.
[159] B. D., 17 October 1943.
[160] B. D., 25 October 1943.
[161] Sherrod, Robert. *Tarawa*. Duell, Sloan and Pearce, 1944, pages 1 – 2.
[162] B. D., 26 October 1943.
[163] B. D., 27 October 1943.
[164] Sherrod, pages 7 – 8.
[165] Sherrod, pages 9 – 12.
[166] B. D., 2 November 1943.
[167] B. D., 7 November 1943.
[168] B. D., 8 November 1943.
[169] B. D., 18 November 1943.
[170] B. D., 19 November 1943.
[171] B. D., 20 November 1943.
[172] B. D., 22 November 1943.
[173] B. D., War Diary, *U.S.S. Tennessee*. 22 November 1943 (National Archives, College Park, Maryland).
[174] B. D., 23 November 1943.
[175] Sherrod, page 123.
[176] B. D., 30 November 1943.
[177] B. D., 12 December 1943.
[178] Sherrod, page 119.
[179] B. D., 10 January 1944.
[180] B. D., 12 January 1944.
[181] B. D., 22 January 1944.
[182] B. D., 24 January 1944.
[183] B. D., 28 January 1944.
[184] B. D., 1 February 1944.
[185] B. D., 4 February 1944.
[186] B. D., 5 February 1944.
[187] B. D., 6 February 1944.
[188] B. D., 9 February 1944.
[189] B. D., 14 February 1944.
[190] B. D., 27 February 1944.
[191] B. D., 28 February 1944.
[192] B. D., 5 March 1944.
[193] B. D., 31 March 1944.
[194] B. D., 3 April 1944.
[195] B. D., 5 April 1944.
[196] B. D., 7 April 1944.
[197] B. D., Loving, Charles. Oral History, 17 July 2012.
[198] Ibid.
[199] Wilson, Robert. Oral History, 31 January 2013.
[200] B. D., 4 July 1944.
[201] Loving, Charles. Oral History, 17 July 2012.
[202] B. D., 6 July 1944.
[203] Ibid.
[204] B. D., 26 July 1944.
[205] B. D., 27 July 1944.
[206] B. D., 30 July 1944.
[207] B. D., 17 August 1944.
[208] B. D., 24 August 1944.
[209] B. D., 8 September 1944.
[210] B. D., 17 September 1944.
[211] B. D., 23 September 1944.
[212] BB-48 BOOKLET OF GENERAL PLANS. BU. SHIPS NO. BB-48-S0103-193296.
[213] Siebold, Donald. Oral History, 21 January 2013.
[214] Umbenhour, Russell. Oral History, 23 January 2013.

215 Winford, Frontis. Oral History, 24 January 2013.
216 Loving, Charles. Oral History, 12 July 2012.
217 Tazewell,John. Oral History, 12 July 2012.
218 Ibid.
219 Ibid.
220 Ibid.
221 Umbenhour, Russell. Oral History, 23 January 2013.
222 Loving, Charles. Oral History, 17 July 2012.
223 Tazewell, John. Oral History, 12 July 2012.
224 Loving, Charles. Oral History, 17 July 2012.
225 Ibid.
226 Ibid.
227 Variot, J. V. Oral History, 17 September 2009.
228 B. D., 5 October 1944.
229 B. D., 14 October 1944.
230 B. D., 15 October 1944.
231 Ibid.
232 B. D., 17 October 1944.
233 B. D., 18 October 1944.
234 B. D., 19 October 1944.
235 B. D., 21 October 1944.
236 Ibid.
237 B. D., 22 October 1944.
238 War Diary, *U.S.S. West Virginia (BB-48)*, 21 October 1944 (National Archives, College Park, Maryland).
239 B. D., 24 October 1944.
240 War Diary, *U.S.S. West Virginia (BB-48)*, 24 October 1944 (National Archives, College Park, Maryland).
241 Action Report, *U.S.S. West Virginia (BB-48)*, 1 November 1944 (National Archives, College Park, Maryland).
242 Morison, S. E. *The Two Ocean War: A Short History of the United States Navy in the Second World War.* Boston: Little, Brown and Company, 1963, pp. 447 – 449.
243 B. D., 24 October 1944.
244 War Diary, *U.S.S. West Virginia (BB-48)*, 25 October 1944 (National Archives, College Park, Maryland).
245 B. D., 25 October 1944.
246 B. D., 28 October 1944.
247 B. D., 4 November 1944.
248 B. D., 23 November 1944.
249 B. D., 24 November 1944.
250 B. D., 25 November 1944.
251 B. D., 12 December 1944.
252 Ibid.
253 B. D., 13 December 1944.
254 B. D., 14 December 1944.
255 B. D., 15 December 1944.
256 B. D., 16 December 1944.
257 B. D., 17 December 1944.
258 B. D., 20 December 1944.
259 B. D., 25 December 1944.
260 B. D., 31 December 1944.
261 B. D., War Diary, *U.S.S. West Virginia (BB-48)*, 6 January 1945 (National Archives, College Park, Maryland).
262 B. D., 6 January 1945.
263 B. D., 7 January 1945.
264 B. D., 9 January 1945.
265 War Diary, *U.S.S. West Virginia (BB-48)*, 11 January 1945 (National Archives, College Park, Maryland).

[266] B. D., 23 January 1945.

[267] B. D., 26 January 1945.

[268] B. D., 29 January 1945.

[269] B. D., 30 January 1945.

[270] B. D., 31 January 1945.

[271] War Diary, *U.S.S. West Virginia (BB-48)*, 31 January 1945 (National Archives, College Park, Maryland).

[272] B. D., 5 February 1945.

[273] Ibid.

[274] B. D., 16 February 1945.

[275] B. D., 19 February 1945.

[276] War Diary, *U.S.S. West Virginia (BB-48)*, 19 February 1945 (National Archives, College Park, Maryland).

[277] B. D., 19 February 1945.

[278] B. D., 20 February 1945.

[279] B. D., 21 February 1945.

[280] B. D., 22 February 1945.

[281] War Diary, *U.S.S. West Virginia (BB-48)*, 27 February 1945 (National Archives, College Park, Maryland).

[282] B. D., 27 February 1945.

[283] War Diary, *U.S.S. West Virginia (BB-48)*, 28 February 1945 (National Archives, College Park, Maryland).

[284] War Diary, *U.S.S. West Virginia (BB-48)*, 5 March 1945 (National Archives, College Park, Maryland).

[285] B. D., 5 March 1945.

[286] Ibid.

[287] Ibid.

[288] B. D., 8 March 1945.

[289] B. D., 9 March 1945.

[290] B. D., 11 March 1945.

[291] B. D., 15 March 1945.

[292] B. D., 21 March 1945.

[293] B. D., 26 March 1945.

[294] B. D., 27 March 1945.

[295] War Diary, *U.S.S. West Virginia (BB-48)*, 27 March 1945 (National Archives, College Park, Maryland).

[296] War Diary, *U.S.S. West Virginia (BB-48)*, 31 March 1945 (National Archives, College Park, Maryland).

[297] B. D., 1 April 1945.

[298] Winford, Frontis. Oral History, 24 January 2013.

[299] B. D., 1 April 1945.

[300] War Diary, *U.S.S. West Virginia (BB-48)*, 1 April 1945 (National Archives, College Park, Maryland).

[301] Ibid.

[302] B. D., 2 April 1945.

[303] Deck Log, *U.S.S. West Virginia (BB-48)*. Revised Form for Reporting AA Action by Surface Ships, 1 April 1945 (National Archives, College Park, Maryland).

[304] Ibid.

[305] Battle Damage Report, *U.S.S. West Virginia (BB-48)*, 27 April 1945 (National Archives, College Park, Maryland).

[306] Ibid.

[307] B. D., 6 April 1945.

[308] B. D., 7 April 1945.

[309] B. D., 9 April 1945.

[310] B. D., 17 April 1945.

[311] B. D., 19 – 23 April 1945.

[312] B. D., 1 May 1945.

[313] B. D., 2 May 1945.

[314] War Diary, *U.S.S. West Virginia (BB-48)*, 2 May 1945 (National Archives, College Park, Maryland).

[315] B. D., 8 May 1945.

[316] B. D., 10 May 1945.

[317] B. D., 16 May 1945.

[318] B. D., 28 May 1945.

[319] War Diary, *U.S.S. West Virginia (BB-48)*, 30 May 1945 (National Archives, College Park, Maryland).

[320] B. D., 1 June 1945.

[321] B. D., 2 June 1945.

[322] B. D., 16 June 1945.

[323] War Diary, *U.S.S. West Virginia (BB-48)*, 27 June 1945 (National Archives, College Park, Maryland).

[324] B. D., 16 June 1945.

[325] War Diary, *U.S.S. West Virginia (BB-48)*, 16 June 1945 (National Archives, College Park, Maryland).

[326] Umbenhour, Russell. Oral History, 23 June 2013.

[327] B. D., 21 June 1945.

[328] B. D., 27 June 1945.

[329] B. D., 7 July 1945.

APPENDICES

APPENDIX I - Dramatis Personae

In the preparation of his "Shellback" book, "THE USS WEST VIRGINIA CROSSES THE EQUATOR AGAIN", Lt. Baumrucker took photographs of the officers and crew of the ship for inclusion. The availability of this book offers an opportunity to identify many of the men who were mentioned in the present work. Following is a list of these men. This exercise allows the reader to know what these men looked like during their wartime service. The page numbers given refer to the pages of the Shellback book visible on the lower inner corner.

Captain H. V. Wiley, Commanding Officer, U. S. S. West Virginia. Page 4, top image.

Commander G. J. King, Executive Officer, U. S. S. West Virginia. He was much respected by Baumrucker but he was later promoted and replaced by Fitzgibbon as Executive Officer. Fitzgibbon became Baumrucker's nemesis. Page 4, bottom image and page 41, top image, front row, fourth from left..

Lt. Robert O. Baumrucker. Page 60, top image.

Lt. Commander Thomas Lombardi. He wrote a memoir of his personal experiences during the attack on Pearl Harbor and he was in charge of Spot I during the battle of Surigao Strait. Page 48, bottom photo, second row, fourth from left.

Gunnery Commander C. M. Hardison. Page 40, front row, far left.

Lt. Soderberg, Baumrucker's friend and "acey-ducey" opponent. Page 41, top image, front row, third from left, and page 59, top image, second row, fifth from left.

Seaman Charles Loving. He ran to the crash site of the kamikaze plane and removed the Japanese body flag from the dead pilot. Guarding this souvenir closely, he has kept it in a safe deposit box in his local bank since 1945. His oral history launched this author on an adventure that led to the writing of this book. Page 45, bottom image, third row, left end.

Lieutenant Tazewell. He received the Bronze Medal for his performance in the battle of Lingayen Gulf and was in charge of the 5" batteries during the battle of Surigao Strait. His oral history gave valuable insights to events affecting Lt. Baumrucker. Page 58, bottom photo, front row, sixth from left.

Chaplain, Lt. Comdr. (Ch. C.) M. F. Williams. Page 40, back row, third from left.

Ensign Donald Siebold. Page 44, top photo, second row, fourth from left.

Ensign Russell Umbenhour. Page 62, bottom photo, second row, fourth from left.

Ensign Joseph Variot. Page 49, top photo, back row, second from left.

Lieut. Comdr. F. H. White. Page 40, front row, far right.

APPENDIX 2 – Fair Weather Fishing

Appendix 2 is a copy of the article written by Baumrucker titled, "Fair Weather Fishing". He mailed the manuscript on November 14, 1942 and The Southern Sportsman published it in its September 1943 issue. The article is a humorous account of his journey from home to report aboard the U. S. S. Mississippi with a focus on his fishing exploits and with a taste of his life aboard ship.

FAIR WEATHER FISHING

By Lt. (jg) R. O. Baumrucker

This has been written in short snatches. Some of it a hundred feet in the air, as my battleship drives on through the sea and coveys of flying fish skim out of the way and finally flip down behind a wave crest. Some of it fathoms below the surface, surrounded by mechanisms, undreamed of by civilians, that lay the fire of our main battery — guns that would not only pluck but probably roast any duck that flew close enough to show his bill. And now, as I revise it in port, the chipping hammers are going like crazy, yard workmen are swarming over us for repairs, and my perspective is such that I wonder if its apparently trivial content will interest you who are free to go fishing more or less whenever you want.

Let's see. It's the story of how I tried for one last fling at a fishing trip before I joined my ship in the Pacific Fleet.

We got a few weeks' training in Chicago—fourteen of us to a small hotel room. Reveille at 6, lights out at 10, while we crammed in navigation, seamanship and gunnery —— basic training to be refined while cruising at sea.

Sundays were our own—until 7:30 p. m.—and on one of our last weekends together Marshall and Bennie Moe and I decided to try some fishing. Me, because I knew of a preserve out near the Fox River where they had lots of game and bass and trout. I'd shot pheasants out there some years before, and thought it was very much like shooting chickens in a barnyard. But I'd always had a hankering to try their trout since they claimed—even though the poor devils were crowded to death in their tiny pools and streams—that it was very sporty fishing. Bennie Moe's wife had just bought them a summer place up in New Hampshire which he had never seen, and he was interested in getting some fingerlings to stock its water. And Marshall, I guess he just wanted to see what it was like to get a good sound sleep out in the sun again. (I hope he hurries up and answers my letter — plenty has happened since his carrier disappeared over the horizon weeks ago.)

Anyway, if any of you have ever fished for cannery trout you know how we made out. Particularly when you think back to the contrast with streams in Idaho, or even the skinny, starving squaretails in White Mountain rivulets.

Marshall promptly found a grassy spot and fell asleep. He was wisest. Bennie Moe and I had conformed to regulations and worn our whites —— enough to scare the fish out of their eight inches of water and up onto the banks.

We snuck up on them from behind bushes and trees, and on the first toss of the fly they'd roar upstream so fast the water nearly foamed with spray. And before we moved on to where they'd gone I always looked back to see if some weren't floating behind, killed in the rush. Finally, down in a pool that was a little muddy, I snagged a little fellow who put up a very fine struggle—not taking out any line, but using up most of the slack I gave him. Marshall even woke up to watch. When the fish finally got too tired to play I brought him in, to find he had been foul-hooked outside a gill. Then Bennie caught one the old-fashioned way, and we paid the cashier $5 or some such sum for our sport and got back to town for our final week at the Naval Officer's Incubator.

Suddenly I was out on the West Coast. There I found my ship had sailed the day before, and I had a week —maybe two—while they figured out some way to get me to her. Maybe I could get some fishing done now. So I checked out to Lake Tahoe for a few days. There wasn't much choice of where to go—no time to pack in anywhere to the good fishing that must be back there. And anyway, Tahoe seemed like a good place even if there wasn't much chance of finding my ship up there.

The morning ride through the mountains as we approached the lake was swell, the best mountains I had seen in the West. Up, up, up we went, and then through many snowsheds and past the Sugar Bowl, where Reg and I had nearly decided to go from Sun Valley for some skiing last winter. Lots of good-looking water, though how well

(Continued on Page 22)

Emerald Bay and Deadman Isle, Lake Tahoe (1)

Crystal Cove, Lake Tahoe (2)

Marshall asleep in the sun.

Muchie and his parasol.

Myself—and some of the Mackinaws we kept at Lake Tahoe.

NEWS OF THE GUN WORLD

(Continued from Preceding Page)

facilities. The idea that "the far fields are always greener" is not entirely true. Many sportsmen live adjacent to excellent hunting areas which they have overlooked in the past in favor of a cross-country trek. This year the slogan should be, "Hunt near home and save transportation."

(3) We all know that some recreation is vital in wartime, particularly for war workers who need short periods of time in the open to recharge their physical and mental energies. The recreational value of hunting alone, therefore, is sufficient to justify such hunting as may be possible under war conditions, without considering the value of the food taken. Nevertheless, during the 1942-43 season, hunters took 255,-404,000 pounds of usable meat for home consumption. This annual crop of wildlife, so needed to help out in the present meat shortage, cannot be harvested except by recreational hunting.

(4) Hunters who live close to areas where wild game is too thick should concentrate their hunting efforts in such regions with the twofold purpose in mind of helping to reduce an overabundant wildlife population which may be doing damage to farm crops, and at the same time easing the hunting pressure in other areas so as to allow game stocks to build up.

(5) The great game of hoarding, which so many Americans participated in before food rationing went into effect, extended also to the hoarding of shotgun shells. Greedy individuals, fearing their cupboards would be bare this season, filled them with stocks entirely too large for personal use. Such actions, of course, were entirely unsportsmanlike. I feel that you, through the columns of your magazine, can make an appeal to good sportsmanship and fair play, and can achieve considerable success by starting a campaign to get local sports groups to collect these large ammunition stocks and redistribute them equitably. Every man who wants to go hunting this season should have his chance to do so. By spreading shells around evenly, every man will have his chance.

(6) As the final point in this national campaign, I am urging that you appeal to sportsmen to take mallards, widgeons, and pintail ducks, where possible, in preference to the other species of ducks which are still comparatively low in numbers, and which cannot stand the heavy hunting pressure that the three mentioned species can. Concentrate on mallards, widgeons, and pintails—give the other species a chance to come back!

All of us who are interested in wildlife want to see sportsmen of America take a reasonable share of big and small game when the hunting seasons open next fall. To accomplish this some new rules must be observed.

Ithaca Gun Company Man Wins Citation

Harry E. Howland, factory manager of the Ithaca Gun Company, has won a citation for evolving a method of saving strategic raw materials and critical machine tool capacity in the production of war weapons.

Howland collaborated with two other men on the suggestion that the triggers of the .45 calibre army automatic pistol be stamped instead of machined. There's a whale of a lot of difference between the two methods.

This innovation resulted in the saving of hundreds of thousands of pounds of critically needed steel in the Rochester, New York, ordnance zone, and paved the way for even more beneficial results by releasing men and machines for other duties. Skilled man power is a prime essential in the winning of the war, and every time a machine can be substituted for skilled workmen, that means more nails for Hitler's and Hirohito's coffins.

Howland, a personal friend of this writer, has been associated for many years with Lou Smith, Executive Vice-President of the Ithaca Gun Company and its subsidiaries, Lefever Gun Company, and Western Gun Company, and the two men make a great team. Wherever shotguns are known, there also Lou Smith is known, and no gun executive is more popular with the gun trade or with shooters.

The Ithaca Company produces several thousand .45 caliber automatic pistols per month, and that's bad for the Axis brigands.

Poison Holds First Place on Bear's Menu

Up in Illinois there's a town, I believe, by the name of Elgin—yes, I'm positive there is—it's the home of Elgin watches or somethin'. Well, anyway, the Elgin Park Department has a bear and her name is Lulu. There's a story behind Lulu and it's a lulu.

While in hibernation last winter, with nothing to do but suck her paw, Lulu fell to brooding over her solitary state, and it soured her normally sunny disposition, so when spring rolled around she came out with a disposition almost as bad as Hitler's, and she was condemned to death—via the poisoned food route.

When 6-year-old Lulu came ambling out of her winter hibernation, the first thing she tried to do was to grab a few whiffs of fresh air—and the next was to grab a hunk of flesh from the seat of Keeper Paul Petschows' pants.

"We can't have our keeper chewed up, the man-power shortage being what it is," said city officials, in effect, if not in those exact words. Parks Commissioner John Zimmerli sought advice on the best way to ease the shrewish Lulu out of this troubled world.

Very simple, said the experts. Just slip her some cyanide of potassium in an apple. She'll never know what hit her. It'll be practically instantaneous and it'll be humane.

They tried that. Lulu never batted an eye. They fed her a bigger dose. No effect, except possibly Lulu got a little more vicious.

Then they switched to strychnine, mixing two cubes with a delectable combination of popcorn and honey. Ah, that was swell, Lulu indicated as she licked it up greedily.

(Continued on Page 24)

FAIR WEATHER FISHING

(Continued from Page 14)

I could do without a car was yet to be seen. (Wow! Betty Grable at the movie tonight!)

I checked in at the Tahoe Tavern because it was right near the bus stop. And, as if they'd seen me coming, a sign in the lobby read: "For Fishing see Johnnie and Muchie at the Wharf."

Well, Muchie and Johnnie were out fishing, so I walked back on the road to a bridge near the village, and fed bread to the trout in the stream below. There were thirty or forty beauties down there — three to five pounds apiece. Only, fishing was not allowed—it was too near a dam, and the fish were sort of community pets who earned their keep by lolling in the current and snapping at bread for tourists. A very pleasant thing to see, nevertheless.

That evening Muchie and Johnnie were there, like a couple of old muskrats sitting in front of their shack at the end of the wharf. And very decent citizens they are, too. Summers they spend up here. Earlier they had spent their time fishing for salmon for the government. And in the fall they hunt ducks in the ricefields of the Sacramento Valley. I must try that some time.

Well, they didn't hold out much hope for stream fishing, unless I could allot a couple of days to pack back into the mountains. Those lunkers at the bridge were smart—they never moved away from the dam, and no one ever caught anything much over five inches long for many miles downstream. They had a trout rod I could use if I wanted to try it, though they didn't know how to use it themselves. Their specialty was to troll in deep water, with copper lines, for mackinaws.

Yes, they said, the fishing had been pretty good. We'd probably get two or three good ones in a morning. I was rather dubious about the rig, having spent some dull days on the Gulf Stream with sails on heavy tackle, but after all, fish were fish—and here was a new way to go after them. So Muchie and I went out the next morning.

I had noticed Muchie's lips were like raw hamburger, and wondered why. When I saw him rig the parasol I knew the answer. Poor guy! His skin couldn't stand the sun. We filled the well in the boat with chubs, cranked the motor, and steamed out for the center of the lake. Except for no slave girls, it was the nearest thing to Cleopatra's barge I had ever seen.

We used three or four chubs hooked behind a four-inch spoon on the end of a hundred yards of copper cable, and hand-fished it as the natives bottom-fish off Nassau. My first three or four bites were either rocks on the bottom or else I jerked their heads off. Muchie told me I was doing both, alternately. But pretty soon I caught on, and hauled in one that weighed about two pounds. Then I missed again, on a beautiful strike, and pulled in my bait to find the chubs all torn to shreds.

From then on we had plenty of fish, but mostly let them go because Muchie wanted only a few for himself.

It was quite a chore to haul in all

that wire simply to rebait or to clean off occasional weeds (which smelled precisely like a very fresh salvo of skunk). And when we had the bottom of the boat full of loosely coiled wire and flopped an active six-pounder into the middle of it, Muchie worried about the line getting kinked. For when it was gone he'd be out of the fishing business until we get our work done out here. (Ah! The ventilation blowers are fixed at last!)

One step removed from market fishing or not, this was turning out to be a good day. The sun was bright and not too warm—and the lake must be very deep. It was the clearest, bluest fresh water I had ever seen. All around us were the California and Nevada mountains, still topped with snow in late summer and streaked with avalanches. Lots of bear and deer, said Muchie.

Well, I'd caught some mackinaws and, reasonable as his charges were, I had to forego any more of Muchie's company in his boat. Junior naval officers aren't exactly overpaid, and don't get paid at all until they catch up with their ship. That is, unless they've got shore duty. But that, I hear, is not a story for a fishing magazine.

So, after a day of swimming and general recuperation from the strenuous training program in Chicago, I came down to the pier in the evening. Muchie and Johnnie had been feeding bread too, I found, and here were half a dozen stropping rainbows snapping up the crumbs with great gusto. They'd start their run from about six feet under, fifteen feet away, and bang! they'd hit the surface like a depth charge!

Altogether too much power going to waste, I thought. So I slipped into the shack and got the rod and line. In thirty seconds I had a honey on the other end. Here was no business of paying out slack—he took what he wanted. For a bread eater he sure had plenty of vitamins—I think he broke out six times before we got him in the net. And then, as we held and admired him, someone quietly said: "Let him go." So, plop, back into the lake he went! Then we all looked at each other in amazement, and no one would admit he had said to let him go.

I wish I'd quit my trout fishing right there, because in the next four days I must have spent twenty hours down there trying to catch another. Nobody can tell me now that fish aren't smart. I even tried twenty-five feet of the finest leader I could buy, and laid the baited hook out there among a dozen similar pieces of bread. Snap! Snap! Snap! They'd take all the chum. But when only the baited piece was left they'd swim 'round and 'round below, squinting up at it once in awhile but never touching it. They must have figured that they'd already paid the cover charge, and the next time somebody might not say "Let him go."

Later on a future shipmate and I got in a few more days at Carmel and Monterey to see the cedars, the seals and birds on the rocks, and the very picturesque community. And we caught a few bluefish off the rocks, though I think I can still smell the sardine bait

on my hands.

Then, late one night, a long distance phone call—and soon we slipped out under the Golden Gate one misty morning for a rendezvous at sea. It was a slow convoy, and for several days we trailed a line off the stern. But we got no bites.

Since then the only fish I've seen have been silver ones, streaking at me under a row of bubbles, straight as an arrow. There have been bigger, black ones, too, that I don't see because I'm at battle stations down at the controls. But I know they're there. Have you ever felt a depth charge rock a ship?

APPENDIX 3 – Shellback Book

Appendix 3 is a complete copy of the "Shellback Book" *USS West Virginia Crosses the Equator Again – October 1944.*

USS WEST VIRGINIA

CROSSES THE EQUATOR AGAIN

OCTOBER 1944

USS WEST VIRGINIA

Crosses the EQUATOR *Again*

OCTOBER 1944

CAPTAIN H. V. WILEY, U. S. NAVY, *Commanding Officer*

COMMANDER G. J. KING, U. S. NAVY, *Executive Officer*

Edited by

R. O. BAUMRUCKER, LIEUT., USNR

Cartoons by

D. L. JOHNSON, MUS3C, USNR

ENTIRE PUBLICATION CLEARED FOR PUBLICATION BY FLEET CHIEF CENSOR

USS WEST VIRGINIA, DECEMBER 7, 1941

USS WEST VIRGINIA, OCTOBER, 1944

CAPTAIN H. V. WILEY, U. S. NAVY

Commanding Officer

USS WEST VIRGINIA

"Captain Wiley, it is a great pleasure to see you once more. When last we met you were commanding the destroyer squadron of the Asiatic Fleet, and I recall with pride the way you and your trusty Shellbacks gave the Japs hell at Makassar Straits, off Bali, and in the Java Sea. May your successes follow you on the USS WEST VIRGINIA."

—NEPTUNUS REX

COMMANDER G. J. KING, U. S. NAVY

Executive Officer

USS WEST VIRGINIA

"Commander King, on your first visit to my domain you were aboard the USS NEW MEXICO, when the fleet cruised to Australia in 1925. Well do I remember your battle against unsurmountable odds at Bataan in 1942. Gratified I am that I was there to guide the submarine out when you made your escape at the last possible moment, for now I see you are bringing back a worthy crew to exterminate those dastard Japs from the Royal Domain."

—NEPTUNUS REX

[4]

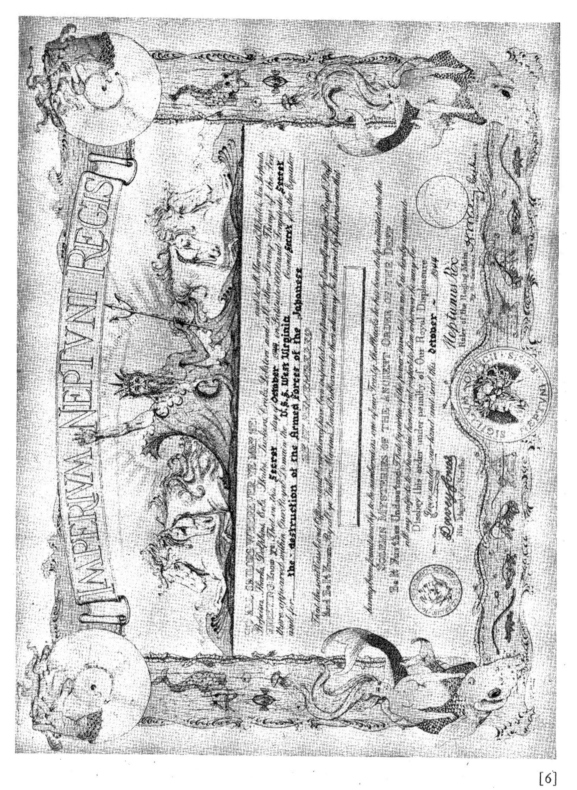

[6]

CROSSING THE LINE

FROM: DAVY JONES
TO: COMMANDING OFFICER,
      USS WEST VIRGINIA
      CINCPAC ORDERS WILL NECESSI-
      TATE CROSSING THE LINE X YOUR
      ATTENTION IS INVITED TO THE
      ROYAL EDICT WHICH STATES NO
      SLIME SEASLUGS SKATES SQUID
      SCUTS PANSEYS PULERS PEWKERS
      PIKERS PANHANDLERS WORMS SAND
      FLEAS FISH LICE JELLYFISH SEA
      LAWYERS OR POLLYWOGS MAY ENTER
      THE ROYAL DOMAIN OF NEPTUNUS
      REX X BEWARE X

With that sobering despatch, received over a secret radio channel, nearly two thousand pollywogs were suddenly brought face to face with their impending doom. For it was now clear that there was to be no free ride across the line for them. War or no war, King Neptune's displeasure was not to be trifled with. No gold-brickers would enter his domain on *this* vessel without benefit of the enlightenment conferred by a thorough initiation.

On her way to one of the most important missions of the war to date, the Wee Vee's course lay through dangerous waters, through territory controlled by the enemy only a few months previous and well within range of still potent bases. In fact, for an hour during the morning when the initiation was at its height, an unidentified plane was circling on the horizon, snooping on this new menace moving out toward the setting sun. But part of the crew was alert and on watch; our guns were manned and ready to send him plunging into the sea if he dared to come within range. Little did he know with what disrespect we treated his Emperor's henchmen. For Captain Wiley had ordered a ceremony unrestrained by the grimmer activity that lay just ahead, and in spite of the handicaps of a ship stripped for action, such an initiation as transpired has seldom if ever been equalled by a ship crossing the line even in peace time.

The ceremonies, outwardly lighthearted, were conducted under the stern realities of this order: "No man shall leave his watch station to take part in the initiation. No man shall be removed from his watch station either forcefully or voluntarily to take part in the initiation. Each gadget and contrivance used in the initiation will be inspected by either the Executive Officer or the Engineering Officer. No knives or scissors will be permitted under any circumstances. It is reiterated that the initiation is a lot of good clean fun, and unnecessary roughness is absolutely forbidden. We don't want to come out of this thing with a Sick Bay filled to overflowing. Above all, *do not relax vigilance in watch standing; you'll get your chance when you are off watch.* It is realized there will be difficulty while you are on watch to resist seeing the show put on on the forecastle, but we must be alert every minute. The Nips have never been known to either give or take time out."

The following despatch arrived soon afterwards:

FROM: TASK FORCE COMMANDER
TO: ALL SHIPS PRESENT
ACTION: USS WEST VIRGINIA
        ALL SHIPS THIS COMMAND MAKE
        PROPER PREPARATIONS FOR THE
        RECEPTION OF HIS IMPERIAL
        MAJESTY NEPTUNUS REX X ALL
        SHIPS IMMEDIATELY ESTABLISH
        AN ADEQUATE LOOKOUT WATCH
        FOR DAVY JONES X DUE TIME
        SHOULD BE ALLOCATED TO THE
        INSTRUCTION OF ALL NOVICES
        OTHERWISE KNOWN AS POLLYWOGS
        WHO ARE APPROACHING THE
        DREADFUL MYSTERIES IN ORDER
        THAT THEIR MINDS SOULS AND
        BODIES MAY BE STEELED TO THE
        ORDEAL THAT AWAITS THEM X

Three or four days in advance of the event there were outward signs of the impending clash. Mysterious apparatus was being rigged and tested under guard on the forecastle. A large salt water "swimming pool," with gismos alongside which had no apparent function other than to flip pollywogs backwards into the tank, was being built,

[7]

On Watch for the Line

plus a platform, podiums and torture racks. Matters of grave importance between Senior Shellbacks from each division were discussed in dignified meetings on the fantail, and were attacked with streams of water by revolting pollywogs. Officers and men turned up with unique and strictly non-regulation haircuts, and the safest precaution of all was taken by some in shaving their hair completely off.

King Neptune was evidently somewhat alarmed, for though he knew the Shellbacks aboard were trusty and tested he also knew they were greatly outnumbered, and the following message was received:

HEAR YE! HEAR YE! HEAR YE!

It has been brought to His Royal Majesty, Neptunus Rex, through his trusty Shellbacks, that certain of ye Box Car Tourists, Park Statues, Hay Makers and Other Landlubbers, attached to the good ship WEST VIRGINIA and soon to enter my Royal Domain, are treating His Royal Majesty with contempt, and are committing

Acts of Insurrection and Sedition. KNOW YE and take due notice accordingly, that such Words and such Acts meet with His Royal Majesty's profound displeasure, and will be punished by eternal pickling or such other torment as His Royal Highness may deem appropriate.

NEPTUNUS REX

But the pollywog advantage was only in numbers. The Worthy Shellbacks were able to retain complete control of the situation, and on the day preceding the crossing of the line everything was proceeding according to plan. That morning this message was deciphered:

FROM: NEPTUNUS REX
TO: USS WEST VIRGINIA
     TO ALL MY FAITHFUL AND ILLUS-
     TRIOUS SUBJECTS CAPTAIN H V
     WILEY AND ALL THE ANCIENT
     SHELLBACKS UNDER HIS COMMAND
     GREETINGS AND SALUTATIONS X I
     WISH TO EXPRESS MY APPRECIA-
     TION TO YOU FOR BRINGING ONCE
     MORE INTO MY DOMAIN THE GOOD

[8]

SHIP WEST VIRGINIA X MY JOY IS INTENSE AT THE PROSPECT OF MAKING ROYAL SUBJECTS OUT OF YOUR CARGO OF LANDLUBBERS DRUG STORE COWBOYS TADPOLES AND ALL SUCH SCUM CALLED POLLYWOGS X REST ASSURED THAT OUR METHODS OF TORTURE HAVE PROGRESSED WITH MODERN METHODS OF WARFARE X MY ILLUSTRIOUS EMISSARY ONE DAVY JONES WILL BOARD THE WEST VIRGINIA SOMETIME DURING THIS AFTERNOON AND I EXPECT HIM TO BE ACCORDED A FITTING AND PROPER RECEPTION X I ALSO DIRECT THE SO-CALLED SEMPER SEVENTY-SIX BE GIVEN THE ROYAL WORKS DURING THE PROCESS OF CLEANSING WHICH MUST BE APPLIED TO ALL MARINES TO MAKE THEM FIT SUBJECTS OF THE SEA X EVEN SO I FEAR THE LATTER TASK WILL BE NIGH TO IMPOSSIBLE AS NO HORSE BLANKET WAS EVER FIT TO TAKE TO SEA X THEIR NAMES HAVE BEEN PLACED ON MY BLACK-LIST AND SHALL BE PRESENTED AT THE PROPER TIME X I SHALL BE WAITING AT THE BORDER LINE OF LATITUDES WHEN YOU CROSS THAT WORLD FAMOUS EQUATORIAL LINE AND THEN OFFER MY PERSONAL GREETINGS AND RULE FOR THE DAY OVER THE ROYAL COURT X

This despatch was promptly followed by:

USS WEST VIRGINIA
C/O DEEP SEA POST OFFICE
REALM OF NEPTUNUS REX

From: Senior Shellback, USS WEST VIRGINIA
To: Senior Pollywog, USS WEST VIRGINIA
Subject: ORDERS
Ref: (a) Despatch from Neptunus Rex, King of the Deep
Encl: (a) Watch List
    1.   The USS WEST VIRGINIA is approaching the Kingdom of the Sovereign of the Seas and his emissary

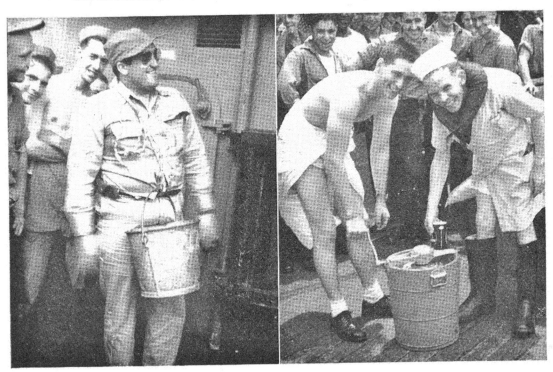

Give Me Your Butts, Please   Gedunks for Shellbacks

[9]

of good will may be expected within hail at any time.

2.   The correct course has been laid and it is essential that contact be made to avoid incurring the displeasure of the Distinguished Ruler.

3.   You will, therefore, maintain a pollywog watch in accordance with the list attached as enclosure (a), to proclaim the arrival of this vessel within hail of that Eminent Navigator Davy Jones, Ambassador Plenipotentiary to Neptunus Rex, King of the Briney Deep.

4.   The watches will be stood in a military manner in the places designated. Watch standers without previous military experience will be properly instructed prior to taking over the watch. The prescribed uniform is mandatory. Leaving post of duty without being properly relieved is a serious offense. Reliefs will be prompt and punctilious. This watch takes precedence over all other duties.

5.   The importance of your task is emphasized by information that the object of your search is a conch shell boat, so small that it may be easily passed up.

6.   Do not miss Davy Jones at the risk of the Royal Displeasure.

H. V. WILEY

The first real overture to the ceremonies was evidenced just after the noon meal, when the band broke out with a concert on the quarterdeck. Nothing unusual about that, except that the Chief Bandmaster was conducting in luxurious locks of flowing pink hair. Soon an ensign came pattering up the deck, dressed in simulated diapers, and pitifully begging everyone he met for a bottle opener so he could get to his bottle of coke.

The lieutenant commander Supply Officer mounted a ventilator on the fantail, dressed in rubber boots and a smock over a kapock life preserver, grinding the handle of a gallon ice cream freezer and loudly proclaiming that he was making gedunks for Shellbacks. Further aft on the fantail, ensigns instead of airplanes were being catapulted, with paddles to take the place of powder charges, and a lieutenant from the First Lieutenant's office was dutifully sweeping up Shellback's butts from a deck that normally is scrupulously clean.

Back against a turret housing the 16-inch guns a solitary Ghandiesque jg was piping a clarinet at a coil of rope stiffened by wire, which feinted in the breeze like a fascinated cobra, and the watch was posted in ridiculous attire throughout the ship for Davy Jones and his assistant, Peg Leg, who were to come aboard late that afternoon to pave the way for King Neptune and his Court.

It was a show for the enlisted men, and in this

Jam Session   Want to See Action?

[10]

Gosh I'm Confused!

What Comes Next?!!!

preliminary hazing the pollywog officers were shown no mercy. High on turret three the Casanova of the Junior Officers' Mess was demonstrating his famous technique on a convincingly attractive but not too willing siren, and persuasion wasn't abetted by glasses of a foul tasting beverage concocted by the ship's doctor. In fact, as the would-be seducer started to shift his chair around the table, "she" leapt to her feet and screamed: "You make one pass at me and I'll slap the lunch out of you!"

The Assistant Navigator wandered around, taking sights with an amazingly intricate but altogether inadequate array of instruments and charts, proclaiming the distance to Tokio in inches, while an odd-looking character circled the decks and mournfully quacked like a duck.

Then suddenly, amid a fanfare of trumpets, Davy Jones and Peg Leg were seen rising out of the sea on the bow, and the Junior Officer-of-the-Deck hurried down from the bridge to greet them.

J. O. O. D.: "Ahoy, there!"

DAVY JONES: "Davy Jones, the Royal Envoy of His Royal Majesty Neptunus Rex, and his assistant, Peg Leg."

J. O. O. D.: "Come aboard, Davy Jones and Peg Leg, and follow me to the bridge, where Captain Wiley awaits you."

CAPTAIN WILEY: "Welcome aboard, Davy Jones and Peg Leg."

DAVY JONES: "Captain Wiley, I bring you the greetings of His Royal Highness Neptunus Rex, and I bid you welcome once again to the Realm of the Briney Deep. It is a great pleasure to see you once more. When last we met you were commanding a destroyer squadron and we recall with pride the way you and your trusty Shellbacks gave the Japs hell at Makassar Straits, off Bali, and in the Java Sea.

"I am especially glad to come aboard this vessel. I am particularly pleased to find that the Japs did not succeed in keeping the West Virginia out of the fight, and it is good to know she will be in there pitching again to rid the Royal Domain of those dastard Japs.

"It has come to the Royal Ears of my Royal Master that all is not perfect on the West Virginia. Therefore he has ordered me to meet the ship before you enter the Royal Domain and declare His Royal Will.

"Sir, Neptunus Rex and His Royal Party will board your ship tomorrow at 0700. I request that the ship break out the Jolly Roger at that time, and all hands prepare to welcome the Royal Party. In the meantime, Captain, I request that the pollywogs be assembled on the forecastle and nearby parts of the ship and listen to the Royal Proclamation and hear the Royal Summons."

J. O. O. D.: "Pass the word for all hands to attend the Royal Proclamation!"

At this point the emissaries descended to the platform on the forecastle and read this proclamation:

[11]

Davy Jones Reading the Proclamation, with Peg Leg

Proclamation!

BY HIS IMPERIAL MAJESTY,

NEPTUNUS REX

HEAR YE! HEAR YE! HEAR YE!

I bring tidings from HIS ROYAL MAJESTY, EMPEROR OF ALL THE SEAS and MOST GRACIOUS RULER OF ALL THE INHABITANTS OF ALL THE MIGHTY OCEANS!

Therefore do I, DAVY JONES, Minister Plenipotentiary and Envoy Extraordinary from his IMPERIAL HIGHNESS NEPTUNUS REX IMPERATOR, bring Royal Greetings to His Majesty's Most Distinguished Subjects, Captain H. V. Wiley and Commander G. J. King, and to all the Loyal Shellbacks entering the Imperial Domain on board the United States Ship WEST VIRGINIA.

ALL HAIL! ALL HAIL! ALL HAIL!

And to all ye miserable pollywogs and landlubbers do I, the Representative of the King, bring fearful warnings. Grovel on the deck in fear and trembling, Oh ye insignificant tadpoles, and spend ye the night in serious meditation and prepare ye well the defense that ye will present to the Royal Court in contemplation of your grievous sins, and pray ye mightily that ye be finally accorded the Great Privilege of Entrance Into the Royal Domain.

And to all those scurvy scoffers, that miserable riffraff from the beach, those unmentionables who by means of their insidious but futile mouthings have endeavored to bring discredit upon the Realm of the Mighty Ruler of the Sea, to this scurrilous scum of the earth I bring dire warnings of their impending doom. Shiver and shake, ye spurious spawn spewed by the filthy earth, as ye contemplate the fearsome punishment that awaits.

Notwithstanding this dastardly attack upon the Realm of the Mighty Ruler of the Deep, His Imperial Majesty in all His Graciousness and Justness has decided to accord to these miserable malefactors the Great Privilege of a Defense, and therefore has had prepared a summary of the charges to be answered before the Royal Court. Look ye well to your defense, and seek ye Mercy of His Most Royal Majesty, the King.

Deputy of the Royal Scribe, serve ye the Royal Subpoenas to the Senior Shellback of each division.

Peg Leg then delivered the subpoenas, and the pollywogs, now sensing for the first time the real import of their fate, spent the night in fear and trembling, meditating on such crimes as these which had been uncovered by the Royal Detectives:

"Aroused much Royal Displeasure by singing 'Deep in the Heart of Texas'."

"Did try to consume beer at various times and places faster than it could be made."

"Claims to be a Romeo—says he has 1000 women."

"Is a mattress-back Commando, and prefers to sleep catty-wampus."

"Said 'No' instead of 'No, *Sir!*' to a Shellback."

"Never shares food, candy or women with Shellbacks."

[12]

Subpoena and Summons Extraordinary
The Royal High Court of the Raging Main

Region of the South Seas }
Domain of Neptunus Rex } ss.

To Whom May Come These Presents—Greetings and Beware!!

Whereas, The Good Ship WEST VIRGINIA, bound southward of the Equator, is about to enter our domain; and

Whereas, The aforesaid ship carries a large and loathsome cargo of landlubbers, beach-combers, guardo-rats, sea-lawyers, lounge-lizards, parlor-dunigans, plow-deserters, park-bench warmers, chicken chasers, hay-tossers, four-flushers, crossword puzzle bugs, dance-hall sheiks, drug store cowboys, asphalt arabs, and all other living creatures of the land, and last but not least he-vamps, liberty-hounds, San Pedro and Long Beach Caballeros masquerading as seamen, of which, low scrum, you are a member, having never appeared before us; and

Whereas, THE ROYAL COURT of the RAGING MAIN will convene on board the good ship WEST VIRGINIA in October, 1944; and

Whereas, An inspection of our Royal Muster shows that it is high time your sad and wandering nautical soul appears before our August Presence; and

Be It Known, That we hereby summon and command you,_____

_____,

now a_____, U. S. Navy,
to appear before the Royal High Court and Our August Presence on the aforesaid date at such time as may best suit OUR pleasure. You will accept most heartily and with good grace the pains and penalties of the awful tortures that will be inflicted upon you to determine your fitness to be one of our Trusty Shellbacks, and answer to the following charges:

CHARGE I. In that you have hitherto wilfully and maliciously failed to show reverence and allegiance to Our Royal Person, and are therein and thereby a vile landlubber and a pollywog.

CHARGE II.

CHARGE III.

CHARGE IV.

Disobey this summons under pain of our swift and terrible displeasure.
Our vigilence is ever wakeful, our vengeance is just and sure.

Given Under Our Hand and Seal
  DAVY JONES
    Scribe

  NEPTUNUS REX
    Ruler of the Raging Main

[13]

Delivering the Subpoenas

"Fading too much Shellback cabbage in crap games."

"Resisting the advances of an Honorable Shellback CPO."

"Trying to give ship's camel a drink and pitch woo with the starboard cat-walk, the U. S. then being in a State of War."

"Impersonating a boatswain's mate."

"Giving a certain group of Shellbacks a bum time."

"Complains about Navy chow."

"Says Navy chow is good."

"Gross impersonation of a man-of-warsman."

"Using vile and ungentlemanly language while scrubbing a Distinguished Shellback's clothes."

"Permitting various and numerous girls to call him 'Baby'."

"Stealing eggs from the crow's nest and oil from the smoking lamp."

"Concealing an inflated lift belt and having a medicine ball in his possession at all times."

Davy Jones and Peg Leg, having finished their duty for the day, obtained permission from the Captain to leave the ship.

But dawn came all too soon for those whose fate lay in the balance. The following message had been dispatched during the night:

```
From: Captain H. V. WILEY
To:   NEPTUNUS REX
      With permission of your Royal
      Majesty, the USS WEST VIRGINIA
```

```
will enter your domain about
0730 in the morning. You and
your Royal Court will be re-
ceived on board with full cer-
emonies. I have directed that
all pollywogs be paraded and
be presented for initiation
into the mysteries of the
deep. My compliments and best
wishes to you and to your
Queen.
```

The reply was quick in coming:

```
FROM: NEPTUNUS REX
TO:   CAPTAIN H. V. WILEY
      CAPTAIN WILEY ON YOUR LAST
      VISIT TO MY DOMAIN YOU WERE
      COMMANDER DESTROYERS ASIATIC
      FLEET CHASING THE NIPPERS
      AROUND MAKASSAR STRAIGHT X MY
      ENVOY PLENIPOTENTIARY INFORMS
      ME THAT YOU ARE BRINGING A
      LARGE NUMBER OF LOUNGE LIZARDS
      LATE FROM POPCORN GULCH IN
      LONG BEACH AS WELL AS A GOODLY
      NUMBER OF SAN PEDRO CABAL-
      LEROS X I SHALL BOARD YOU
      ABOUT 0700 ASSUME COMMAND AND
      BREAK MY FLAG X YOUR MIGHTY
      SLOOP OF WAR IS ACCEPTED X THE
      ROYAL NAVIGATOR WILL BE AT THE
      HELM AND YOU MAY REST ASSURED
      THAT SHE WILL BE PROPERLY
      HANDLED X WE WILL THEN PROCEED
      WITH THE INSPECTION OF THIS
      MOTLEY LOAD OF LANDLUBBERS
      BEACHCOMBERS LOUNGE LIZARDS
```

[14]

[15]

PARLOR DUNIGANS PLOW DESERTERS AND LONG BEACH COWBOYS FALSELY MASQUERADING AS SEAMEN AND MAN O WARS MEN X

At 0705 the Royal Party was sighted on the line, rising up through a haze of mist and seaweed, and the Jolly Roger was broken at the fore as they came aboard. They then proceeded to the quarter-deck to be received with honors. First came King Neptune in his Royal Robes, with the Royal Consort, followed by the Royal Princesses and the Royal Baby. Then came Davy Jones, Peg Leg, the Royal Navigator, the Royal Judges, Royal Prosecutors, Royal Counsellors, Royal Executioners, Royal Chief of Police and the Royal Cops, the Royal Barbers, the Royal Undertaker, Electricians, Torturers, Docs, Cook, Sea Hag, Conchubine and the Royal Polar Bears, plus dozens of strikers to bring up the rear. Captain Wiley descended from the bridge to receive the Distinguished Party in these terms:

CAPTAIN WILEY: "Your Imperial Majesty, I welcome you and your court aboard my ship. The United States Navy needs men with strength of will, courage, and ability to learn the Mysteries of the Sea.

"We bring you today, for initiation into the Order of Shellbacks, an extraordinarily large group of officers and men, some of age and experience, some young and innocent and new to life at sea.

"We ask that you try them, to test them, with the hope that many will be found worthy of the name Shellback."

NEPTUNUS REX: "I request permission to take over the ship, Sir."

CAPTAIN WILEY: "You have the ship."

NEPTUNUS REX: "Royal Navigator, take the conn! Two block the Jolly Roger! Inform the Royal Judges to prepare to open court! Call the candidates to Quarters for inspection!"

These ceremonies completed, the Captain returned to the bridge and, to put it mildly, all hell broke loose. The wild ensuing melee would be impossible to describe in full detail in the short space of a book, for the Royal Party was adequately manned. All that can be attempted is to trace the route taken by each of the nearly two thousand pollywogs. What actually transpired is best left to the worst possible imaginings of the reader.

Each member of the Royal Party carried a wooden paddle, and demonstrated a Royal Technique in using them in the inspection. Grease, lampblack and graphite appeared as if from nowhere, and was soon transferred to faces, arms, backs and—especially—hair. As soon as the Royal Party completed its tour of inspection it moved up to the scene of the Royal Court to convert these landlubbers into fit subjects for His Majesty's Great Domain.

Each candidate approached the throne from the starboard side of the forecastle, through a brief but efficient receiving line. Here he was taken into custody by the Royal Cops, and brought to trial before the Royal Judges by the Royal Prosecutors, Counsellors and Executioner.

A careful subsequent examination of the findings of the Court fails to produce a single instance of a pollywog not being found guilty of every count, and more. With resounding raps of their gavels the Royal Judges meted out justice—found each and every pollywog guilty—and sentenced them to "The Works," "The Royal Works" or "The Royal Double Works." Special Friends of the Cops received Extra Special Attention.

From the Court it was but a surprisingly short trip to the excruciating rack of the Royal Torturers, where the candidate's body was paddled into shape, his joints thoroughly examined, and his landlubber's dust dusted off. His tonsils were effectively sprayed before he was permitted to enter into the presence of His Majesty and Royal Consort, and he was allowed but a brief instant to gaze upon the Exotic Splendour of the Court, the Beauty of the Royal Princesses, the Enticing Dancing Girls, and the Sultry Royal Conchubine.

A selected few were permitted to kiss the chubby stomach of the Royal Baby. Then all were hastened to the Royal Barbers, for most hair was too long and many whiskers needed lathering. The situation was, indeed, so drastic that an unfamiliar and especially viscous type of deep sea lather was required. Fortunately the Royal Barbers had been forehanded enough to see that plenty of grease was available.

Then, head over heels into the pool and the arms of the Royal Polar Bears, who had patiently waited shoulder deep in the sacred portion of the Briney, where they faithfully executed their duty in rins-

[16]

[17]

[18]

NEPTUNE CHARACTERS

KING NEPTUNE . . . . J. A. Prewitt, CBM
ROYAL CONSORT . . . . J. A. Aldrich, CCM
ROYAL PRINCESSES . . . . F. P. Abbott, Cox
                        J. L. Radford, Y1c
                        R. R. Rodgers, Lieut.
ROYAL BABY . . . . W. J. Yackly, BM2c
ROYAL GUEST OF HONOR . . . . Captain H. V. Wiley
           Commanding USS WEST VIRGINIA
DAVY JONES . . . . A. A. Siewert, CSM
PEG LEG . . . . . . G. Pasquariello, Chief Boatswain
ASSISTANT TO DAVY JONES . . . J. Wasilkowski, Ensign
           E. J. Greene, Chief Electrician
ROYAL NAVIGATOR . . . . W. J. Lucik, CQM
ROYAL JUDGES . . . . L. C. Crowder, CGM
           F. A. Sines, Lieut-Comdr (DC)
           L. E. Votaw, CCS
ROYAL PROSECUTORS . . . J. H. Brownfield, Commander
           J. A. Cunningham, Machinist
ROYAL COUNSELLORS . . . C. M. Hardison, Commander
           S. Martin, CCk
ROYAL EXECUTIONERS . . . . . . J. W. Booth, BM2c
           G. J. Egland, GM1c

ROYAL CHIEF OF POLICE . . K. H. Barrett, Chief Gunner
ROYAL BARBERS . . . . . . E. J. Fruechtl, Lieutenant
           F. Krivasich, CPhM
           T. L. Shealy, CSK
           E. W. Smith, CSK
STRIKERS . . . . E. L. English, CFC
           J. H. Forrester, CFC
           J. B. Fowler, BM2c
           B. H. Shelton, CTC
ROYAL UNDERTAKER . . . . . E. L. Bingamon, CMM
ROYAL ELECTRICIANS . . . . M. Brown, CEM
           E. J. Hickman, CEM
         N. L. Keefe, Chief Electrician
           O. Osheim, Lieutenant
ROYAL DOCS . . . . J. D. Atkins, EM1c
           G. R. Conrad, CWT
           A. L. Lynch, CWT
           R. R. MacGregor, CB
ROYAL COOK . . . . J. Lutrell, CFC
ROYAL CONCHUBINE . . . . G. Gutnik, PFC
SEA HAG . . . . . . E. N. Castleberry, Machinist

ROYAL COPS

R. E. Brown, WT2c
O. S. Brown, MM1c
J. M. Bruner, RT2c
J. B. Fowler, BM2c
W. Fredricksen, Cox
L. S. Garafano, WT2c
D. V. Hill, Cox

R. Y. Holmes, GM3c
E. W. Juntunen, S1c
G. L. Kent, Lieut.
G. J. Klaske, EM2c
S. C. Knopp, GM2c
C. E. Lewis, WT3c
R. L. Lynn, Cox

M. O. Marvig, WT1c
R. J. Malloy, Cox
A. H. Marvin, S1c
E. B. McMahon, GM3c
C. H. Mears, EM1c
W. L. Meinecke, Mach.
C. V. Miller, CTC

G. F. Overbee, GM2c
D. C. Parker, Cox
G. W. Pomplin, MM1c
J. B. Thurmond, RT3c
C. F. Stutsy, Cox
M. R. Vonderlinde, GM1c
C. A. Young, CMM

ROYAL POLAR BEARS

M. F. Baron, MM2c
E. R. Gardner, MM2c

A. B. Hopper, CMus
R. W. Nicholson, GM1c
M. W. Whatley, MM2c

F. H. White, Lieut.-Comdr.
F. W. Zech, SK1c
R. C. F. Reinicke, M2c

F. Scarberry, BM2c
J. E. Shreffler, RT3c

ROYAL TORTURERS

A. T. Bagwell, CM
J. N. Ballantyne, Lieut. (jg)

G. J. Boroff, FC2c
J. B. Camm, CSF
C. O. Fanslow, CBM

L. E. Gregson, CEM
L. H. Hegarty, FC3c
R. G. Manthei, Lieut.

L. E. Warner, CGM
D. F. Wingate, Lieut.

[19]

189

ing off the last distasteful vestiges of each polly-wog. From there it was out-of-the-pool, for a quick trip down Lover's Lane.

Some pollywogs were so unworthy that they were seen to falter occasionally as they scurried aft on the port side, to be greeted by their Shell-back shipmates. This was especially disappointing to some of the Shellbacks and difficult to understand, for no tripping was allowed—though most of the pollywogs received a stimulating blast of water in the face just as they neared their goal. But all were duly qualified.

As the last new Shellback joined our ranks, King Neptune took his leave, and "clean sweep down,

fore and aft" was piped. The First Lieutenant buried his face in his hands and wept as all hands went to the showers and the supply of fresh water fell to a new low.

It was not long afterwards, in the Philippines, that the West Virginia met the supreme test. Flying the same colors she had flown when she went to the bottom on December 7, she paved the way for the successful landing of our forces by a precise and terrific shore bombardment. Then, in company with her sister ships, she sank and defeated a considerable portion of the Japanese Fleet.

Neptunus Rex must have been well pleased with the initiation.

"Just a Lot of Good Clean Fun"

CONVERTED POLLYWOGS

OFFICERS

Lieut.-Commander . . . . T. A. Lombardi	Ensign . . . . T. E. Redstone
Lieutenant . . . . J. W. Lawson	Ensign . . . . S. Nachlas
Lieutenant . . . . F. J. Bitterman	Ensign . . . . E. E. Kovachek
Lieutenant . . . . L. D. Brown	Ensign . . . . S. C. Bennett
Lieutenant . . . . R. M. Rocktaschel	Ensign . . . . R. N. Catledge
Lieutenant . . . . K. D. Talley	Ensign . . . . F. J. Devine
Lieutenant . . . . H. Mattlage	Ensign . . . . W. W. Gordon
Lieutenant . . . . R. R. Mayer	Ensign . . . . D. Haweeli
Lieutenant . . . . W. E. Nelson	Ensign . . . . R. P. Crossley
Lieutenant . . . . L. M. Crandall	Ensign . . . . C. H. Colpitt
Lieutenant . . . . H. B. Wands, Jr.	Ensign . . . . R. S. McCarty
Lieutenant . . . . J. A. English	Ensign . . . . R. K. Plumb
Lieutenant . . . . J. H. Brinker, Jr.	Ensign . . . . C. R. Scott
Lieutenant . . . . H. R. Busby	Ensign . . . . T. M. Jarmon, Jr.
Lieutenant . . . . E. F. Coombs	Ensign . . . . C. A. Goebel, Jr.
Lieutenant . . . . W. F. Marquardt	Ensign . . . . W. M. Rosson
Lieutenant . . . . C. Sherman	Ensign . . . . R. I. Brabets
Lieutenant . . . . J. A. Soderberg, Jr.	Ensign . . . . D. W. Seibold
Lieutenant . . . . C. A. Taylor, Jr.	Ensign . . . . R. E. Umbenhour, Jr.
Lieutenant (jg) . . . . J. J. Crowley	Ensign . . . . P. A. Adams
Lieutenant (jg) . . . . A. F. Hughes	Ensign . . . . J. T. Batte
Lieutenant (jg) . . . . J. P. Floyd, Jr.	Ensign . . . . F. T. Kleber
Lieutenant (jg) . . . . W. W. Marsh	Ensign . . . . W. G. Pledger
Lieutenant (jg) . . . . T. E. Rooney	Ensign . . . . H. D. Williams
Lieutenant (jg) . . . . R. B. Tillinghast, Jr.	Lieut. Commander . . . . . . W. M. Porter (SC)
Lieutenant (jg) . . . . F. R. Cooper	Lieutenant . . . . D. A. Mutchler (SC)
Lieutenant (jg) . . . . C. F. McNamara	Lieutenant . . . . D. R. Kohli (MC)
Lieutenant (jg) . . . . P. R. Bechtolt	Lieutenant . . . . H. B. Henderson (DC)
Lieutenant (jg) . . . . H. B. Gist, Jr.	Lieutenant . . . . W. C. Reiner (MC)
Lieutenant (jg) . . . . E. N. Brodhagen	Lieutenant (jg) . . . . C. F. Shea (SC)
Lieutenant (jg) . . . . N. B. Servoss	Captain . . . . T. C. J. Whedbee (USMC)
Ensign . . . . R. G. Wilson	First Lieutenant . . . . J. Lovell (USMC)
Ensign . . . . R. C. Shirley	First Lieutenant . . . . . H. C. Steffens (USMC)

[22]

CONVERTED POLLYWOGS

Name	Rate	Name	Rate	Name	Rate
Alexander, C. H.	GM3c	Miller, M. M.	S2c	Esposita, T. J.	S1c
Allen, C. E.	S2c	Miniea, S. J.	S2c	Evans, R. B.	GM3c
Anderson, C. H.	S1c	Miner, L. V.	S2c	Fitzwater, C. W.	S1c
Anderson, F. D.	S2c	Mann, E. H.	S2c	Franco, J. R.	S1c
Anderson, H. H.	S1c	Mourning, L. R.	BM2c	Frank, J.	S1c
Ashley, J. M.	S2c	Myers, C. L.	GM1c	Gezik, R. C.	S1c
Baer, H. M.	S2c	Nelson, E. J.	BM1c	Goad, O. H.	S1c
Bertles, L. B.	S1c	Ostoin, J. J.	S2c	Green, W. E.	S1c
Bowen, J. J.	S1c	Pedersen, W.	S2c	Green, W. H.	S1c
Brock, D. D.	S1c	Rayburn, E.	S1c	Harper, W. A.	S1c
Brocklesby, P.	S1c	Reidy, W. D.	S1c	Harrison, R. A.	S1c
Canfield, A. M.	S2c	Remillard, E. J.	S2c	Hatfield, W. J.	S1c
Carlyle, H. H.	S2c	Roth, C. W.	S1c	Heinrich, D. B.	S1c
Felty, R. L.	S1c	Ruiz, H. H.	S1c	Henry, M. E.	S1c
Fields, W. H.	S2c	Rumfelt, L. W.	S2c	Henry, R.	S2c
Finnegan, P. E.	S2c	Smith, J. M.	S2c	Henson, R. E.	S1c
Fincher, L. P.	S1c	Sheller, E. J.	GM3c	Hersman, G. L.	S1c
Flores, W. M.	S1c	Stokes, H. O.	S2c	Highland, W. H.	S1c
Foley, Z. H.	S1c	Thirtle, G.	GM2c	Hill, F.	S1c
Foss, H. M.	S1c	Thompson, P. K.	S1c	Hitt, W. H.	S1c
Foster, G. E.	S1c	Wiggington, C. J.	S2c	Ireton, R. R.	S2c
Frame, R. H.	S1c	Williston, J. A.	S2c	Jenkins, R. E.	S2c
Fredericksen, E. B.	S1c	Wood, J. A.	Cox.	Kendgiora, L. J.	S1c
Frost, H. A.	S1c			Levendusky, T.	S2c
Garner, G.	S1c			McDonald, R. R.	S2c
Gardner, L. P.	S1c			Mikortis, J. J.	S2c
Garrison, J. H.	S2c	Name	Rate	Millwee, R. E.	S2c
Gautreau, R. L.	S1c	Appanaitis, B. E.	S2c	Moore, M. E.	S2c
Gonzales, M. C.	S1c	Bachman, E. C.	S2c	Olson, M. S.	S2c
Goodman, K. F.	S2c	Bannister, D. G.	BM2c	Olson, H. S.	GM3c
Graham, G. W.	S2c	Bartrug, O. L.	S1c	Penley, J. W.	S1c
Hite, H. W.	S1c	Bartrug, S. B.	S1c	Pickett, F. D.	S2c
Holm, E. J.	GM2c	Beck, J. W.	S1c	Popejoy, J. W.	S1c
Johnson, D. G.	S2c	Bible, F. D.	S1c	Printice, R. A.	S1c
Livingstone, D. I.	S2c	Bothern, H. R.	BM1c	Proctor, B. S.	BM2c
Loberg, C. C.	S2c	Brand, H. N.	GM1c	Reeve, V. W.	S1c
Longshore, J. M.	S2c	Briones, J.	S2c	Roberts, W. E.	S2c
Love, J. W.	S2c	Brown, J. C.	S2c	Robinson, C. L.	S1c
Lucero, R. N.	S2c	Brown, R. N.	S2c	Schilreef, J.	S1c
Mackintosh, R. G.	S2c	Cross, R. R.	Cox.	Schneider, R. E.	S2c
Maki, R. V.	S2c	Crutchleo, C. C.	S1c	Sharp, C. W.	S2c
Martinez, R.	S1c	Demmon, B. G.	S2c	Shephard, W. L.	S2c
Matkins, H. K.	S2c	Denslow, F. H.	S1c	Smith, F. W.	S1c
McDonald, J. F.	S2c	Emmons, D. D.	S1c	Shively, B. O.	GM2c
Medina, J. A.	S2c			Soland, L. W.	S2c

[23]

CONVERTED POLLYWOGS

Name	Rate
Soule, W. L.	S1c
Stone, L. F.	S1c
Sutter, O. H.	Cox.
Syring, I. A.	S2c
Uzee, V. J.	S1c
Valentine, J. S.	S1c
Vosberg, E. R.	Cox.
Westholder, L. F.	S2c
Whitaker, A. L.	S2c

Name	Rate
Bacon, D. F.	S2c
Baker, L. V.	S2c
Benson, L. M.	S2c
Bingham, P. L.	S2c
Dalessio, N. E.	Cox.
Daniels, M. L.	S2c
Ditlevson, E.	S2c
Foggia, D.	BM1c
Grimes, F. H.	S1c
Kumpula, G. A.	S1c
Lambert, R. H.	S1c
La Rue, A. C.	S1c
Laws, D. C.	Cox.
Leach, J. N.	S2c
Lemley, H. N.	S1c
Lewis, A. D.	S1c
Magistro, J.	S1c
Maria, J. B.	S2c
Marino, J. R.	S2c
Marshall, H. I.	S2c
McCartney, A. W.	S1c
McClain, C. B.	S1c
McClure, E. F.	S1c
McCreary, W. E.	S1c
Moody, F. L.	S1c
Morgan, J. L.	S2c
Mucgynski, B. S.	S1c
Oneill, J. D.	S1c
Olsnewski, A. J.	S1c
Oshenic, E. A.	S1c

Name	Rate
Perkins, C. F.	S2c
Perille, C. J.	S1c
Poling, E. W.	S1c
Ray, F. W.	S1c
Razgavieus, J. A.	S1c
Rechlitz, F. J.	S1c
Riddle, J. L.	S1c
Riley, J. J.	S2c
Rine, E. J.	S1c
Roberts, C.	S2c
Roberts, W. F.	S1c
Rogus, J. M.	S1c
Rowen, N. P.	S2c
Saieva, S. B.	S1c
Schmidgall, J. A.	S1c
Schmitt, A. J.	S1c
Seay, J. R.	GM3c
Shell, E. L.	S2c
Simmons, R. E.	S1c
Sloan, A. W.	GM2c
Smith, N. E.	S1c
Specht, E. J.	S1c
St. Arnold, B. J.	S1c
Stephens, E. D.	S2c
Stevens, B. S.	S1c
Stratman, R. K.	S1c
Sullenger, F. A.	S2c
Symonds, L. H.	Cox.
Taggert, E. H.	S2c
Tibbetts, A.	S2c
Trean, P. C.	S2c
Tucker, L.	GM2c
Van Horn, E. E.	S2c
Walcavich, E. N.	BM2c
Waldow, H. R.	S1c
Walker, C. J.	S1c
Walsh, J. A.	BM1c
Webb, D. C.	S2c
Wittenberger, E. E.	S1c
Wright, M. L.	GM2c
Wright, L. D.	S1c
Wyatt, W. H.	S1c

Name	Rate
Aiello, N. M.	S2c
Asbell, E. C.	S2c
Aubry, R. J.	S2c
Ballard, C. E.	BM2c
Barcus, I. I.	S2c
Bechtel, R. E.	S2c
Bennet, L. A.	S2c
Brockway, R. M.	S2c
Childress, M. T.	S2c
Denkhaus, G. H.	S1c
Ditty, G. R.	GM2c
Guilbeaux, E. J.	S1c
Hale, L. Jr.	S1c
Hammond, H. D.	S1c
Harmon, J. I.	S2c
Hawkins, G. R.	S2c
Hermann, E. J.	S1c
Hernandez, A. P.	S1c
Hicks, J. W.	S1c
Hileman, R. J.	S1c
Hill, B. T.	S1c
Karas, P. G.	S2c
Kendrick, R. R.	GM2c
Linn, C. J.	BM1c
Lutz, R. E.	S1c
Mascarenas, H. J.	S2c
McGill, D. L.	S2c
McGuckin, F. J.	BM2c
Milholland, M. B.	S2c
Miller, Y. A.	S2c
Partyka, J. S.	S2c
Pilarczyk, E.	S1c
Reiter, A. J.	S2c
Rellergert, A. C.	S2c
Roberson, R. B.	S2c
Robinson, C. J.	S2c
Rome, D. J.	S1c
Rose, L. S.	S1c
Ross, C. V.	S1c
Rough, E. A.	S1c
Ruddick, S. R.	S1c
Rudman, J. S.	S1c
Stephenson, F. P.	S2c
Stidham, M. M.	S1c
Tadgerson, E. D.	S1c

[24]

CONVERTED POLLYWOGS

Name	Rate	Name	Rate	Name	Rate
Terry, H. E.	S1c	Dixon, W. M.	S2c	Thompson, P.	S1c
Thoms, G. R.	S2c	Foy, J. H.	BM2c	Trevethan, A. S.	S2c
Thorpe, J. H.	S2c	Haney, R. D.	S1c	Variot, J. D.	S2c
Turek, W. C.	S2c	Hassell, T. J.	BM1c	Willis, M. L.	S2c
Vickers, L. H.	S1c	Hedrick, R. V.	S2c	Wing, E. I.	S2c
Vitellaro, E. W.	Cox.	Julian, A. T.	S2c	Witucki, R. F.	S2c
Wadley, W. W.	S1c	Justice, T. L.	S1c	Woltman, A. G.	S2c
Walazek, E. C.	S2c	Lechich, C. R.	S2c	Zettle, C. W.	Cox.
Watters, M. E.	S2c	Linowiecki, F. J.	S2c	Zimaga, R. R.	S2c
Weadick, T. F.	S1c	Magliolo, S.	S2c		
Webster, C. S.	S1c	Marshall, L. C.	S2c		
Wethington, L. O.	S1c	Mathison, D. M.	S2c		

Name	Rate
Wibbenmeyer, A. T.	S2c
Williams, D.	S2c
Williams, S. L.	S2c
Winkle, W. P.	S1c
Winsted, E. G.	S1c
Wipper, H. A.	S2c
Witt, J. W.	S1c
Wolf, R. E.	S1c
Wright, E. M.	S2c
Wroblewski, B. U.	S1c
Yeager, E. P.	S2c
Yeargin, W. A.	S1c

Name	Rate	Name	Rate
		Mohr, F. H.	S2c
		Mollenkopf, B.	S2c
		Muri, M. P.	S2c
		Nelson, K. P.	S2c
		Newton, C. W.	S2c
		Niedermeyer, L. E.	S2c
		Oswald, D. H.	S2c
		Poulson, B. G.	S2c
		Purser, J. W.	S1c
		Quick, C. D.	S2c
		Quinnelly, G. L.	S1c
		Ras, E. S.	S1c
		Ricker, A. A.	S1c
		Rittinger, C.	S1c
		Robbons, C. R.	S1c
		Roberts, J. M.	S1c

Name	Rate
Augustine, C. J.	S2c
Baker, M.	S2c
Banjanin, T. T.	S2c
Barbieri, P.	S2c
Barry, B.	S2c
Bergen, H. B.	S2c
Blanford, V. E.	S2c
Blum, M. E.	S2c
Clingman, H. F.	S2c
Cole, G. H.	S2c
Comella, W.	S2c
Decker, J. C.	S2c
DeHolt, R. B.	S2c
Denton, N. R.	S2c
Des Marais, D. L.	S2c
Dixon, J.	S2c

Name	Rate
Roby, H. C.	S1c
Robinson, G. W.	Cox.
Robinson, R. A.	S2c
Robinson, R. H.	S1c
Romano, R.	S1c
Rudnick, J.	S1c
Sauer, W.	S2c
Scarboraugh, S. J.	S2c
Schultz, S. H.	S2c
Siskin, H. L.	S1c
Slane, A. D.	S1c
Stedman, E. R.	S1c
Steiner, G. F.	S2c
Stewart, W. W.	S2c
Stuber, L. R.	S2c
Szymborski, A. J.	S1c

Name	Rate
Alberico, W. V.	S2c
Andler, R. J.	S2c
Auberry, J. H.	S2c
Balbinot, L. E.	S2c
Billington, B. E.	S2c
Brady, H. E.	S2c
Bravebull, J.	S2c
Brinkerhoff, B. M.	S2c
Buckner, H. D.	S2c
Buffo, J.	S2c
Burrows, R. J.	S2c
Chadwick, B. W.	S2c
Chaney, C. G.	S2c
Conosenti, A.	S2c
Coogan, J. H.	S2c
Cook, E. M.	S2c
Durham, H. B.	S1c
Fitchett, R. D.	S2c
Geci, G.	S1c
Gibson, E.	S1c
Godar, J. R.	S2c
Grandstaff, C. M.	S1c
Green, L. B.	S1c
Gudeman, R. H.	S2c
Hren, J. F.	S2c
Iverson, N. E.	S1c
Justice, R. L.	S2c
Kartes, C. J.	S2c
Kellner, E. J.	S2c
Kling, W. J.	S1c

[25]

CONVERTED POLLYWOGS

Name	Rate	Name	Rate	Name	Rate
Knox, C. B.	BM1c	Cummings, D. A.	Pvt.	Riesing, R. L.	Pvt.
Legore, D. D.	S1c	Dal Santo, R. N.	FMC.	Rogers, D. R.	ACk.
Le Juhn, P. J.	S2c	Decker, W. A.	PlSgt.	Rowe, D. E.	PFC
Liebert, V. H.	S1c	Doss, H. A.	PFC	Satterla, G. F.	PFC
Lorenson, H. C.	S2c	Druten, P. R.	PFC	Schimmelpfennig, G. A.	Corp.
Martin, E. F.	S2c	Du Boise, J. E.	PFC	Shatto, L. M.	Pvt.
Moff, E. C.	S1c	Dykhius, C. A.	PFC	Sherman, R. C.	PFC
Molzahn, L. V.	S2c	Easter, L. L.	PFC	Spears, R. L.	PFC
Morris, H. A.	GM2c	Evans, J. M.	PFC	Spurgeon, C. O.	PFC
Nard, L. R.	S1c	Farnsworth, R. D.	PFC	Stewart, J. O.	Corp.
O'Connor, W. H.	S2c	Forcha, D. M.	PFC	Strawn, E. O.	PFC
Overby, G.	S2c	Gootee, D. A.	PFC	Suttle, J. F.	PFC
Paul, L. L.	S2c	Gradick, J. E.	FM1c	Theisen, C. N.	PFC
Peer, S. A.	S1c	Herold, D. H.	PFC	Thompson, W. S.	PFC
Pouncey, E. A.	S1c	Hooton, D. R.	PFC	Thomsen, H. A.	Corp.
Reisch, C. E.	S2c	James, H. T., Jr.	PFC	Von Tobel, F. E.	Corp.
Ripperger, B. F.	S2c	Jenner, R. S.	PFC	Weinel, R. P.	Pvt.
Shephard, H. J.	S2c	Jurchick, P. G.	PFC	Wells, J. C.	PFC
Shields, B. L.	S1c	Kabza, L. P.	PFC	Wheat, H. L.	PFC
Sloderbeck, J. E.	S2c	Kimble, H. L.	PFC	Whitten, L. A.	Pvt.
Smith, C. G.	S1c	Lakness, N. A.	1stSgt.	Wilson, C. F.	PFC
Smith, D. L.	GM2c	Lynch, R. E.	PFC	Wooten, A. M.	PFC
Snuggs, A. P.	S1c	Martinez, F. C.	PFC	Zastrow, B. J.	PFC
Thieme, B. J.	S2c	Martinez, M. G.	PFC	Ziel, W. B.	PFC
Thomas, R. F.	S2c	Maynard, J. A.	PFC		
Tretter, C. J.	S2c	McMurray, T. B.	PFC		
Trout, B. A.	S2c	Mekulich, S. H.	PFC		
Uhrich, D.	S2c	Mikkelson, C. W.	Sgt.		
Urbanski, S. J.	S2c	Millard, K. E.	PFC	Name	Rate
Vignery, E. C.	S2c	Moon, J. C.	Corp.	Beyer, V. A.	S2c
Wallace, W. A.	S2c	Much, R. W.	Corp.	Biever, E. H.	S1c
Whitemore, B. E.	S2c	Mulford, S. R.	PFC	Boston, N. A.	S2c
Williams, R. J.	S2c	Nelson, C. C.	PFC	Bowen, D. N.	S2c
Wilson, F. W.	S2c	Noyes, R. A.	PFC	Burwell, F. S.	S2c
		Ott, K. W.	PFC	Cales, R. W.	S1c
		Parypa, L., Jr.	PFC	Caza, D. R.	S2c
		Peckels, J. R.	PFC	Cox, R. M.	S2c
		Perry, W. C.	PFC	Craver, J. R.	S2c
Name	Rate	Peterson, R. W.	Corp.	Crews, C.	S1c
Akers, R.	PFC	Plaisance, J. J.	PFC	Hartog, K. H.	S2c
Barclay, J. A.	PFC	Powell, G. K.	PFC	Hicks, W. D.	GM3c
Bayer, R. Jr.	Sgt.	Ragsdale, J. C.	PFC	Hitchcock, S. F.	S1c
Betson, W. A.	PFC	Raiche, J. R.	Sgt.	Holder, J. G.	S1c
Burden, C. Y.	PFC	Reed, E.	PlSgt.	Howard, C.	S2c
Cook, W. T.	PFC	Renois, J. B.	Sgt.	Hudson, F. E.	S2c
Correll, E.	PFC				

[26]

CONVERTED POLLYWOGS

Name	Rate
Jeziorski, C. J.	S2c
Karr, G. G.	S2c
Kershuk, M.	S1c
Killian, W. L.	S2c
Kulikowski, A. J.	S2c
Larson, P. V.	S1c
Leidall, P. D.	S2c
Little, H. L.	S2c
McCulloch, D. L.	S2c
McMillin, J.	GM3c
Marschel, B. W.	S2c
Marshall, L. C.	S2c
Martin, J. A.	S2c
Matney, A. T.	S2c
Miller, W. K.	S2c
Molina, J.	S2c
Parkinson, R. J.	S1c
Paull, R. W.	S1c
Phernetton, I. C.	S1c
Pulver, M. J.	S1c
Reed, L. A.	S1c
Robbins, R. E.	S2c
Robinette, M. B.	S2c
Robinson, G. W.	GM3c
Ross, L. W.	S1c
Rowland, R. V.	S1c
Rushin, R. R.	S2c
Schembari, A. J.	S1c
Schwartzler, R. C.	S1c
Schweigart, A.	S2c
Shaffer, H. H.	S2c
Sharp, E. E.	S1c
Shelton, C. C.	GM3c
Shelton, J. T.	S2c
Sherrod, L. K.	S2c
Sholos, S.	S1c
Sielky, F. J.	S1c
Skrapke, H. J.	S2c
Sloan, A. E.	S1c
Smith, A. D.	S2c
Smith, O. L.	S2c
Snider, R. I.	S1c
Sparks, J. W.	S2c
Sparks, M. D.	S2c
Spence, C. H.	S2c

Name	Rate
Spriggs, D. F.	S2c
Szymanski, R. J.	S1c
Tart, P. H.	S1c
Vigil, N.	S2c
Waszak, V. M.	S2c
Wauford, J. D.	BM1c
White, R. A.	S2c
Wiggins, G. L.	S1c
Wiggs, A.	S2c
Wilkins, L. W.	S2c
Zwirchitz, E. J.	S2c

Name	Rate
Anderson, N. E.	S2c
Arnholz, C. A.	S1c
Baker, T. W.	S1c
Barney, L. A.	S1c
Barcus, M. L.	S2c
Beckstrom, G. E.	S2c
Benson, R. C.	S2c
Bernard, H. D.	S1c
Bevan, R. O.	S2c
Birkland, H.	S2c
Blahut, J. J.	S2c
Boome, A. T.	S2c
Brinch, J. A.	S1c
Cassell, H. O.	S1c
Collins, J. D.	S1c
Cooper, J. O.	S2c
Cornett, G. C.	S2c
Coston, B. E.	S2c
Fischesser, F. A.	GM3c
Garmon, H. E.	S1c
Hayes, J. B.	BM1c
Leagans, H. W.	S2c
Lemond, E. F.	S2c
Marshall, V. E.	S2c
Martineau, L. D.	S1c
Matlock, W. E.	S1c
May, J. C.	S2c
McDowell, B. F.	S2c

Name	Rate
Moldenhauer, C. C.	S2c
Morris, P.	S1c
Mudrack, R. L.	S2c
Niswanger, S.	S2c
Oglesby, J. R.	S2c
Ostrom, A. W.	S2c
Outlaw, E. V.	S1c
O'Hagan, A. C.	S2c
Pagac, G.	S2c
Paxton, D. S.	Cox.
Peterson, R. N.	S2c
Poland, H. D.	S1c
Pomykala, W. J.	S2c
Poulson, J. M.	S2c
Powell, B. R.	S2c
Prather, P. H.	S2c
Ramey, H. E.	S2c
Rapoza, J. J.	S2c
Rasmussen, D. C.	S2c
Rasmussen, R. G.	S1c
Reed, S. E.	S2c
Reitter, J. J.	S2c
Renfroe, G. C.	GM2c
Setterberg, C. J.	S2c
Skelton, D. J.	S1c
Smith, F. L.	S2c
Smith, W. A.	S1c
Stanfill, H. C.	S2c
Stevenson, C. C.	S2c
Stops, C. L.	S2c
Stroehmar, H. E.	S2c
Tattina, A.	GM2c
Turner, J. P.	S2c
Varnado, A. B.	S2c
Vanwey, M. D.	S2c
Warner, E. E.	S2c
Weinzierl, F. L.	S2c
Welker, J. T.	S2c
Wheeler, O. O.	S1c
Wiggins, C. M.	S2c
Wigginton, V. D.	S2c
Wilson, G. I.	S2c
Young, R. V.	S1c

[27]

CONVERTED POLLYWOGS

Name	Rate	Name	Rate	Name	Rate
Agnew, D. E.	S1c	Roylance, J. O.	S1c	Lee, D. L.	S2c
Bailey, C. E.	S2c	Russell, E. L.	S2c	Manning, R. E.	S2c
Bauman, H. E.	S2c	Rutherford, E.	S1c	McMahon, T. H.	S2c
Bears, K. D.	S2c	Scantlin, C. E.	S1c	Melior, H. E.	S2c
Bettencourt, A. H.	S2c	Schaffner, R. I.	S2c	Medlin, G. E.	S2c
Bezinque, C. J.	S1c	Schlegel, B. H.	S2c	McGechie, M. F.	S2c
Bigshield, N.	S1c	Schlenk, R.	S2c	Musser, R. W.	S2c
Bone, C. D.	S2c	Schmidt, E. L.	S1c	McQuaid, J. D.	S2c
Boos, L. H.	S1c	Schneider, E.	S2c	Mannerelli, F. J.	S2c
Braden, L. O.	S2c	Schulte, E.	S2c	Marshall, S. E.	S2c
Breitkreutz, H. H.	S2c	Schuster, W. F.	S2c	McClure, M. T.	S2c
Bryan, W. D.	S1c	Serafini, P. J.	S2c	Noyes, T. I.	S2c
Burchett, R. E.	S2c	Stracener, E.	S2c	Petermann, L. A.	S2c
Couture, L. V.	S2c	Stetz, M.	S1c	Pranin, S. H.	S1c
Crudo, W. J.	Cox.	Thomas, D. C.	S1c	Palach, V. E.	S2c
Curtis, B. D.	S2c	Walker, C. O.	S1c	Pacatte, N. V.	S1c
Dawson, E. B.	S1c	Whitcomb, M. F.	GM3c	Pemberton, R.	S2c
Holt, D. E.	S2c	Whitworth, W. C.	S1c	Peters, W. F.	S2c
Keck, W. U.	S1c	Widmeier, J. J.	S1c	Peddicord, J. B.	BM2c
Kiralla, J. S.	S2c	Wilson, G. J.	S1c	Powell, K.	S1c
Kleinfeldt, H. T.	GM2c	Vanover, C. M.	S2c	Pickett, A. D.	S1c
Lashon, L. R.	S2c	Vercellino, R. J.	S2c	Prentice, J. A.	S1c
Lundin, R. C.	S2c			Pitt, D. J.	S1c
Manke, G. O. A.	S1c			Priest, H. C.	S1c
Marks, W. D.	S2c			Riker, M. O.	S1c
Martin, J. L.	S2c	Name	Rate	Reeves, J. N.	S1c
McLane, W. A.	S2c	Albiston, E. J.	S2c	Roy, J. B.	S1c
Meyer, G. E.	S2c	Behrnes, C. B.	S1c	Richter, H. F.	S2c
Morse, F. E.	S2c	Bright, R. F.	GM2c	Roberts, R. E.	S2c
Mugge, D.	S1c	Brown, C.	S1c	Reynolds, J. D.	S1c
Olsen, A. C.	S1c	Cauthron, E. C.	S2c	Ruppert, F. C.	S1c
Parks, C. W.	S1c	Childs, W. D.	S2c	Rose, W. P.	S2c
Pedersen, H. W.	S1c	Chladik, F. J.	S2c	Rogusky, C. C.	S1c
Phillips, D. A.	S2c	Cicale, A. S.	S2c	Romero, E.	S2c
Pifer, W. F.	S1c	Deeds, R. E.	S1c	Ruppel, H.	S2c
Pindar, L. D.	S1c	Engle, D. A.	S1c	Robar, R. B.	S1c
Posey, M. R.	S1c	Huffstetler, W. H.	S1c	Raymond, F. L.	S1c
Price, G. L.	S1c	Hunsaker, L.	S2c	Roseboom, W.	S1c
Qualset, H. G.	S2c	Jacobson, O. V.	Cox.	Reyes, J. C.	S2c
Rebell, W.	S1c	Klein, A. M.	S2c	Szmborski, L. J.	S1c
Regueiro, R. J.	S1c	Kitchen, M. J.	GH3c	Snyder, C. M.	S2c
Rhodes, W.	S2c	Klobucar, E. J.	S1c	Spence, H.	S2c
Rodarmel, W. A.	S1c	Locker, N. L.	S1c	Saragusa, J. A.	S2c
Rogers, L. R.	S1c	Larson, L. H.	S1c	Simoneaux, I. E.	S1c
Rohrbaugh, J. A.	S1c				

[28]

CONVERTED POLLYWOGS

Name	Rate	Name	Rate	Name	Rate
Schallert, C. E.	S1c	Eastman, R. H.	FC3c	Tidrick, R. E.	FC3c
Szwejk, L.	S1c	Edlin, R. D.	FC1c	Tollison, W. T.	S2c
Schnurbusch, W. W.	S2c	Evans, E. H.	FC3c	Tougas, D. L.	S2c
Todd, R. F.	Cox.	Ferland, J. R.	FC1c	Trites, E. F.	FC2c
Van Sickle, H. W.	S1c	Green, L. A.	S1c	Tyer, J. A.	FC3c
Weatherman, C.	Cox.	Hammond, D. F.	FC2c	Van Dolah, R. L.	S2c
Woodland, W. L.	S1c	Hannaford, T. W.	S1c	Warner, D. W.	S2c
Wilson, G.	S2c	Hayes, F. J.	FC3c	Williams, R. T.	S1c
Williams, A. T.	S1c	Hess, C. J.	FC3c	Wittich, G. W.	S1c
Wallace, C. R.	S2c	Hill, R. D.	S1c	Wilcox, W.	S1c
Walker, J. S.	S1c	Juhas, C. J.	FC3c	White, J. H.	S2c
Wilhelm, J. R.	S2c	Kern, J. D.	S1c	Winger, H. M.	FC3c
Trujillo, F. E.	S1c	Klappauf, R. V.	FC3c	Woodruff, W. E	S1c
Pridgen, A. W.	S2c	Kroll, A. L.	S1c	Wray, E. P.	S2c
		Kyte, M. L.	S2c	Wright, R. E.	S1c
		Macias, J. D.	S2c		
		Martin, D. F.	FC3c		

Name	Rate	Martin, R. E.	S1c	Name	Rate
Alderson, M. L.	S2c	Mason, J. R.	FC3c	Bender, A. J.	ARM2c
Anderson, C. D.	S1c	Mathis, R., Jr.	FC3c	Drone, C. L.	ARM3c
Anderson, D. L.	S2c	Matteson, H. L.	S1c	Fox, L. W.	CAMM(PA)
Anderson, R. W.	S2c	McKenna, E. A.	S1c	Kuplack, J. E.	AOM1c
Andreason, B. P.	S2c	McPherson, W. A.	FC1c	Ladson, M. E.	S1c
Baughman, L. H.	S2c	Millar, R. C.	S2c	Nimie, C. J.	S2c
Berry, J. E. O.	CFC	Munro, H.	S2c	Rehkop, F., Jr.	S2c
Brannon, M. C.	S1c	Murrah, C. J.	S2c	Salazar, L.	S1c
Brucks, C. J.	FC3c	Nelson, R. L.	S2c	Scheer, L. W.	S2c
Buffington, M. G.	S1c	Nolan, R. W.	S2c	Schirmer, M. L.	S1c
Burbury, N. E.	S2c	O'Connor, J. T.	S2c	Schlaefer, H. H., Jr.	AMM1c
Calvin, G. W.	S1c	Olsen, C. H.	FC3c	Schoenrock, C. R.	S2c
Campbell, M. H.	FC2c	Owen, C. P.	S1c	Shelton, N. E.	PR2c
Carson, M. L.	S1c	Page, G. E.	S1c	Thompson, J. W.	AM2c
Cavin, G. C.	S2c	Pawlirzyn, M.	S1c	Thorson, R. R.	AMMI3c
Cherpeske, D. F.	S1c	Pridgen, A. W.	S2c	Wilder, J. C.	S1c(AMM)
Cobble, R. C.	S1c	Routh, C. H.	FC3c	Van Dine, J. W.	S1c(AMM)
Collins, J. P.	S2c	Rinetti, A. H.	FC3c		
Curry, R. J.	S1c	Schneider, R. F.	S1c		
Custance, H. F.	FC3c	Seale, R. P.	FC3c		
Deerfield, W. Y.	S1c	Skomski, N. A.	S2c	Name	Rate
Diehl, J. L.	FC3c	Smith, A. L.	S2c	Beene, C. E.	S1c
Downing, J. L.	FC2c	Smith, J. W.	BM1c	Beyer, P. W.	S2c
Dyment, D. R.	S1c	Soranno, R. A.	FC3c	Bonosoro, A. J.	GM3c
Eastman, F. H.	S1c	Stienman, E. R.	S2c		
		Teaford, L. W.	S2c		

[29]

CONVERTED POLLYWOGS

Name	Rate
Clardy, C. T.	GM2c
Hayward, D. E.	GM2c
Hottinger, F. J.	GM3c
Jaeger, E. W.	GM3c
Lucas, W. I.	S2c
Martinson, W. F.	S2c
Payette, K. L.	S2c
Perry, M. E.	S2c
Pinkerton, J. E.	S2c
Reed, E. F.	S2c
Reinhardt, M. A.	S2c
Renfrow, O. C.	S2c
Renfroe, J. W.	GM3c
Ropp, J. A.	S2c
Rude, G. R.	Y1c
Shaughnessy, J. F.	S2c
Valle, E.	S2c
VanCleave, J. H.	S2c
Wadley, D. C.	S2c
Webb, A. J.	S1c
Welch, H. A.	S2c
Widdowson, F. K.	S2c
Wigington, D. R.	S2c
Wilson, M. G.	S2c
Wood, D. O.	S2c
Yannotti, A. V.	S2c
Youmans, W. F.	Y3c
Ziudema, L.	S1c

Name	Rate
Avril, W. B.	S2c
Banks, S. W.	S1c
Barrett, W. T.	Rdm3c
Cupp, H. G.	S1c
Erney, A. E.	Rdm3c
Evans, E. D.	Rdm3c
Forson, W. W.	S1c
Hale, J. R.	S1c
Hartung, C. V.	Rdm3c
Hawkins, G. L.	S1c
Holloway, B. R.	S1c

Name	Rate
Lee, C. T.	S1c
Martin, V. L.	S1c
McCaffrey, J. B.	Rdm3c
McClelland, R. N.	S1c
McFarland, J. I.	S1c
Mitchell, J. R.	S1c
Morlan, L. A.	S1c
Nesbitt, C. E.	S1c
Newsome, R. L.	S1c
Paden, R. G.	Rdm3c
Parker, J. F.	Rdm3c
Petschow, A. P.	S1c
Pike, G. C.	S1c
Plesha, G. M.	S1c
Pusheck, C. C.	S1c
Quirt, W. C.	Rdm3c
Reeves, R. D.	S1c
Rightmer, A. D.	S1c
Robinson, W. T.	Rdm3c
Rogers, W. T.	S1c
Shields, M. H.	S1c
Shipperly, W. W.	S1c
Smith, B. L.	RT2c
Spaustainitis, L. I.	Rdm1c
Squire, F. J.	S1c
Thomas, A. J.	S1c
Trout, J. K.	S1c
Twilley, W. E.	S1c
Wright, J. P.	RT1c

Name	Rate
Badowsky, W. J.	F1c
Baker, A. H.	F2c
Benak, H. J.	MMS3c
Black, A. W.	F2c
Bloemers, P.	F1c
Boehm, W.	MMS3c
Boroznoff, M.	F1c
Bottlinger, A. M.	MM2c
Brasili, A. J.	F1c
Brown, F. A.	MM2c

Name	Rate
Brudzynsky, A. R.	F2c
Bush, C. H.	F1c
Binder, G. W.	F2c
Care, E. A.	MM1c
Cowden, J. W.	Y1c
Crask, H. G.	M3c
Crowder, J. P.	F1c
Dike, H. F.	MoMM3c
Dougherty, E. A.	F1c
Edwards, J. B.	MM3c
Ferebee, L. L.	MoMM1c
Flotow, S. L.	MM2c
Forest, A. J.	MM2c
Fuller, M. T.	MM3c
Gagliardi, J. D.	F1c
Gardner, E. R.	MM2c
Gefel, J. B.	MM3c
Grubb, J. L.	MMS3c
Hairell, S. F.	MM1c
Halladay, F. M.	F1c
Hamment, R. D.	Y3c
Hibbs, C. J.	F2c
Hirkaler, J. M.	F1c
Hodges, W. F.	MM2c
Hutchins, J. E.	F1c
Jaworski, E. A.	MM1c
Jones, D. J.	F1c
Jorgenson, R.	MoMM3c
Juenger, A. E.	F1c
Kruger, L. L.	F1c
Koch, G.	F2c
Landry, W. H.	F1c
La Rosa, H.	MM1c
Lash, W. H.	MM2c
Love, L. B.	F2c
Loving, C. W.	F2c
Luebbert, E. J.	MM2c
Lucas, H.	F1c
Lumbert, W. F.	MM2c
Lyday, C.	MM2c
Maloney, R. L.	M1c
Mangiarcina, P.	MM1c
Marks, W. J.	F2c

[30]

CONVERTED POLLYWOGS

Name	Rate	Name	Rate	Name	Rate
Marlatt, W. R.	F2c	Austin, J. C.	F1c	Hester, R. N.	F1c
Marpert, C. D.	F2c	Ayres, F., Jr.	F1c	Hlebinsky, G.	F1c
Martin, W. A.	F1c	Baker, C. L.	F1c	Hooten, H. E.	F1c
Mask, H. C.	CMM	Baker, N. A.	F2c	Hudson, C. H.	WT1c
McGinnis, H. L.	F2c	Ballman, C. E.	F1c	Hutto, W. W.	WT1c
Miller, R.	MM3c	Barton, L. E.	F1c	Johnson, L. F.	F2c
Mullinex, D. C.	F1c	Beach, H. P.	F2c	Johnson, W. G.	WT2c
Murray, B. B.	MoMM3c	Becich, W. G.	WT3c	Jones, E.	F1c
Myers, A.	F1c	Bergen, M.	F2c	Kaminski, J.	F1c
Panus, R. J.	MM2c	Bianco, A. N.	F1c	Keziah, J. B.	F2c
Peairs, C. J.	F1c	Bills, H. E.	F2c	King, B.	WT1c
Pittman, E. S.	F2c	Blezard, G. M.	WT3c	King, G. P.	WT3c
Poisson, P. R.	MM3c	Blomster, W. W.	F1c	Knapp, R. D.	F1c
Puntigam, S. V.	F1c	Boudreaux, L. P.	F2c	Kosar, J.	F1c
Racioppi, C. J.	MM1c	Boyle, V. M.	F1c	Kosinski, E. J.	WT1c
Ramirez, W. M.	F1c	Bradford, H. E.	F2c	Kristan, A. G.	F1c
Robbins, F.	F2c	Brinkerhoff, L. G.	F2c	Large, C. O.	WT2c
Rock, J. J.	F1c	Brinkman, M. H.	F2c	LaRocca, J.	F1c
Rogers, W. G.	F1c	Broadaway, C. L.	F2c	LeClair, L. C.	F2c
Rupnick, W. J.	MM2c	Chambers, B. M.	WT3c	LePre, B. A.	F1c
Schippers, H. H.	MMS3c	Cowser, J. A.	F2c	Luckiesh, F. J.	CWT(AA)
Sherer, L. E.	MM2c	Davis, A. M.	WT1c	Mabrey, T. J.	WT2c
Skates, J. R.	MoMM3c	Dean, R. O.	WT1c	Malone, J. L.	F1c
Smith, J. B.	MoMM3c	Deck, H. E.	F1c	Manville, E. E.	F2c
Thibeault, J. B.	F1c	Dold, W. B.	WT2c	Mashura, A.	F1c
Turley, R. J.	CMoMM	Donaldson, M. G.	WT3c	McCabe, A. L.	MM1c
Turner, J. L.	MM3c	Doremus, J. R.	F1c	McGarrigle, R. J.	F1c
Von Blon, W. A.	MoMM3c	Dowdy, R. W.	F1c	McKeen, W. H.	F1c
Walker, R. H.	MM3c	Dube, R. S.	F1c	Moss, H. L.	F1c
Weber, W. G.	MoMM3c	Eisworth, K. R.	WT1c	Olson, W. C.	WT1c
Woods, J. C.	M3c	Ek, G. L.	F1c	Parker, G. W.	F1c
Woodward, N. H.	F1c	English, L. B.	WT2c	Pecard, J. D.	B1c
Warren, W. E.	Y3c	Faulk, H. G.	WT3c	Pedersen, E. W.	F2c
		Frain, R. J.	F1c	Pelissier, P. L.	CWT(PA)
		Frease, A. F.	WT3c	Pepper, L. W.	WT2c
		Furst, H. W.	WT3c	Peterson, E. A.	B3c

Name	Rate	Name	Rate	Name	Rate
Accardi, J. V.	WT3c	Gardner, R. E.	F2c	Peterson, L. E.	F2c
Adams, S. C.	F1c	George, J. B.	F1c	Piatek, E.	WT2c
Albanese, S. A.	WT3c	Gould, J. K.	F1c	Pike, J. L.	WT1c
Amann, K. B.	F1c	Hacker, C. B.	F1c	Pringle, H. E.	F1c
Ancion, A. F.	F1c	Hall, D. W.	F2c	Pritchard, E. E.	WT1c
Anstett, W. C.	WT3c	Hegeman, D. L.	F1c	Rapes, D.	F2c
				Reckner, C. H.	F1c

[31]

CONVERTED POLLYWOGS

Name	Rate	Name	Rate	Name	Rate
Richard, C. W.	WT2c	Edwards, A. J.	EM3c	Pickard, M. R.	S2c
Ruhs, C. W.	MM2c	Erlandson, R. N.	EM3c	Presnall, W. E.	F1c
Schwartz, M.	F1c	Eschner, P. G.	EM3c	Richards, H. T.	F1c
Shingler, J. D.	WT3c	Ethington, B. W.	F1c	Rowberg, H. D.	F1c
Sparks, H., Jr.	F1c	Fall, C. B.	EM1c	Ruhl, A. D.	F1c
Steinhauer, R. F.	CWT(AA)	Ferson, R. B.	EM3c	Sabo, J. W.	F2c
Thompson, F.	MM3c	Finnegan, R. E.	EM1c	Salminen, L. E.	F1c
Tiffany, W. B., Jr.	WT3c	Fredricksen, E. T.	F1c	Sanchez, G.	EM3c
Tober, R.	F1c	Freeman, J. J.	F2c	Sands, J. D.	EM3c
Totten, H. J.	WT2c	Fravor, D. F.	F2c	Schafman, R. R.	EM3c
Walsh, J. F.	F1c	Glover, E. C.	F2c	Schow, M. R.	F1c
West, D. E.	WT3c	Grandy, C. L.	F2c	Schymich, W.	F1c
Youngberg, G. B.	F1c	Gregson, L. E.	CEM	Shouse, J. B.	EM3c
Zdravesky, G. M.	WT2c	Haase, E. S.	F1c	Shultz, R. L.	F1c
Zilius, W. G.	F1c	Hammond, G. B.	F2c	Sievers, D. H.	F2c
		Hefner, G. J.	S2c	Sledge, J. W.	EM3c
		Helvaty, J. J.	EM3c	Silski, F. S.	EM3c
		Hetherington, J. C.	S2c	Snodgrass, K.	EM3c
		Hetherton, J. G.	F2c	Snyder, W. K.	F2c

Name	Rate	Name	Rate	Name	Rate
Allsup, J. F.	EM3c	Hilton, C. S.	EM3c	Sorenson, R.	F1c
Baker, V. W.	EM3c	Howard, P. D.	F1c	Stephenson, R. J.	F1c
Barnhart, W. J.	EM3c	Howe, R. E.	S2c	Stevens, J. E.	EM3c
Berry, J. M.	EM2c	Huffman, R. W.	F1c	Stevenson, E. P.	EM3c
Brinzea, G.	EM3c	Ingram, R. J.	EM3c	Steinbicer, J. O.	EM2c
Brooks, D. R.	EM3c	Johnson, E. G.	EM1c	Stone, L. W.	F2c
Brown, M.	CEM	Johnson, O. F.	EM3c	Stose, R. J.	F1c
Brunet, D. P.	EM3c	Kelly, T. F.	S2c	Taylor, E. L.	F1c
Butler, H. C.	EM2c	King, J. W.	F1c	Taylor, W. H.	F1c
Capin, R. W.	F1c	Klaske, G. J.	EM2c	Thurman, W. H.	F2c
Cerny, J. J.	F2c	Kline, R. F.	EM3c	Trabert, H. R.	F2c
Chambers, M. O.	EM2c	Koehler, F. V.	F1c	Turman, G. W.	EM1c
Christy, R. L.	EM3c	Kruzan, L. M.	F1c	Tysdal, C. B.	EM2c
Clymer, W. V.	EM3c	Lemberger, J.	EM1c	Urban, F. A.	F1c
County, A. J.	F2c	Maddox, C. O.	F2c	Vierra, J. S.	EM3c
Crites, F. T.	F2c	Martha, J. J.	F1c	Volz, J. A.	F1c
Crowder, G. W.	F2c	Mauldin, R. B.	EM3c	Walsworth, H. J.	EM1c
Day, J. S.	F1c	McArthur, D. P.	EM1c	Ward, H. E.	EM3c
Dea, J. F.	F2c	Mears, C. H.	EM1c	Ward, J. E.	F1c
Depke, T. R.	F2c	Miller, T. W.	EM2c	Warner, L. M.	F1c
Dodge, R. W.	F1c	Monroe, J. R.	EM3c	Warren, D. B.	F1c
Doyle, R. J.	EM3c	Moore, A. L.	EM3c	Washer, F. R.	F2c
Dull, J. E.	EM3c	Moyer, E. W.	EM1c	Westcott, R. H.	F1c
		Murphey, C. J.	EM2c	White, K. H.	EM2c
		Newberg, P. L.	EM2c	Williams, J. A.	F1c

[32]

CONVERTED POLLYWOGS

Name	Rate	Name	Rate	Name	Rate
Young, E. C.	EM3c	Gossage, J. M	MM1c	Paur, T. W.	MM2c
Young, S. M.	EM3c	Griner, S. M.	F1c	Pence, H. E.	MM2c
Youngberg, G. B.	F1c	Grunow, H.	MM1c	Plummer, G. W.	MM3c
Yule, A.	F2c	Hall, M. J.	MM3c	Potter, W. G.	F1c
Zale, P. J.	F1c	Harris, J. H.	MM2c	Ramsey, J. A.	MM1c
		Harris, E. L.	F1c	Rasmussen, G. E.	MM1c
		Hausch, J. C.	F1c	Redden, A. E.	F1c
		Hayth, J. T.	F1c	Rummel, R. A.	F2c
		Hensley, D. A.	F2c	Scranton, T. M.	F1c

Name	Rate	Name	Rate	Name	Rate
		Hinzman, F. F.	F2c	Simkus, F. J.	F1c
Akins, O. L.	CMM	Hochradel, D. G.	F2c	Simons, K. L.	F1c
Benetti, J. G.	MM3c	Horton, G. W.	MM3c	Sloat, W. S.	F1c
Beuselinck, A. C.	MM3c	Hostetter, M. J.	F1c	Smith, H. L.	F1c
Brewer, P. L.	F2c	Hylton, E. E.	MM2c	Soika, C. A.	F1c
Brown, K. W.	MM2c	Ierien, N. R.	MM1c	Stiefel, E. M.	F1c
Brundidge, H. W.	F2c	Jarley, L. M.	MM2c	Stamper, J. A.	F1c
Bruton, B. L.	F2c	Jarley, W. J.	MM3c	Swan, G., Jr.	F1c
Bryant, R. E.	F2c	Jefferson, H. W.	F1c	Syriac, L.	MM3c
Burleson, P.	F1c	Justice, F. J.	MM2c	Thews, C. B.	F1c
Butcher, J. J.	F2c	Keels, A. W.	F1c	Thompson, A. W.	F1c
Caferio, J. C.	F1c	Kelley, H. A.	MM1c	Treichel, E. E.	F1c
Caldwell, W. I.	F2c	Kennedy, W. C.	MM3c	Van Alstine, E. H.	F1c
Carlson, C. H.	F2c	Kesterson, H. L.	MM3c	Van Toorn, R. B.	F1c
Chappei, E. D.	MM3c	Kizel, W.	F1c	Vickers, A. K.	F2c
Chittester, N. E.	F2c	Knight, C. H.	F1c	Wiemert, C. A.	F1c
Coats, P. E.	F2c	Larson, J. L.	F1c	Wierson, A. O.	F1c
Davis, H. W.	F1c	Lindell, R. C.	MM1c	Wilson, C. G.	F1c
Dewalt, R. S.	F2c	Long, R. E.	F1c	Wiseman, W. H.	F1c
Dicola, D. W.	F1c	Martin, R.	MM2c	Whitaker, J. C.	F1c
Domienik, E. K.	MM2c	Matley, A. W.	MM3c	Whitelock, R. S.	F1c
Dorn, J. F.	MM3c	Maurice, L. L.	F2c	Wright, L. H.	F1c
Dourdis, H. J.	MM2c	McGill, A.	MM1c	Zager, E. N.	F1c
Dusick, H. R.	MM3c	McKinney, C. E.	MM3c		
Dykes, R. A.	F1c	McMurrain, R. L.	MM1c		
Ellenburg, J.	MM3c	Monaghan, J. A.	F1c		
Ferguson, D. M.	F1c	Moore, J. J.	MM2c	Name	Rate
Fielding, F.	CMM	Mycue, A. B.	MM1c	Alcala, R.	Bug1c
Flaherty, T. F.	CMM	Napolitano, R. W.	F1c	Anderson, B. H.	Mus3c
Foster, L. T.	CMM	Olson, O. O.	MM2c	Baker, D. H.	Bgmstr3c
Freeland, M. W.	MM2c	Ondus, F. J.	F2c	Baker, J. R.	Bug1c
Gaskins, J. L.	MM3c	Ossenfort, E. C.	F1c	Beasley, N. M.	S1c
Gifford, W. H.	MM2c	Parker, E. G.	MM3c	Bender, W. A.	Mus2c
Gleeson, R. J.	MM2c	Pathman, H. W.	F2c	Bentley, R. D.	Mus3c
Gorenflo, D. L.	F2c				

[33]

CONVERTED POLLYWOGS

Name	Rate	Name	Rate	Name	Rate
Biddle, L. O.	Mus3c	McPhail, G. R.	S1c	Van Allen, K. F.	Mus2c
Clemmitt, J.	Mus3c	Mettler, A. J.	S1c	Vogel, R. L.	S2c
Conrath, A. E.	QM3c	Miller, G. F.	Mus3c	Wahlstrand, C. E.	QM3c
Gensman, C. O.	S2c	Milne, D. R.	S1c	Wheeler, R. B.	Mus3c
Goforth, J. E.	S2c	Neill, W. L.	Mus3c	Wicks, H. A.	S2c
Greenley, G. L.	Mus2c	Osmer, W. A.	Mus3c	Wing, C. M.	Mus3c
Hanks, W. H.	Mus2c	Prazenica, C. C.	AcrM3c	Wood, R. G.	S2c
				Worrow, E. J.	S2c

ALFRED   by **FOSTER HUMFREVILLE**

"Alfred wants to know if he couldn't wait and be initiated the next time we cross the equator"

—*Courtesy Collier's Magazine*

Name	Rate
Benning, R. L.	S1c
Blaylock, C. M.	S1c
Brown, B. J.	S1c
Brunick, L. M.	RM3c
Burchard, M. R.	S1c
Burke, P. E.	S2c
Burnes, R. L.	RM3c
Campagna, C. E.	S2c
Cassyre, C. A.	RM3c
Chamberlain, R. G.	S1c
Conradt, J. F.	S1c
Conrelio, F. A.	RM3c
Cornell, A. C.	RM3c
Demrow, R. C.	S1c
Dragoo, H. P.	S1c
Ford, W. P.	RM3c
Fowler, C. L.	S1c
Freden, E.	S1c
Furphy, J. J.	S1c
Furse, G. S.	S1c
Gillespie, J. W.	RT3c
Imming, M. F.	S1c
James, C. E.	RM3c
Kane, G. J.	S1c
Kase, E. J.	S1c
Mallat, J. P.	S2c
Mangum, C. E.	RM2c
Mount, I. G.	RM2c
Paul, L. L.	RM2c
Pederson, W. A.	S1c
Pithan, N. W.	S2c
Pollock, C. W.	S1c

Name	Rate	Name	Rate
Hatchel, H. L.	Bug1c	Pyne, M. E.	Bgmstr3c
Hawley, R. C.	Mus3c	Quinn, J. P.	QM3c
Hendrick, C. D.	S1c	Rea, R. E.	QM2c
Henyecz, J.	Mus2c	Ruiz, A. J.	QM3c
Johnson, D. L.	Mus3c	Sax, A. E.	S1c
Kangas, G. R.	S1c	Shetler, H. E.	S1c
Kleinberg, G. E.	Mus3c	Simpson, W. H.	Mus3c
Kuhnle, J. G.	S1c	Slota, L.	Mus3c
Manzler, C. S.	PhoM1c	Swanson, W. C.	QM3c
May, J. R.	QM3c	Thompson, B. F.	Mus1c

[34]

CONVERTED POLLYWOGS

Name	Rate
Pottorff, R. E.	S1c
Ray, J.	S1c
Reed, J. W.	S1c
Reese, I. G.	RM3c
Roe, C. K.	S1c
Salantai, S.	S1c
Sherman, J. G.	S2c
Simson, D. B.	RM3c
Slate, W. J.	RM2c
Stirewalt, G. W.	S1c
Sullivan, J. J.	RM3c
Sutherland, R.	RM2c
Weller, R. E.	RT2c
Wright, W. A.	RT2c
Will, C. H.	RM3c
Yuska, E. E.	S1c
Zaleski, E. W.	S1c

Name	Rate
Albers, R. F.	S1c
Babcock, R. P.	S1c
Bierman, W. D.	S1c
Brauer, E. R.	S1c
Buckley, J. B.	S1c
Burke, C. R.	S1c
Burns, J. M.	SM3c
Colegate, V. C.	S1c
Darby, W. G.	S1c
De Smet, A. P.	S1c
Dinterman, R. M.	S1c
Dunning, R. E.	S1c
Epperheimer, H. C.	SM2c
Freedman, B.	SM2c
Gebhardt, J. J.	S1c
Herrin, T. W.	S1c
Hollingsworth, C. R.	S1c
Kemper, G. E.	S1c
Landenberger, H., Jr.	S1c
Leo, C. A.	S1c
Martinez, W. A.	S1c
McLaughlin, J. F.	S1c

Name	Rate
McNally, J. F.	S1c
Ray, C. R.	S1c
Romans, R. N.	S1c
Scharer, H. J.	SM1c
Schaub, R. E.	S1c
Schindler, L. A.	S1c
Spencer, L. W.	S1c
Stadtman, W. L.	S1c
Stultz, H. O.	S1c
Torr, N., Jr.	S1c
Waddell, T. J.	S1c
Whorton, B. D.	S1c
Wies, C. E.	S1c
Wivholm, J. F.	S1c

Name	Rate
Bannister, O. E.	Y1c
Bishop, A. M.	Y3c
French, J. B.	BM2c
Gentry, C. C.	S1c
Grant, D. N.	CY
Hoeper, J. F.	S1c
Kittle, J. R.	CY
Miller, J. L.	Cox.
Moore, G. Y.	Y2c
Pahre, R. E.	S1c
Paul, R. D.	S1c
Rieser, W. R.	S1c
Robinson, G. B.	BM2c
Tubbs, C. M.	Y3c
Wasepka, L. K.	S1c

Name	Rate
Abbott, F. P.	Cox.
Abbott, R. K.	S1c
Banning, W. A.	S2c
Bearden, E. M.	S1c
Bennet, V. R.	S1c

Name	Rate
Blood, C. L.	S1c
Bloodworth, W. F.	CM1c
Breakey, C. T.	S1c
Bridwell, W. H.	S1c
Brock, H. E.	S1c
Bruckler, C.	SF1c
Carpenter, W.	Ptr2c
Carter, E.	S1c
Christoffel, H. J.	SF1c
Curtis, E. O.	SF2c
Dalrymple, M. F.	SF2c
Dendy, E. B.	S1c
Denton, E. R.	SF3c
Doty, W. T.	SF2c
Edwards, P.	S1c
Feltz, F. H.	SF1c
Ghant, L. R.	S2c
Gibson, J. C.	S2c
Gill, E.	SF3c
Girard, E. L.	S2c
Gomes, E. D.	SF2c
Gridley, J. C.	PM3c
Griffin, J. B.	SF1c
Hackenberry, W. R.	S1c
Hawxwell, J. E.	SF3c
Hendren, J. D.	S1c
Herndon, J. H.	SF3c
Hickey, P. R.	S1c
Howard, C. A.	S1c
Jones, W. E.	S1c
Kaiser, K. R.	S1c
Kelly, T. F.	S1c
Leimbacher, G. A.	S2c
Leitner, J. W.	S1c
Likavec, F.	CM3c
Lundstrom, J. L.	S1c
Michaelis, B. J.	S1c
May, S. H.	S1c
Mayo, W. C.	S1c
Martinez, G. W.	S1c
Mazur, F. M.	S2c
McElroy, W. S.	SF1c
Miller, J. V.	S1c
Milckovich, G. T.	SF3c
Mountney, C. L.	S1c

[35]

CONVERTED POLLYWOGS

Name	Rate	Name	Rate	Name	Rate
Morgan, L. R.	SF3c	Bentley, M. M.	S1c	Jackson, J. N.	Bkr3c
Morris, L. W. G.	S1c	Blizzard, J. G.	S1c	Jackson, L. V.	StM2c
Olson, C.	S2c	Bonde, E.	S1c	Jacobson, A. P.	S1c
Phillips, W. H.	S1c	Booker, S. B.	StM2c	Jackson, R. N.	SK3c
Poluka, S.	S1c	Borja, A. A.	StM1c	Johnson, B. L.	StM2c
Powers, L. J.	SF3c	Bourn, E.	StM2c	Johnson, C.	StM1c
Rassmussen, L. F.	S2c	Boyd, T. J.	SK2c	Johnson, W. E.	StM3c
Robatcek, A. J.	CM1c	Brady, F.	StM2c	Jones, W. L.	StM2c
Roberts, T. J.	S1c	Carney, C. H.	S1c	Jordan, T.	StM2c
Romero, C. J.	S1c	Carr, L.	StM1c	Kader, L. F.	F1c
Rose, J. W.	S1c	Caudle, A. B.	SC1c	Kellogg, J. D.	Bkr3c
Rospotynski, H. A.	S1c	Chancey, R. E.	F2c	Kennard, C. C.	S1c
Russell, D. M.	SF3c	Cherpergi, J. P.	S1c	Knous, D. L.	F1c
Ryan, J. A.	SF1c	Clark, L. T.	S1c	Lamar, F., Jr.	StM3c
Senkbeil, A. F.	S2c	Cobb, D. P.	S1c	Matthews, R. P.	SC3c
Seifman, W. E.	S1c	Cook, R. W.	SC3c	McDonald, O. C.	StM2c
Scally, J. W.	SF2c	Cook, W. T.	S1c	McNeill, J. M.	SK1c
Stiltner, G. O.	CM1c	Crew, G. L.	SC3c	Messendrink, R. L.	SC3c
St. Pierre, A. J.	S1c	Dahlstrom, C. C.	CCS	Miller, R. L.	S1c
Strovers, C. E.	S1c	Downing, D. E.	Bkr3c	Miller, R. J.	F1c
Shepherd, C. P.	SF1c	Drake, R. S.	SK2c	Moran, J.	SK3c
Sistek, C. A.	S1c	Essex, F. L.	SC3c	Neisler, A. W.	SK1c
Sullivan, H. A.	S1c	Fleming, W. H.	SK3c	Orth, L. M.	SC3c
Taylor, A. R.	S2c	Flores, J. C.	St2c	Owens, H. C.	CSK
Thomas, I. J.	SF2c	Gackle, G. D.	SK3c	Pappagallo, J. A.	S1c
Underwood, D. W.	CM2c	Gladney, M.	StM2c	Passy, I. V.	S1c
Wallington, W. D.	SF3c	Glenn, A.	StM2c	Peden, F. B.	S1c
Walston, R. D.	SF1c	Graves, R. L.	SK3c	Perry, D. E.	Bkr3c
Ward, D. E.	S1c	Gray, T.	StM1c	Peterson, L. E.	F2c
Washburn, G. H.	S1c	Green, J. A.	S1c	Pollack, F. L.	SC1c
Wahl, G.	BM2c	Green, W. K.	S1c	Powers, J. F.	SK3c
Youngerman, R. F.	SF3c	Grimes, R. J.	SC3c	Primm, A. M., Jr.	SK3c
		Haack, A. C.	S1c	Purslow, H. R.	Cox.
		Hampton, B. B.	S1c	Quichocho, J. Q.	StM2c
		Hanna, A. J.	S1c	Randolph, M. F., Jr.	S1c
		Hannah, L. P.	S1c	Reinicke, R. C. R.	M2c

Name	Rate	Name	Rate	Name	Rate
Allerton, K. R.	Bkr2c	Hawkins, W. W.	SC3c	Rende, S.	SC3c
Alston, J. C.	S1c	Heard, E. B.	SK3c	Rhoden, J. C., Jr.	S2c
Anderson, W. F.	S1c	Hedrick, C.	StM2c	Rigsby, W.	StM2c
Baker, R. E.	F2c	Hellstrom, G. A.	S1c	Rippeto, M. C.	SC1c
Beamon, P. D.	StM2c	Hemmingway, R. W.	SK3c	Robertson, J. L.	StM2c
Belfry, E. A.	SC1c	Hewell, T. A.	S2c	Robertson, J. H.	SC3c
Benish, R. J.	S1c	Howell, J. H.	StM1c	Rocco, A. L.	S1c
		Hume, H. C.	S1c		

[36]

CONVERTED POLLYWOGS

Name	Rate
Rodzon, J. T.	S1c
Rogers, H. L.	StM2c
Rogers, S. L.	StM1c
Rome, J. B.	StM1c
Ross, C.	StM1c
Russell, C. B.	SC3c
Sapato, E.	CST
Satterlee, D. E.	S1c
Schoen, H. L.	Bkr3c
Scott, L.	StM2c
Sertich, G., Jr.	S1c
Shannon, L. C., Jr.	StM2c
Sharp, R. A.	S1c
Sheldon, J. D.	Bkr2c
Sherrer, J. G., Jr.	StM1c
Shinn, W. R.	Bkr3c
Shoffner, C. L.	StM2c
Shufflebarger, E. R.	S1c
Sikes, W. A.	SK3c
Simmons, M.	StM2c
Simpson, H.	StM2c
Sims, L.	StM2c
Sims, R. T.	SK2c
Smith, A. F.	StM2c
Smith, H. A.	StM2c
Smith, M.	StM2c
Snitkin, W. W.	SK3c
Speidell, N. B.	Bkr1c
Stanger, D. B.	S1c
Stanhouse, E. P.	SC3c
Starks, H. G.	StM2c
Stathas, G., Jr.	S1c
Steffey, G. W.	SK2c
Stevens, R. L.	S1c
Stuart, D. R.	SK1c
Stuart, G. R.	Bkr2c
Sweetman, P. V.	S1c
Tallent, J. E.	SK2c
Terry, H. J.	S1c
Thompson, W.	StM1c
Throm, C. G.	Bkr3c
Utley, E. M., Jr.	SC2c
Vance, P. A.	StM2c

Name	Rate
Walker, E.	StM2c
Wall, D. W.	SK3c
Wallace, B. L.	StM2c
Walters, A. A.	SC3c
Wann, L. L.	S1c
Washington, L.	StM2c
West, A. G.	SC3c
White, G. E.	SC3c
Wick, A. B.	SK3c
Williams, L.	StM1c
Williams, D. A.	StM1c
Whittington, L. J.	SK3c
Young, L. H.	S1c
Zech, F. W.	SK1c

Name	Rate
Ball, J. G.	PhM3c
Behr, F. W. F.	H.A.1c
Boggess, D. E.	PhM3c
Carroll, H. J.	PhM3c
Dean, M. W.	PhM2c
Durst, G. O.	H.A.1c
Ferrington, A. E.	H.A.1c
George, V. R.	PhM2c
Glover, M. E.	PhM2c
Graff, M.	H.A.1c
Hall, T. C.	PhM2c
Hays, B. J.	PhM2c
Herring, F. D.	PhM3c
Inserra, L. S.	H.A.1c
Lewis, L. B.	PhM3c
Lyons, C. L.	H.A.1c
Nelson, E. T.	S1c
Orr, W. R.	PhM1c
Overton, L. W.	PhM1c
Owen, R. E.	PhM3c
Schmoll, C. H.	PhM2c
Sullivan, R. J.	H.A.1c
Tindal, A. S.	PhM1c
Valdez, E. F.	H.A.2c

Name	Rate
Wheeler, S.	PhM2c
Yelverton, T. B.	PhM2c

Name	Rate
Akin, M. J.	S2c
Anaya, T. M.	S2c
Ankrun, W. C.	S1c
Audette, C. E.	S2c
Blake, C. F.	S2c
Blanchard, L. E.	S2c
Bergmann, E. B.	S1c
Brown, E. S.	S2c
Cannon, R. M.	S2c
Cardenas, A. H.	S2c
Chavez, I. J.	S2c
Costa, D.	S1c
Jones, S. F.	S2c
Lappin, E. A.	S1c
Martin, A. J.	S2c
Martinie, B. K.	S1c
Martinez, R.	S2c
Mayeux, J. S.	S1c
Moran, L. E.	S2c
Mohrland, E.	S1c
Mortimeyer, E. R.	S1c
Nelson, R. A.	S1c
O'Leary, H. E.	S1c
Orr, D. M.	S2c
Owen, T. A.	S2c
Posey, C. Y.	S1c
Price, H.	S1c
Reeves, C. L.	S1c
Revel, N. D.	S1c
Ring, R. R.	S1c
Rivera, P.	S2c
Roehrer, S. G.	S1c
Rollar, R.	S1c
Sanders, D. R.	S2c
Sarkozi, J.	S2c
Savage, P. J.	S1c
Schemel, J. S.	S2c
Schneider, T. L.	S2c
Scott, C. O.	S2c

[37]

CONVERTED POLLYWOGS

Name	Rate	Name	Rate	Name	Rate
Serrano, S. G.	S2c	Woodward, A. G.	S2c	Doyle, R. C.	CSp(A)
Spencer, H. O.	Cox.	Young, G. N.	BM2c	Harrow, E. E.	WT1c
Stellmach, M.	S2c			Haubert, S. R.	BM1c
Tang, F. Q.	S2c			Hensley, O. A.	Cox.
Thomas, J. A.	S2c			Hockstrasser, J. J.	BM1c
Topp, R. F.	S1c			Hurd, P. V.	CSp(A)
Watts, M. H.	S2c	Name	Rate	Jansen, E. F.	MM1c
White, W. H.	S2c	Althouse, D. G.	BM1c	Koser, R. B.	S2c
Willander, E. V.	S2c	Burton, W. K.	BM1c	Ramirez, W. M.	S1c
Wilson, R. K.	S2c	Deletkanich, P.	BM2c	Stephens, H. L.	Cox.
				Taylor, F. M.	BM2c

★

CONVERTED MOUNTAINEERS

Front Row: Lombardi, Hayes.
Second Row: Foggia, Haubert, Reed, Ditty.
Back Row: Rainey, Rieschl, Wadley, McGuckin, Birkland, Vickers, Terry, Bennett, Winsted, Brand, Street.

[38]

SHIPMATES

Front Row: Comdr. Hardison, Comdr. Brownfield, Comdr. Sugarman, Lieut. Comdr. White.
Back Row: Lieut. Comdr. Wiggins, Lieut. Arendts, Lieut. Comdr. Williams, Lieut. Comdr. Porter.

HEADS OF DEPARTMENTS

ENGINEERING . . . . Comdr. J. H. Brownfield

NAVIGATION . . . . Comdr. C. M. Sugarman

GUNNERY . . . . Comdr. C. M. Hardison

SUPPLY . . . . Lieut. Comdr. (SC) W. M. Porter

MEDICAL . . . . Lieut. Comdr. (MC) H. E. Wiggins

CHAPLAIN . . . . Lieut. Comdr. (ChC) M. F. Williams

FIRST LIEUTENANT . . . . Lieut. Comdr. F. H. White

COMMUNICATIONS . . . . Lieut. S. C. Arendts

Front Row: Althouse, Hurd, Lieut. Soderberg, Comdr. King, Warner, Doyle, Burton.
Second Row: Whatley, Stephens, Taylor, Hensley, Harrow, Jansen.
Back Row: Haubert, Yackly, Deletkanich, Thompson, Ramirez, Hill.

Front Row: Miller, W. K., Phernetton, Hitchcock, Wilkins, Zwirchitz, Little, Howard, Parkinson.
Second Row: Robbins, Sielky, Snider, Shaffer, Paull, Waszak, Burwell, Kulikouski, Rowland, Szymanski.
Third Row: Sholos, Vigil, Larson, Leidall, Kershuk, Marshall, Sherrod, Martin, Sutton, Cox.
Back Row: Crews, Schembari, Hudson, Molina, Spriggs, Craver, Biever, Schweigart, Pulver, White.

[41]

Front Row: Mangum, Ford, Reese, Mount, Sutherland.
Second Row: Snell, Slate, Lieut. (jg) Exton, Lieut. Busby, Lieut. Arendts, Lieut. Marquardt, Lieut. (jg) Alldredge, Ens. Nachlas, Ch. Radio Elec. Reed, Williams, Winslow.
Third Row: Imming, Kase, Stirewalt, Pottorff, Chamberlain, Pithan, Sherman, James, Paul, Bass.
Back Row: Demrow, Furphy, Brunick, Ray, Conradt, Will, Benning, Reed, Pollock, Salantai.

Front Row: Brown, Jones, Reeves, Young, Lieut. Wands, Ens. Jarmon, Ring, Martinez, Akin, Bergmann.
Second Row: Mortimyer, Mayeux, Mohrland, Ankrum, Cannon, Lappin, Scott, Roehrer, Stellmach, White.
Back Row: Thomas, Willander, Owen, Nelson, Rivera, Tang, Sanders, Sarkozi, Topp, Chavez, Moran.

[42]

Front Row: Radford, Kittle, Chief Ship's Clerk O'Brien, Grant, Bell.
Second Row: Tubbs, Stoney, Troudt, Youmans.
Back Row: Moore, Paul, Bishop, Pahre, Rieser.

Front Row: Smith, M., Smith, A., Beamon, Ford, LaMar, Baker, Johnson, W., Williams, L., Johnson, B.
Second Row: Ross, Bourne, Williams, D., Thompson, Gray, Rigsby, Robertson, Hedrick, Rogers, H.
Back Row: Shannon, Simms, McDonald, Carr, Brady, Vance, Glenn, Gladney, Scott, Schoffner.
Inset: Simpson, Sherrer.

[43]

Front Row: Warner, Richards, Dea, Youngberg, Fravor, Stose, Hammond, Grandy, Martha, Hetherton.
Second Row: Gregson, Brown, Ch. Elect. Keefe, Ens. Seibold, Lieut. Osheim, Ens. Jones, Ch. Elect. Greene, Ch. Elect. Nickerson, Gleaves, Hickman.
Third Row: Murphey, Charrier, Walsworth, Lemberger, Sands, Chambers, Barnhart, Snodgrass, Steinbicer, Moyer, Monroe.
Back Row: Ingram, Ferson, Vierra, Young, S. M., Mears, Young, E. C., Berry, Mauldin, Sledge, Edwards, Miller.

Front Row: Wilson, Scranton, Burleson, Maurice, Pathman, Griner, Whitaker, Hochradel, McGill, Dykes.
Second Row: Paur, Chappel, Lindell, Rasmussen, Mach. Kubow, Ens. Brabets, Brown, O. L., Lukas, Hylton, Ramsey.
Third Row: Knight, Dorn, McKinney, Matley, Baron, Freeland, Brown, K. W., Hayth, Bauselinck, Sloat.
Back Row: Kizel, Gifford, Whitelock, Treichel, Bruton, Domienik, Benetti, Cafiero, Ellenburg, Keels.

[44]

Front Row: Cornelio, Burnes, Kane, Hollingsworth, Schindler, Roe, Sullivan, Simson.
Second Row: Robinson, French, Miller, Lieut. (jg) Gist, Ens. Scott, Ens. Kleber, Lieut. (jg) Cooper, Ens. Shirley, Ens. Wilson, Thomas, Stadtman.
Third Row: Yuska, Whorton, Smith, Waddell, DeSmet, Fulton, Freden, Spencer, Blaylock, Burke, P. E.
Back Row: Zaleski, Wies, Reed, Herrin, Furse, Epperheimer, Pederson, Brauer, Dragoo, Cornell, Cassayre.

Front Row: Rock, Lucas, Woodward.
Second Row: Jorgenson, Crowder, Fuller, Racioppi, Cowden, Hodges, Brown, Bottlinger, Lyday, Brudzynsky.
Third Row: Loving, Skates, Gefel, Marks, Warren, Laws, Hibbs, Smith, Bush, Schwartz.
Back Row: Rupnick, Badowsky, Juenger, Turner, Ramirez, Koch, Walker, Black, Borozhnoff, Jones.

[45]

Front Row: Torr, Wivholm, Alexander, Scharer, Siewert, Lieut. Cohn, Hisey, Burns, Young, Landenberger.
Second Row: Dunning, Dinterman, Romans, Albers, Burke, McNally, Ray, Babcock, Colegate, Martinez.
Back Row: Leo, Buckley, Stultz, Kemper, Gebhardt, Carr, Darby, McLaughlin, Schaub, Bierman.

Front Row: Terry, Ballard, McGuckin, Vitellaro, Rose, Wibbenmeyer, Winkle, Roberson, Wilson.
Second Row: Kendrick, Sumners, Streett, Ditty, Linn, Hodges, Lieut. Talley, Ens. Devine, Reitzel, Fields.
Third Row: Wright, Williams, S. L., Hicks, Denkhaus, Wipper, Turek, Robinson, Milholland, McGill, Lotz.
Back Row: Wroblewski, Tadgerson, Pucksar, Wethington, Childress, Hale, Harmon, Hammond, Rough, Stidham, Brockway.

[46]

Front Row: Gross, Knox, Guarino, Williamson.
Second Row: Smith, D. L., Morris, Welsh, Valine, Lieut. Sherman, Lieut. (jg) Marsh, Ens. Williams, Murray, Scarberry, Townsend.
Third Row: Buffo, Conosenti, Tretter, Shephard, Snuggs, Kartes, Bravebull, Auberry, Burrows, Uhrich.
Back Row: Smith, C. G., Legore, Hren, Whitemore, Andler, Moff, Martin, Lorenson, Grandstaff, Chadwick.

Front Row: Bothern, Lieut. English, Ens. Gordon, Ens. Rosson, Crawford, Brand.
Second Row: Bannister, Latas, Evans, Vosberg, Sutter, Schneider, Cross, Shively, Proctor.
Third Row: Robinson, Emmons, Bible, Hodge, Hersman, Ireton, Hitt, Roberts, Bartrug, O. L.
Back Row: Uzee, Smith, F. W., Jenkins, Sharp, Beck, Gczik, Mikottis, Harrison, Esposita.

[47]

217

Front Row: Walsh, Lieut. Crandall, Ens. Plumb, Ens. Cupp, Miller, Foggia.
Second Row: Holmes, Seay, Tucker, Sloan, Wright, Laws, D'Alessio, Parker, Symonds, Walcavich.
Third Row: Lemely, Olsnewski, Taggart, Walker, Waldow, Roberts, Tibbets, Marshall, Marvin.
Back Row: Schmitt, Poling, Ray, McClain, Saieua, Van Horn, McCreary, Lambert.

Front Row: Wheeler, Fishesser, Wiggins, Cooper.
Second Row: Paxton, Tattini, Renfroe, Lombardi, Lieut. (jg) Floyd, Lieut. Manthei, Ens. Goebel, Hayes, Wilk, Detilla.
Third Row: Arnholz, Poulson, Niswanger, Pagac, Bevan, Wigginton, Brinch, Martineau, Ostrom, Moldenhauer.
Back Row: Wilson, Skelton, Rasmussen, D. C., Varnado, Prather, Smith, W. A., Rapoza, Stroehmar, Boome, Oglesby.

[48]

Front Row: Robinson, G. W., Zettle, Foy, Gennera, Hassell.
Second Row: Clingman, Schultz, Roberts, Ens. Pledger, Lieut. Caulfield, Lieut. (jg) Redstone, Jennings, O'Riley, Hedrick, Sauer.
Third Row: Dixon, W. M., Woltman, Siskin, Mathison, Robbins, Robinson, R. A., Muri, Stewart, Mohr, Rittenger.
Back Row: Niedermeyer, Variot, Rudnick, Thompson, Dixon, J., Cole, Willis, Des Marais, Quick, Stuber.

Front Row: Green, Brinckerhoff, Alberico, Buckner, Kellner, Pouncey, Gibson, DeFrancesco.
Second Row: Billington, Durham, Iverson, O'Connor, Wallace, Sloderbeck, Cook, Coogan, Geci, Liebert.
Third Row: Kling, Nard, Brady, Justice, Vignery, Thomas, Reisch, Williams, Paul, LeJuhn.
Back Row: Balbinot, Overby, Rainey, Gudeman, Shields, Ripperger, Fitchett, Urbanski, Chaney, Trout.

[49]

Front Row: Nelson, Burden, Ziel, Theisen, Betson, Akers, Jurchich, James.
Second Row: Bayer, Raiche, Decker, Lakness, Lt. Lovell, Capt. Whedbee, Lt. Steffens, Reed, Renois, Rogers, Mikkelson.
Third Row: Peterson, Much, Mekulich, Thomsen, Schimmelpfennig, Dal Santo, Moon, Stewart, Von Tobel.
Back Row: Lynch, Dykhius, Farnsworth, Wells, Ragsdale, Parypa, Plaisance, Ott, Cummings, Wooten.

Front Row: Hopper, Kleinberg, Clemmitt, Johnson, Van Allen, Bender, Greenly, Neill, Hawley, Thomson.
Second Row: Miller, Anderson, Bentley, Wing, Osmer, Wheeler, Henyecz, Slota, Biddle.

[50]

Front Row: Vincent, Schwartzler, Killian, Robinson, G. W., Shelton, C. C., Hicks, Ellison, Sharp, Bowen.
Second Row: McMillin, Pearson, Thomas, Zyzneski, Rieschl, Ens. Sahlin, Lieut. (jg) Ballantyne, Wauford, Butterfield, Reynolds, Newby.
Third Row: Karr, Hartog, Ross, Smith, Shelton, J. T., Robinson, J., Jr., Sparks, M. D., Skrapke, McCulloch, Beyer, Miller, H. A.
Back Row: Robinette, Spence, Marchel, Sloan, Jeziorski, Sparks, J. W., Cales, Wiggs, Rushin, Tart, Wiggins.

Front Row: Rea, Ruiz, Rogers, Lucik, Lieut. (jg) Tillinghast, Ens. Batte, Manzler, May.
Second Row: Wahlstrand, Sax, Goforth, Swanson, Hendrick, Gensman, Kuhnle, Hoeper, Quinn, Pyne.
Back Row: Alcala, Vogel, Shetler, Wicks, Worrow, Mettler, McPhail, Prazenica, Wood.

[51]

221

Front Row: Salazar, Wilder, Fox, Ens. Kovachek, Lieut. Rodgers, Ens. Walker, Schlaefer.
Second Row: Thorson, Schirmer, Shelton, Byrne, Schoenrock, Van Dine, Rehkop.
Back Row: Thompson, Scheer, Drone, Nimie, Bender, Kuplack.

Front Row: Schmidgall, Maria, St. Arnold, Moody, Rogus, Treon, Perkins, Razgavicus.
Second Row: Wittenberger, Ditlenson, Daniels, Shell, Speckt, Grimes, Lewis, Leach, Oshenic, Muczynski.
Third Row: Morgan, Smith, Simmons, Wyatt, Rowen, O'Neil, Stephens, McClure, Stratman, Riley.
Back Row: LaRue, Rine, Perrile, Stevens, McCartney, Kumpula, Webb, Bacon, Marino, Rechlitz.

[52]

Front Row: Ashley, Flores, Mackintosh, Livingston, Brockelsby, Finster, Frame, Miniea.
Second Row: Frost, Gautreau, Green, Foss, Ruiz, Anderson, C. H., Brock, Bertles, Miller, McDonald.
Third Row: Ostoin, Fields, Frederiksen, Rayburn, Roth, Allen, Garner, Juntunen, Stokes, Felty.
Back Row: Lucero, Carlyle, Baer, Martinez, Loberg, Remillard, Love, Williston, St. Clair, Fincher.

Front Row: Penley, Harper, Kendgiora, Shephard, Brown, J. C., Denslow, Heinrich, Henry, R.
Second Row: Demmon, Green, W. E., Brown, R. N., Soule, McDonald, Hatfield, Fitzwater, Moore, Schilreff.
Third Row: Popejoy, Henry, M. E., Pickett, Smith, A. D., Syring, Franco, Valentine, Hill, Goad, Crutchleo.
Back Row: Frank, Olson, M. S., Reeve, Stone, Whitaker Westholder, Briones, Bartrug, S. B., Highland, Henson.

[53]

Front Row: Purser, Julian, Trevethan, Marshall, Nelson, Denton, Lechich.
Second Row: Ricker, Oswald, Quinnelly, Baker, Haney, Steiner, Witucki, Justice, Augustine, Stedman.
Third Row: Swineford, Ras, DeHolt, Wing, Slane, Bergen, Blum, Romano, Barry, Scarboraugh.
Back Row: Robinson, R. H., Banjanin, Poulson, Magliolo, Comella, Roby, Linowiecki, Zimiga, Barbieri, Blandford.

Front Row: Frye, Warner, Blahut, Pomykala, Matlock, Peterson, Mudrak, Bernard, Cassell, Garmon.
Second Row: Anderson, Rasmussen, R. G., Marshall, Morris, Le Mond, Cornett, Barney, Benson, Smith, F. L., Baker.
Third Row: Stevenson, Birkland, Young, McDowell, Barcus, Weinzierl, Anders, O'Hagan, Van Wey, Welker.
Back Row: Stops, May, Poland, Standfill, Coston, Collins, Reed, Turner, Ramey, Setterberg.

[54]

Front Row: Walaszek, Thomas, Asbell, Aiello, Rome, Hileman, Weadick, Thrailkill.
Second Row: Stephenson, Ross, Hill, Williams, D., Karas, Reiter, Pilarszyk, Watters, Webster, Wolf.
Third Row: Winsted, Wadley, Vickers, Guilbeaux, Bechtel, Aubry, Thorpe, Miller, Mascarenas, Ruddick.
Back Row: Hernandez, Hermann, Rudman, Hawkins, Witt, Partyka, Barcus, Rellergert, Bennett, Yeager.

Front Row: Thomas, Schaffner, Bryan, Boos, Widmeier, Wilson.
Second Row: Kiralla, Schlegel, Sabbatini, Fredericksen, Kleinfeldt, Lynn, Whitcomb, Manke, Marks, Posey.
Third Row: Schuster, Martin, Holt, Phillips, Scantlin, Rutherford, Bigshield, Qualset, Russell, Rodarmel.
Back Row: Schneider, Rebell, Keck, Parks, Rogers, Stetz, Schmidt, Curtis, Vercellino, Vanover.

[55]

Front Row: Childs, Raymond, Engle, McGechie, Locker, Pemberton, McClure, Brown, Spence, Richter, Williams.
Second Row: Taylor, Marsden, Jacobson, Lieut. (jg) Brodhagen, Lieut. Nelson, Lieut. Brown, Lieut. (jg) Servoss, Bright, Bronecki, Kitchen, Peddicord.
Third Row: Romero, Albiston, Medlin, Wallace, Lee, Dearing, Roy, Reeves, Prentice, Szwejk, Georgie, Couthron, Huffstetler, Marshall, Robar.
Back Row: Riker, Pacatte, Hunsaker, Van Sickle, Musser, Mannarelli, Manning, Roberts, Deeds, Pitt, Snyder.

Front Row: Whitworth, Rohrbaugh, Schulte, Mugge, Pedersen, Schlenk, Bears, Agnew.
Second Row: Bailey, Crudo, Knopp, Ens. Colpitt, Lieut. Wingate, Lieut. (jg) Rooney, Booth, Stutsy, McMahan, McLane.
Third Row: Price, Breitkreutz, Rhodes, Braden, Bone, Dawson, Regueiro, Walker, Bettencourt, Meyer, Bezinque.
Back Row: Stracener, Rowden, Lashon, Olsen, Couture, Morse, Burchett, Bauman, Lundin, Roylance, Serafini.

[56]

Front Row: Wallington, Mayo, Sullivan, Abbott, Ghant, Lyons, Senkbeil, Rospotynski, Mazur, Gibson.
Second Row: Stiltner, Bruckler, Ryan, Triggs, Prewitt, Lieut. Mattlage, Carp. Ray, Camm, Doty, Curtis, Kerrigan.
Third Row: Russell, Edwards, Blood, Leitner, Banning, Dendy, Herndon, Sistek, St. Pierre, Skiera.
Back Row: Kaiser, Hawxwell, Milekovich, Phillips, Michaelis, Rose, Hendren, Howard, Washburn.

Front Row: Forcha, Gootee, Martinez, F. C., Whitten, Herold, Hooton, Correll, Satterla, Gutnik, Sherman.
Second Row: Weinel, Spurgeon, Kabza, Wheat, Suttle, McMurray, Noyes, Kimble, Du Boise, Druten.
Third Row: Reising, Wilson, Jenner, Spears, Millard, Powell, Strawn, Doss, Evans, Cook.
Back Row: Martinez, M. G., Shatto, Mulford, Peckels, Rowe, Easter, Barclay, Maynard, Gradick, Thompson.

[57]

Front Row: Rupert, Rupple, Schallert, Reyes.
Second Row: Chladek, Powell, Skogberg, Klobucar, Woodland, Simoneaux, Hubbard, Wilson, Wilhelm, Larson.
Third Row: Parris, Rogusky, Walker, Reynolds, Noyes, Saragusa, Pickett, Trujillo, Schnurbush, Melior.
Back Row: Cicale, Weatherman, McMahon, Szymborski, Petermann, Roseboom, Pranin, Palach, McQuaid, Priest.

Front Row: Seale, Annis, Ferland, Berry, English, Lieut. Tazewell, Ens. Horner, Bokum, Hayes, Jordan.
Second Row: Tidrick, McKenna, Hill, Murrah, Cavin, O'Conner, Warner, Williams,
Anderson, C. D., Evans, Mason, Hegarty.
Back Row: Nance, Collins, Page, Nolan, Macias, Pridgen, Owens, Nelson, Alderson, Munro, Kern, Wilcox.

[58]

Front Row: Miller, Roberts, Youngerman, Kelly, Taylor, Jandebeur, Girard, Poluka, Breakey, Carter, Denton.
Second Row: Robatcek, Christoffel, McKnight, Ch. Carp. Hook, Lieut. Soderberg, Lieut. (jg) Jeffs, Ens. Crossley, Aldrich, Fanslow, Walston, Shepherd, Myers.
Third Row: Lambrecht, Seifman, Scally, Gridley, Gill, Bearden, Powers, Morris, Thomas, Mountney, May, Covey, Romero, Likavec, Morgan.
Back Row: Jones, Grossman, Hackenberry, Strovers, Lundstrom, Hickey, Gomes, Bennett, Leimbacher, Brock, Olson.

Front Row: Lewis, Gardner, Brinkman, Hester, Walsh.
Second Row: Richard, Johnson, W. G., Luckiesh, MacGregor, Conrad, Lynch, Dean, Hutto, Davis, Piatek.
Third Row: West, Large, Kosinski, LePre, Donaldson, Hlebinsky, Hardee, Mabrey, Bergen, McGarrigle.
Back Row: Jones, Manville, Kristan, Barton, Brown, G. H., Dube, Ruhs, Thompson, Ballman, Albanese.

[59]

Front Row: Luttrell, Forrester, Ens. Jones, Lieut. Fruechtl, Lieut. Comdr. Lombardi, Lieut. Baumrucker, Ens. Catledge, Ens. Bennett, Owsley.
Second Row: Smith, J. W., Calvin, Wilson, Baughman, Johnson, Hardman, McPherson, Cherpeske, Hess, Steinman.
Third Row: Harrington, Edlin, Licht, Millar, Routh, Ulrich, Ward, Skomski, Meyer, Mathis.
Back Row: Fink, Downing, Eastman, F. H., Stephens, Brucks, Woodruff, Anderson, D. L., Smith, A. L., Rinetti, Winger, Custance.

Front Row: Wigington, Overbee, Vonder Linde, Rude, Ch. Gun. Olmsted, Ch. Gun. Barrett, Crowder, Egeland, Clardy, Hayward, Renfrow.
Second Row: Jaeger, Hottinger, Renfroe, Webb, Wadely, Ropp, Beene, Reinhardt, Widdowson, Yanotti.
Back Row: Bonosoro, Van Cleave, Martinson, Reed, Welch, Beyer, Zuidema, Pinkerton, Shaughnessy, Lucas.

[60]

Front Row: Kyte, Hannaford, Buffington, Carson, Pawlirzyn, Matteson, Wray.
Second Row: Andreasen, Trites, Hammond, Kelly, Ens. Adams, Ens. Morgan, Gossett, Martin, D.F., Cline, Klappauf.
Third Row: Van Dolah, Wright, White, Tougas, Diehl, Anderson, R. W., Martin, R. E., Green, Cobble, Teaford.
Back Row: Perry, Soranno, Burbury, Deerfield, Schnieder, Seversen, Olsen, Miller, Curry, Eastman, R. H.

Front Row: Mathews, Peden, Schoen, Rende, Haack, Stanhouse, Essex, Cook, Grimes, Jackson.
Second Row: Orth, White, Rippeto, Spiedell, Dahlstrom, Acting Pay Clerk McCullough, Votaw, Pollack, Jankoski, Belfry, Caudle, Shinn.
Third Row: Walters, Perry, Kennard, West, Stuart, Russell, Rhoden, Hewell, Downing, Crew, Hawkins, Hume, Kellogg.
Back Row: Utley, Throm, Lauro, Green, Robertson, Sheldon, Carney, Allerton, Rodzon, Passy.

[61]

231

Front Row: Rocco, Boyd, Pappagallo, Sikes.
Second Row: Tallent, Snitkin, Stuart, McNeill, Owens, Acting Pay Clerk Gottfried, Lieut. (jg) Shea, Smith, Neisler, Zech, Jankoski.
Third Row: Primm, Stevens, Wick, Walker, Fleming, Peterson, Heard, Wall, Powers, Steffey.
Back Row: Graves, Whittington, Sims, Gackle, Drake, Stanger, Sertich, Jackson, Randolph, Moccia.

Front Row: Hall, Kaminski, Adams, Marvig, McCabe, Tucker, Brown, R. E.
Second Row: Eisworth, Zdravesky, Steinhauer, Ens. Umbenhour, Lieut. Kent, Ch. Mach. Cunningham, Pelissier, Pecard, Hudson, Dold.
Third Row: Brinkerhoff, Knapp, Pritchard, Becich, Accardi, Pringle, Bills, Peterson, Blomster, Ek, Doremus.
Back Row: Chambers, Totten, King, G. P., Pedersen, Olson, Bianco, Rapes, Anstett, Boudreaux, King, B., Kosar.

[62]

Front Row: Mitchell, Alexander, Heilman, Mourning, Nelson, Lieut. Taylor, Wood, Finnegan, Reidy, Holm.
Second Row: Bowen, Smith, Matkins, Johnson, D. G., Maki, Pedersen, Anderson, H. H., Gardner, Thompson.
Back Row: Longshore, Anderson, F. D., Johnson, J. A., Mann, Hefner, Gonzales, Foster, Canfield, Foley.

Front Row: Posey, Blanchard, Martinie, Lieut. Wands, Ens. Jarmon, Blake, Price.
Second Row: Spencer, Watts, Cardenas, Woodward, Audette, Rollar, Schemel, Martin, Revel.
Back Row: Malloy, O'Leary, Wilson, Serrano, Savage, Costa, Orr.

[63]

Front Row: McGinnis, Hirkaler, Murray, Poisson, Landry, Marpert, Hutchins, Crask, Thibeault, Woods, Schippers.
Second Row: LaRosa, Hairell, Mask, Reichert, Bingaman, Ens. Heatlie, Lieut. Dice, Mach. Castleberry, Giorgi, Turley, Luebbert, Maloney.
Third Row: Benak, Moore, Bloemers, Rogers, Punitigam, Martin, Binder, Myers, Steele, Krueger, Sherer, Miller, Boehm.
Back Row: Flotow, Lumbert, Dougherty, Pinchowsky, Jaworski, Edwards, Mullenix, Lash, Ferebee, Care, Forest.

Front Row: Stone, Shultz, Sievers, Cerny, Stephenson, Snyder, Schow, Salminen.
Second Row: Newberg, Johnson, E. G., White, Tysdal, Klaske, Turman, McArthur, Doyle, Stevens, Helvaty, Allsup.
Third Row: Washer, Hetherington, Shouse, Silski, Presnall, Ethington, Christy, Brunet, Baker, Urban.
Back Row: Freeman, Sanchez, Schafman, Medina, Ward, H. E., Hilton, Thurmon, Maddox, Erlandson, Brinzea.

[64]

SHIP'S LOG

THE LOG OF THE WEE VEE
(To the tune of "California, Here I Come")

In September, one fine day,
  We left the good ol' U. S. A.
    Hawaii, the land of tropical palms,
      Was first stop, but soon we left 'cause that was much too calm.
      And we were heading far out on the blue,
        For our unknown rendezvous;
          Our first attackers then broke through—
            'Twas Neptunus and his crew!

      (Secret) Island, here we come;
        The place the Japs were driven from.
          Next Leyte, and battle with the Jap fleet.
          We beat 'em, and it was really quite a feat.
            And then we left for the New Hebrides,
              For beer and swimming and a life of ease.
              Then, once again, the battle call;
                Back to Leyte—on the ball!

        (Censored) Island, here we are;
          Our convoy won't be very far.
            It's secure, and we are going far away
              To mail call and mem'ries of another day.
              And now we're going back into the fray,
                Headin' towards Manila Bay.
                We kicked the Japs from Luzon, too,
                  You Bataaners, that's for you!

          Lingayen Gulf was where we hit;
            It wasn't long before they quit.
              MacArthur took over and all is well;
                He's giving those Japs all sorts and kinds of hell.
                And now we're going to—who knows where?
                  But suddenly we'll just be there.
                  This ends our story for right now
                    But we'll be coming back—and how!

                                              —Don Johnson

THAT NIGHT AT SURIGAO

ONE COULD SENSE a surge of exhilaration run through the ship as the word was passed over the PA system late that afternoon, four days after the attack on Tacloban. The speakers blared:

"All hands to quarters for a special announcement!"

The invasion attack had been exciting enough, as it was the first action for many of the crew. At least it had provided a welcome stimulant after the grueling days of drill and the many uneventful days

Fantail, December 7, 1941

of steaming to our objective. And it had been an historical day for the West Virginia as she moved in to lead the attack, for she was flying the same colors she flew when she went to the bottom on December 7th.

But it had lacked much of the excitement of Tarawa and Kwajalein; pre-invasion bombardments were almost down to a science by now. On D-plus-one day, with the beachhead firmly established but

with intermittent shore bombardment still going on, the Wee Vee was lying offshore and we were fishing from the quarterdeck in the litter-strewn water of Leyte Gulf. We actually looked forward to the early morning and evening visits of Washing Machine Charlie as a few planes at a time would run the gauntlet of ships in the Gulf, drawing great pyramids of AA fire. They gave us something to look forward to, as we waited around wondering what our next move would be.

What! No Mail?

Mail call was still too vague a date in the future, and it was a little early yet for topside movies.

The planes reminded us of lone mudhens high-tailing across a public shooting ground on the first day of the season, dodging the shots of hundreds of gunners the best they could. Almost inevitably they wound up in a flaming mass, and the crew not on watch took station twice a day to see the performance. Bets were placed as to whether this one or that one would burst into flames in mid-air and disintegrate, or streak into the sea in a column of smoke, or crash in flames in the hills beyond.

But on the morning of D-plus-four day we noticed a change from these light attacks. More planes than usual came over for the dawn run, and our gunners were kept at work long after breakfast time. Then, just as chow was piped for the noon meal, they came again—fifty or sixty of them—and

[66]

kept us at our guns until 3 o'clock before we could eat.

That Old Scuttlebutt

Rumors were running wild through the ship that the Jap fleet was out, on its way from Borneo and Manila and Formosa and even from Japan. Groups of battleships, large groups of heavy and light cruisers and masses of destroyers were escorting their largest carriers, and closing in from all directions. But these rumors were largely laughed at and classed as the usual scuttlebutt—bum dope that helped keep us amused and pass the time of day.

But at quarters we got it straight. Four battleships, six cruisers, a couple of carriers and a large number of cans *had* been sighted, steaming through the Mindanao Sea on their way up to Surigao Strait, and we were going out to meet them! Now we were really going to do some business.

The evening meal was a substantial one, and welcome, for we'd been on lean rations for several days. We were issued K rations to keep on our battle stations, for no one knew when we'd get fed again. As dusk approached there were many little preparations in evidence—jugs of water and blankets were lugged to battle stations, and once in a while a can of fruit that had been "big-dealed" from the commissary issuing room. Charlie didn't draw much of an audience that night, as we had bigger game in mind, and most of the crew was at battle stations long before General Quarters.

The Wee Vee in the Van

The battle line steamed out of Leyte Gulf through a gorgeous red and pink sunset. Our small observation planes were flown off the ship,

[67]

as the expected gunfire would blast them to shreds on the fantail. They would be of little or no use in a night engagement.

The West Virginia was in the van again, leading more of the "victims of Pearl Harbor" and once more flying the colors she'd carried to the bottom. From the hatch in my battle station, in the main battery director on top of the mainmast, I looked down the column of this "scrap iron Navy," and out to the cruisers and destroyers escorting us.

The night came up black. The sea was smooth, with moderate ground swells. There was intermittent AA fire at various points on the horizon, and occasionally unidentified lights flared up on various bearings. Small lightning flashes lit up isolated portions of the sky.

I settled back inside the director and plugged in on the Captain's battle circuit to listen to the dope. My pointer and trainer and others of my crew lounged in the open doorway, laughing and chattering about some liberty back on the coast. I trained the director into the breeze to try to cool it off, for it had been soaking up the hot sun all day.

Watchful Waiting

Back and forth we patrolled, east and west across the northern end of the Strait, waiting for the

Main Battery Bombarding Leyte

enemy to arrive. Then, about 2300, one of our PT boats in the south entrance to the Strait reported a large black shape had entered and turned north, and we went to General Quarters.

Then another report—a *very* large ship had passed through, but still out of range.

Some time later the PT's were ordered to attack, and we wondered if they'd finish them off before we got a crack at the targets ourselves. The reports weren't clear—not all the word came over the circuit. But it seemed as if the PT's hadn't done too much damage, and soon we were tracking out three of our destroyers which were sent to investigate.

We trained the director out on the Strait, and I promised my operator the biggest gedunk I could wangle out of the soda fountain if he picked up the targets before anyone else found them.

Repel Air Attack!

We were facing right down the Strait now, a strip of water about fifteen miles wide and fifty miles long, and we strained our eyes to be sure not to miss the faintest sign of the enemy's approach.

Here They Come!

Several very large vessels were now reported moving up through the murky blackness, and oc-casionally I'd look through my powerful spotting glass or raise up through the hatch to scan the horizon through my binoculars. But all was solid blackness, and the faint glimmer of occasional lightning flashes still only lit up minor areas in the sky. Our destroyers were still moving out.

Suddenly—there they were!

"On target! On target! Commence tracking, plot!" We were trained on a large enemy ship, sneaking up on us through the black of night, hoping to catch us unawares—and here we had him right in the notch!

Soon other targets appeared, some of them large and others obviously the destroyer screen. Still out of range of our guns, they were coming straight at us at high speed. Their T was crossed! And by a lady who'd been rudely mussed up almost three years before, who was now out here for some satisfaction.

We picked up the largest closest target, trained out our guns, and waited for the order to commence firing.

Destroyers Go In First

We watched our three destroyers move in on the enemy's port beam, and checked and rechecked to be sure our range was not fouled by friendly ships. We got a little anxious about who was going to fire on whom first; our target was well within range now, but still no order came from the bridge.

Then things happened in a hurry. We saw the destroyers open up, and the enemy answer back—balls of fire loping across our line of sight—apparently at short range because of the flat trajectory. Then our cruisers commenced firing, and their first salvo was high in the sky and well on its way when—at 0353—we got the word.

[68]

"Commence firing! Commence firing!"

"Fire one," was the calm word from plot, and the Wee Vee rocked back on her side in a great cloud of flame as our first salvo was on its way. My eyes were glued on the spotting glass now, waiting for the signal that tells us when our shots will land —hoping to get a glimpse of the target so as to spot the next salvo on. At this range it was almost too much to hope for a hit or even a straddle on the first salvo. The buzzer sounded, and I saw our balls of fire arcing downward and WHAM!

Right On!

"Ya hit 'im! Ya hit 'im! No change, no change!" Out there on the horizon I saw a tremendous burst of flame. Only a heavily armored target would explode our 16 inch armor-piercing projectiles on impact, and almost immediately we fired again.

Salvo after salvo went out, and nearly all of them were right on. Part of the time I was halfway out of the director hatch, not even conscious of the concussion from the giants below, and part of the time my eyes were glued to the spotting glass to help guide them to their mark. Our cruisers had opened up in rapid fire now, and soon our next battleship in column was firing.

Sheets of flame were bursting from the targets. Sometimes I caught glimpses of a great hulk silhouetted in the flares—other times it looked like Niagara Falls out there from the splashes of the many salvoes. My pointer claims he saw the pagoda superstructure of a battleship. I was too busy on other details to confirm or deny.

Plot reported the target slowing in the water, then turning around—and the Captain ordered "Cease firing."

Why Waste Bullets?

And then I watched the great glowing masses on the horizon, as reports came in that only one of our destroyers had taken a hit, and she was still under

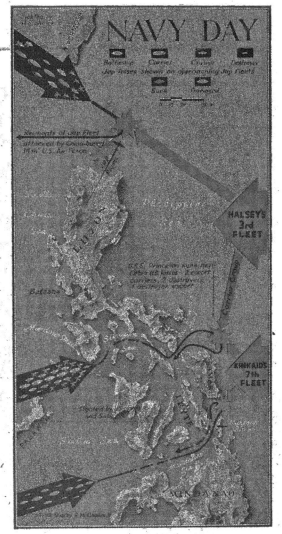

—Courtesy Time Magazine

control. One PT had rammed an underwater obstruction, and the Strait was filled with Nips who had abandoned ship—or whose ships had abandoned them.

The destroyers were picking up survivors—those that would come aboard. A few small targets were escaping out of the southern end of the Strait, but we had word that our planes would be out there to work them over as soon as it was light enough.

Until dawn we watched the great fires burning

[69]

on the horizon—enemy ships ablaze! The largest glow began to die down, when suddenly it loomed up brighter than ever, and we saw great clouds of fire shoot into the sky as the flames evidently reached the powder magazines and blew the remains to smithereens.

The Yamashiro. "So Sorry, Please!"

Bring On Some More!

By 0730 we had secured from General Quarters, and gathered in small groups on the quarterdeck to talk it over. We learned that our escort carriers were engaging another force to eastward, and that our fast carriers had been in action to the north. As this is written we have but fragmentary reports on the action—we don't even know just how large a fleet we'd taken on.

But it was something pretty big, and the "scrap iron Navy" had really done a job. With no air support in our phase of the battle, we'd done more than send them back licking their wounds—we'd sent most of them to the bottom.

The Wee Vee was no longer a virgin—but she was still a lady as she proudly maneuvered with her sister ships awaiting further orders.

[70]

HAIL WEST VIRGINIA

```
                    U. S. S. WEST VIRGINIA
                     ORDERS OF THE DAY

                        WATCH BILL
```

<table>
<tr><td><u>O.O.D.</u></td><td><u>J.O.O.D.</u></td></tr>
<tr><td>08-12 Lt. Carol Landis</td><td>Ens. Betty Grable</td></tr>
<tr><td>12-16 Lt. Betty Hutton</td><td>Ens. Judy Garland</td></tr>
<tr><td>16-20 Lt. Claudette Colbert</td><td>Ens. Ann Rutherford</td></tr>
<tr><td>20-24 Lt. Joan Bennett</td><td>Ens. Linda Darnell</td></tr>
<tr><td>00-04 Lt. (jg) Ann Sheridan</td><td>Ens. Donna Reed</td></tr>
<tr><td>04-08 Lt. (jg) Olivia DeHavilland</td><td>Ens. Lana Turner</td></tr>
</table>

0515 Call Bugler and Police Petty Officer.

0520 Throw well-punctured Bugler and Police Petty Officer over the side.

0530 Wake Officers.

0600 Officers will inspect living compartments to see that men are well-covered.

0630 Muster 500 coolies for stores working party. Take bottled lunch.

0930 Prepare to waken all hands, using chimes and sweet music.

0935 Taps optional.

1100 Brunch is served in bed. Mail, telephone messages, telegrams and flowers to accompany brunch on tray.

1130 MAIL CALL. Liberty and holiday routine. Liberty expires on the dock at 1115 the following week.

1200 Send No. 1 motor launch to dock to pick up women guests.

1300 MAIL CALL. Send No. 2 motor launch to see what happened to No. 1.

1315 Daily plane departs for the States for all hands desiring leave.

1400 MAIL Call. Break out deck chairs, hors d'hoeuvres and lemonade for crew's recreation period. USO shows, band concerts and Happy Hours in customary locations about the ship.

1500 All Officers not actually on watch tour the ship to see that men have sufficient lotion to avoid sun burning. Gentle massage on affected parts will alleviate burning.

1600 MAIL CALL.

1700 Buffet supper in the crew's recreation center.

1730 Compulsory two hour nap and rest period begins. Chamber music.

1930 Ship's crew will be entertained by a group of gorgeous native girls who have seen no man for three years.

2030 DARKEN SHIP. All hands are on their own.

NOTES:

    1. Personnel inspection will not be held. In the event this word is belayed, ALL HANDS are cautioned against being on board.

    2. There has been an alarming increase in the consumption of beer in the past few weeks. Cooling facilities are being over-taxed. ALL HANDS must exert every effort to draw no more than they can reasonably consume that day. Bottles will <u>not</u> be broken on the starboard side of the quarterdeck.

Lieut. Comdr. HEDY LAMARR
Executive Officer.

[72]

Our First Plane

Tom Shealy —
Original Plankowner

Captain's Inspection

George Garner—
First Purple
Heart

Grounds of the Royal

Swimming Call

MAIL!

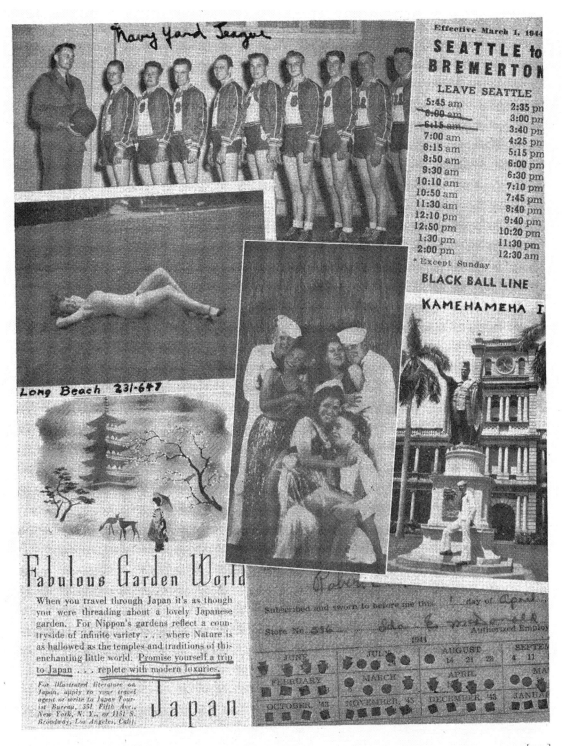

[74]

How Many Times ?!!

"F" Division's Duck

Gedunk Stand

Good pose, eh!

Diamond Head

CROSSROADS of the PACIFIC

ORIENT

N. AMERICA

AUSTRALIA

S. AMERICA

SYDNEY

NEW YORK

MANILA

LOS ANGELES

TAHITI

LONDON

TODAY'S SPECIAL

U.S.S. West Virginia - 1940

[75]

Aloha Tower

aiea beer party

Pilikia!

Domain of the Golden Dragon
THIS IS TO CERTIFY THAT

WAS DULY INITIATED INTO THE
Silent Mysteries of the Far East
HAVING CROSSED THE INTERNATIONAL DATE LINE
ON BOARD THE
UNITED STATES SHIP WEST VIRGINIA
BOUND WEST FOR TOKIO
IN LATITUDE SECRET LONGITUDE 180°
ON 30 September, 1944
H. V. Wiley, Captain, U.S.N.
GOLDEN DRAGON

Royal Hawaiian

[77]

247

[78]

INDEX

20551284R00147

Printed in Great Britain
by Amazon